D1527450

Chevrolet—Racing?

Fourteen Years of
Raucous Silence!
1957–1970

Chevrolet—Racing?

Fourteen Years of Raucous Silence! 1957–1970

Paul Van Valkenburgh

Society of Automotive Engineers, Inc.
400 Commonwealth Drive
Warrendale, PA 15096-0001 U.S.A.
Phone: (724)776-4841
Fax: (724)776-5760

Library of Congress Cataloging-in-Publication Data

A catalog record for this book is available
from the Library of Congress.

ISBN 0-7680-0529-9

SAE Order No. R-271

Contents

Photo Credits

Preface

This is a reprint of a 28-year-old book which revealed the inside story of Chevrolet's early surreptitious involvement in racing, from 1957–1970. I was an R&D engineer (in race car aerodynamics, instrumentation, vehicle dynamics, and computer simulations) at Chevrolet during the years when they were quietly supporting Chaparral, Penske, McLaren, and Smokey Yunick. As the program wound down, I left to become a writer, and decided that all the invisible insiders deserved some credit. I submitted the manuscript to Road & Track Books, who at first gave me a contract and advance, then for some unknown reason got nervous about it and passed me on to a small publisher back East.

When the book was published, John deLorean, the new general manager of Chevrolet, saw a copy and asked, "Who is this guy? Did we really do all this stuff?" When assured it was all true, he reportedly decided that all they could do was ignore it. For some reason, in spite of its eventual recognition as a classic, few automotive magazines at the time would review it.

It became a rare collector's item, going for as much as $300 today (when one can be found), because of its limited print run and the quiet opposition to its incriminating content—the sole published exposé of one of racing's most famous "secret" activities. Ironically, if I had saved 20 books to sell at that price, I would have made more than I did from the entire first printing. A common lament I hear is, "I loaned my copy to someone once, and never got it back."

In spite of the demand, I had little enthusiasm for reprinting it, even though Chevrolet (in a change of heart) actually suggested that possibility a few years back for an anniversary celebration. This is essentially a duplicate of the original book, not a rewrite. Almost nothing has been changed, so as to leave it in its natural context, even though the writing is a little awkward in places. Of course, this preface and an epilogue were added, and the cover and title changed slightly to distinguish it from the original. I added the defining years "1957–1970" to the title to clarify the era to readers who hadn't even been born then, and I changed the equals sign to the dash I originally intended. This error crept in somehow during production, and I didn't notice it until the cover had been printed, and I've hated it ever since, especially when I hear someone say "Chevrolet Equals Racing." And I could finally include an index, which wasn't ready in time for the first printing.

As I proofread this edition, I often found it hard to believe we were doing these things over 30 years ago. Some of the engineering and technology was so advanced at the time, that some professional racing teams have only recently rediscovered it: long-distance race car telemetry, driver analysis, vehicle dynamics analysis, compliance analysis, wind tunnels, chassis shakers, computerized track simulations—exept that our computers didn't even have keyboards and monitors. We had to input on punched cards, and the only output was numerical on fanfold paper. But the basic physics hasn't changed at all.

Knowledgeable race fans will note that the book is often historically quaint, in light of subsequent, sometimes ironic happenings since. It could have been entirely rewritten just based on later technological advancements, especially in aerodynamics, electronics, computers, data acquisition, rules changes, and production cars, not to mention all the career changes, deaths, and changing allegiances. But everything was left the same because it illustrates what the thinking was during auto racing's techno-revolution 30–40 years ago. This is how it all began—the origin of many of the most spectacular discoveries and innovations in racing.

Paul Van Valkenburgh
PVanvalken@aol.com

Dedication

In addition to all of the well-known public names in Chevrolet's racing history, a considerable amount of credit is deserved by the invisible people— many of those Chevrolet and General Motors employees who quietly contributed to Chevrolet's competition successes in some way or another, some time or another, during the years of official disinterest.

My apologies to those not mentioned who were just outside the fringe, or whose efforts were so well-guarded that they were never identified by me or my sources.

To:

Bob Alt, Julian Baranowski, Harry Barr, Jim Bennington, Dean Bedford, Randy Bienke, Al Bodnar, Frank Boehm, Norm Brown, Bob Brown, Frank Burrell, George Caramanna, Leroy Casebier, L.X. Chapin, Jim Chatterly, John Clark, Bob Clift, Ed Cole, Cliff Collins, Tom Collins, Dave Corvin, Don Cox, Ken Cross, Dan DeLonnay, Ernie DeFusco, Carl Dryden, Zora Arkus-Duntov, Ray Eland, Don Elfes, Bill Elliott, Ken Escheback, George Fabyan, Bill Fay, Herb Fishel, George Foltz, Carl Friebel, Fred Frenke, Ray Gallant, Don Gates, Dick Godowski, Bernard Genack, Bob Gervais, John Giacoletti, Tom Goad, Ted Gondert, Bill Gornick, George Hija, Vic Hickey, Leon Hostnick, Bill Howell, Don Hubbard, Gib Hufstader, Clark Irwin, Jack Jaquette, Gary Johnston, Jack Kay, Dick Keinath, Kent Kelley, E.H. Kelley, Bill King, Jim Kinsler, Joe Knable, Semon Knudsen, Ed Krol, Jim Kuhn, Joe Kurleto, Len Kutkus, Len Littleton, Ernie Lummis, Norm Luther, Joe Marasco, Jim Marsh, Jack McLaughlin, Walt MacKenzie, Bob McLean, Bill Meyer, George Miotke, Bill Mitchell, Jerry Mrlik, Jim Musser, Theron Nelson, John Nolte, Ziggy Obidzinski, Charley Peterson, Vince Piggins, Joe Pike, Mike Pocobello, Fred Porter, Paul Pryor, Al Rasegan, Jim Read, Jim Richardson, Dick Rider, Paul Rishel, Earl Rohrbacher, Ken Rose, Mauri Rose, Bill Route, Bob Rubarth, Ed Rudaitis,

Ken Ryder, Joe Samson, Al Schroeder, Vern Schulin, Horatio Shakespear, Larry Shinoda, Milt Simpson, Charley Simmons, Sam Sineni, Charley Smith, Phil Smith, Bob Spilski, Don Stoeckel, Jerry Thompson, Carl Vogel, Bill Weide, Bob Wachowski, Frank Winchell, Walt Zetye, and Bob Zimmerman.

Introduction

Was Chevrolet involved in racing? For fourteen years (from June 7, 1959 through 1970) they never built a complete, running, race-ready vehicle—unless you can consider a Corvette a race car. Nor was the company ever officially represented at a race. Nor did they ever pay a driver to race. And they never claimed credit for Chevrolet product racing wins, nor promoted them in advertising in all those years.

Yet, in that period, Chevrolet probably acquired more successes and more technical knowledge of high performance than any other company in the world.

Was Chevrolet involved in racing? That may be simply a problem of semantics. How did they accomplish what they did? This book finally tells the story.

This is not a review of all the races in which Chevrolet-powered vehicles competed, and it is not a carefully-worded evasion of the true story. Perhaps half of the content of this book is information never before known by the racing public. So much can be said about Chevrolets in competition—race reports, engine specifications, the speed equipment industry, early history—that an apology is hardly necessary for all that has been left out here. This is merely the inside story, a supplement for those who have followed the "outside story" all these years.

I had seen Jim Hall and Roger Penske race on the West Coast, but there was no connection when I was interviewed for a position at Chevrolet Engineering. When I was shown around the department in which I was to work, however, I couldn't keep from laughing out loud. Everywhere I went, I saw all the "evidence" lying around—aluminum monocoque chassis, the automatic transmission, racing tires, aluminum engines ... It was like crash-landing at the North Pole and discovering that there really is a Santa's workshop full of toys there.

It was not to last, though. Eventually, the activity dissolved and we all went our own ways. I happened to become a writer, which is why the story is being told in my words, although it is *our* story—the story of hundreds of us. I was simply a small part of the team at one time. Anyhow, the story will always be Chevrolet's, because the product tends to be more important than the people. But perhaps Chevrolet's strong product reputation will be better understood if this book establishes for the company a strong *engineering* reputation. Chevrolet, as a collection of individuals, deserves it.

The total account is really fascinating as hell. When I began, I thought I knew most of the story. But as I combined my knowledge with the public record, and the pieces all fit together, I couldn't wait to finish the book so I could read it myself. There probably is not a harder automotive book in the world to research, but as I pieced it together from records, recollections, rumors, tips, slips, and discussions with other ex-employees, I was amazed at how simple it all was. Of course, everyone tends to tell his part of the story his own way, but for every incident there were at least two people involved, so that, in many cases, I could take the average of the available opinions and assemble the whole truth as nearly as possible.

No one who is or was involved is going to like *all* my interpretations of the situation. And I fully expect the most noise from those who volunteered the least when the research was in process. There has also been the inevitable, discouraging case of individuals who continually expressed a very low opinion of certain other persons' efforts. But I tried to avoid any vituperation ... since the accuser was just as frequently the accused!

What is humorous to me at this writing is that some people may not believe this book. No one is going to officially verify or refute anything I say, and so it could be a pure fabrication. I certainly present no evidence. For the lack of documentation to reference, the vast majority of this book has come from memories anyhow—my own, and those of other equally fallible people. So there may be a few errors in detail, but not enough to affect the basic plot.

My greatest regret is going to occur when those hundreds of former participants swarm to me saying, "Why didn't you tell me you were writing it? You left out the best part. Didn't you know that ..." Perhaps I'll just have to accumulate all those stories for the sequel: *Chevrolet Returns to Non-Racing.*

It may be difficult to follow the story in places. This is because so much was going on simultaneously, with so many different people and projects, that it was practically impossible to organize the book purely chronologically. If the early parts occasionally seem incomplete ... read on to the finish anyhow.

Paul Van Valkenburgh

1

The Preamble

Total import car registrations passed the 100,000 mark in the U.S., and the year's sales projection was another 40,000. The MG TD was the leading import, with the Jaguar XK 120 in second place. Over in Europe, Alberto Ascari was defending his World Championship title in a Ferrari against Juan Fangio in a Maserati. Everyone was racing in T-shirts, and roll-over bars were unnecessary weight. A man named A.C.B. Chapman was driving and marketing a Lotus kit chassis which used an MG engine. Tazio Nuvolari died. Jaguar took 1, 2, 4 at LeMans, while Mercedes was designing the 300 SLR for a new FIA racing formula.

Elkhart Lake and Bridgehampton were running races on blocked-off highways, while Watkins Glen had just opened a permanent closed circuit. Walt Hansgen won the first race there in a modified Jag, and the XK 120C was the car to beat on airport courses across the U.S. Sebring ran its third AAA-sanctioned race with John Fitch/Phil Walters winning in a Cunningham-Chrysler. Crosley Motors was in deep financial trouble. An Oldsmobile won the Daytona Beach stock car race at 89.5 mph.

At Offut AFB in Omaha, Allards came in first and second, driven by Carroll Shelby and James Hall. Roger Penske was delivering newspapers after high school in Cleveland. Mark Donohue was working as a service station attendant in Martha's Vineyard, because he could get a driver's license at sixteen in Massachusetts.

The year was 1953—not an extraordinarily significant year in automobile racing. And then something moderately unusual happened. Conservative old Chevrolet announced that the company was going into production with an all-American sports car called the Corvette. It wasn't any great surprise, because similar "show cars" had been built in Detroit for years, and fairly accurate rumors preceded the event by many months. The purists were apathetic. As everyone knew, Detroit could not build a good-handling sports car. Chevrolet's inline-six was a reliable old engine, and the stronger truck six would bolt in, but the Corvette was not a "racer"—it had a fiberglass body and an *automatic transmission.*

The original production Chevrolet Corvette on the banked GM Proving Grounds track at Milford, Michigan. A bold step for an American automobile manufacturer, and the first recognition of European influence in Detroit.

Actually, no one at Chevrolet was particularly interested in sports cars. Imports (of any kind) accounted for an infinitesimal portion of automobile sales in America, and Chevrolet was only interested in competing with Ford. It was the people at General Motors Styling who pushed the idea across. Harley Earl, the head of Styling, was aware of the youth trend through his college-age son, and he broke from the traditional "advanced design" concepts of the day. Up to that time, styling exercises and experimental prototype show cars were based on the "bigger-is-better" theme, which resulted in some really monstrous and gaudy examples. Earl took a hard look at the MG and the Jaguar and the Mercedes, added a lot of his imagination, and sketched up the first Corvette drawings.

The internal layout was the responsibility of a Styling engineer named Bob McLean, who was to ensure that the body would actually fit over all the necessary components. The standard procedure for vehicle design was to start with the engine and front suspension and work rearward, allowing a given volume for passengers and luggage. But for this all-new concept, a "tight" design, McLean tried a new technique—designing forward. Starting at the rear axle, he placed the driver as near as he could to the wheel wells, then allowed legroom, then fitted in an engine, and then kept the front suspension in as close as possible. The final drawings and full-size mockup so

The first Corvette chassis was closely adapted from the sedan, except for a shortened wheel-base and increased rear roll understeer. The engine was also moved back 7″ and down 3″. Note the Powerglide automatic transmission.

impressed GM Management that they ordered it built for their annual traveling circus, the GM Motorama. Chevrolet was talked into cooperating, and Maurice Olley, the director of R&D, proceeded to adapt the Chevrolet engine and driveline to fit.

The Corvette is one of very few examples of a show car that developed enough public interest to justify production. At its introduction, the response was so favorable that Chevrolet began thinking seriously about a new kind of image, a performance image. Because the car was designed around production components and the body could be built in fiberglass, tooling costs were low, and so an initial production run of 300 cars was planned. The idea was to test the market at the lowest possible cost, and even if the concept failed, the cars would be good for Chevrolet promotion. To add a little exotica to the mundane "stovebolt-six," it was equipped with three sidedraft Carter carburetors, a stronger cam, and dual exhausts. At that, the performance was still not up to the image, and so at $3,440, the original Corvette came out as an economy sports car.

It might have stayed that way if it weren't for Zora Arkus-Duntov. He had seen the prototype at the New York Auto Show, and because of his previous experience at Allard, he was highly enthusiastic about the potential of Corvette. At first, Duntov's influence was minimal, because there were few people at Chevrolet who cared about high-performance. But gradually his

The 235 cubic inch "Blue Flame Special," equipped with three sidedraft carburetors, 8:1 compression ratio, mechanical tappet cam, and dual exhausts, was capable of 150 horsepower. Engine speeds were "known to exceed 5000 rpm."

enthusiasm convinced Ed Cole (then chief engineer of Chevrolet—now president of General Motors) that successes in competition were an invaluable sales tool. Racing wins, however, would be very difficult to achieve with the eighteen-year-old Chevrolet six-cylinder engine.

The next year, in the summer of 1954, Chevrolet made another incongruous move—it began producing a V-8 economy engine. Ford, of course, had been selling its flathead V-8 for over twenty years, and many other manufacturers had already begun offering overhead-valve V-8's. But Chevrolet's engine was something a little different. Whereas everyone else was getting involved in a horsepower race, Chevrolet set out to produce the most efficient—and *cheapest*—engine possible. That is not to say it was to be a weak or inferior engine, but that it had to be inexpensive to manufacture. To attain that goal, the project engineer, Harry Barr (who was later to become director of GM Engineering Staff), produced a masterpiece of simplicity and functionality which became a benchmark in reciprocating engines. A large part of the credit is also due to E.H. Kelley, the production engineer who concentrated on costs.

The most obvious innovation was the absence of a common rocker arm shaft. With each stamped rocker arm pivoting around a ball on its own stud, a large number of pieces were eliminated. Not only that, the reciprocating weight was reduced, which allowed higher rpm, and it was easier to adjust valve

This cutaway of the original 265 cubic inch engine in 1955 can be distinguished from later engines not only by the relatively small bore and valves, but by the upward-looping exhaust manifolds and the lack of an oil filter boss on the block casting,

clearances. (Ten years later, this design permitted the inclination of valves in the famous "porcupine heads" for the bigblock engine.) The valve chamber cover was eliminated by machining the bottom of the intake manifold to serve that purpose, and the manifold was also used to serve as a common water outlet for both heads. With this design, the cylinder heads could be made interchangeable, and they were also cast with integral valve guides. All separate oil lines were eliminated by circulating oil up through the hollow pushrods and "splashing" the rockers.

Since material costs money, it was also made an extremely light engine. It was compact, with a short stroke and literally no block skirt below the main bearing split line. This not only produced the greatest ratio of displacement per pound, but the short stroke reduced piston speed at higher rpm's as well. The valve train was good to 5600 rpm, and the short stroke meant it could be run there all day. There were some public mutterings about durability, with all these innovations, but Ed Cole announced that it had been run for over 36 hours at 5500 rpm—and history has verified the promise. It was merely an incredibly simple, compact, light engine. There just was not much to go wrong with it. It was rated at 162 horsepower from 265 cubic inches, or 180 horsepower with the optional four-barrel carburetor and dual exhaust. Hardly a *racing* engine.

Walt MacKenzie, left, director of the Chevrolet race team at Daytona in 1956, whose job in later years was to convince auto writers that "Chevrolet is not involved ..." With him is John Fitch, popular Corvette racer of the day.

Herb Thomas brings his Smokey Yunick-prepared Chevrolet across the finish line at Darlington in 1955. While the Chryslers dominated the longer NASCAR races, Chevrolet took the short ones, and played it up grand in advertising.

But then came another unusual occurrence. A few NASCAR drivers took the new '55 Chevrolet V-8's to Daytona Beach in February 1955, to run on the "Beach and Road Course." Jack Radtke finished tenth behind Kiekhaefer's Chrysler 300s and assorted Buicks and Oldsmobiles, and suddenly the Chevrolet looked a little different. This was Grand National racing with the fastest stock cars, and Championship drivers such as Tim and Fonty Flock, Lee Petty, Curtis Turner, Buck Baker, and Junior Johnson. And if that performance was surprising, two weeks later a Chevy V-8 won the season's first NASCAR "short-track" race at Fayetteville, North Carolina. Smokey Yunick had been preparing winning Hudsons for Herb Thomas in Grand National, but for the tighter tracks he built the Chevrolet, and Thomas won the first time out in it. Two weeks later, Smokey tried it against the Grand National cars again at Columbia, South Carolina, and this time Fonty Flock won, beating his brother in one of the Chryslers. The next day at Hillsboro, North Carolina, Fonty was fifth, while Herb Thomas went out with a broken wheel.

The new Chevrolet was a sensation. Its performance was news as far north as Detroit, where people at Chevrolet Engineering and Chevrolet's ad agency, Campbell-Ewald, were getting ideas. Barney Clark and Jim Wangers jumped on the promotion possibilities immediately, and by June, they had Chevrolet NASCAR successes advertised in both *Motor Trend* and Detroit's trade journal, *Automotive News*. Over at Chevrolet, Ed Cole was watching the show from an engineering standpoint, and he promptly dispatched Mauri Rose to the South to find out what was happening. Rose had the most knowledge of racing of any engineer at Chevrolet at the time, with three Indianapolis wins in his recent past, and he knew what to look for. The report was in favor of Smokey Yunick as a base of operations in the South, with necessary parts engineered and supplied by Chevrolet to satisfy NASCAR regulations. So little was allowed in the way of speed modifications in those days, that the primary job—especially on dirt tracks—was durability, and this was an obvious task for Chevrolet Engineering.

Still, the entire operation was seen as sales promotion, and it was placed under Walt MacKenzie, who was given an advertising budget. Rose was engineer in charge, Campbell-Ewald wrote the ads, and Smokey prepared and raced the cars, with Herb Thomas doing most of the driving. It took a little time to get the heavy-duty parts into even limited production, and while they were finding the weak points, they mostly ran on the shorter tracks. The shock wore off the competition in Grand National, and Chevrolet won only one other race in that class that first year. But while Chevrolet was cleaning up in Short Track, and Campbell-Ewald was pushing the fact all over the country, Rose and Cole were going into high-performance to make it a profitable parts business.

Chevrolet wasn't building race cars, they were building production sedans that were suitable for racing ... with the proper optional heavy-duty parts. As the racers broke components—wheels, axles, steering arms, spindles, etc.—Chevrolet

Don't argue with this baby!

All the low-priced cars
and most of the high-priced cars
tried it recently in official NASCAR* trials...
and took a licking!

Meet the champ! The new Chevrolet 180-h.p. "Super Turbo-Fire V8" — the most modern V8 on the road today.

You want facts, don't you? And not ours. Facts instead from an independent, outside source where the only thing that counts is who came in first, second, and so on. Here they are —

Daytona Beach. NASCAR Acceleration Tests Over Measured Mile From Standing Start. Chevrolet captured the 4 top positions in its class! 8 of the first 11! And on a time basis Chevrolet beat every high-priced car, too — but one!

Daytona Beach. NASCAR Straightaway Running open to cars delivered in Florida for $2,500 or less. Chevrolet captured the first two places, 7 out of the first 11 places!

Daytona Beach. NASCAR 2-Way Straightaway Running over measured mile. Open to cars from 250 to 299 cu. in. displacement. Chevrolet captured 3 of the first 5 places! None of its competition (What competition?) even finished "in the money"!

Columbia, S. C. NASCAR 100-Mile Race on half-mile track. Very tight turns. Chevrolet finished first! Way, *way* ahead — as in sales! With a new car, and *no* pit stops!

Fayetteville, N. C. NASCAR Late Model Event. After running the fastest qualifying round — (with a new car) — Chevrolet again finished first. Because of even tighter turns the driver chose to run the entire 150 laps in second gear! Yet no overheating or pit stops!

These facts you can't laugh off. Sales Leader, Road Leader, a crowning achievement of Chevrolet and General Motors. *Try* a Chevrolet and live in a land of going-away where you win all the arguments! Today, maybe? . . . Chevrolet Division of General Motors, Detroit 2, Mich.

*National Association for Stock Car Auto Racing

SPECIAL: *Added power for the Chevrolet "Super Turbo-Fire V8" — the new 195-h.p. Special Power Kit now available at extra cost on special order.*

 SALES LEADER FOR 19 STRAIGHT YEARS

produced heavier ones and made them available to everyone. That doesn't mean that everyone had to *buy* them, though. Advertising was paying the racing bill, and if it looked like a certain driver could win, and he looked good in photographs, he might be able to get all the pieces and a car to put them on, for no more than his signature on a release. However, it wasn't an organized racing team. Everything passed through Yunick's shop, but everyone campaigned his own car.

The cost wasn't all that great in those years, anyhow. The basic running showroom-stock Chevrolet was about $2,000, all the special parts were no more than another $1,000, and everyone took care of his own labor. The system worked so well that by September Chevrolet took seven of the first ten places at the Darlington 500, and from then on, sometimes half the cars entered in stock car races were Chevrolets.

Kiekhaefer's Chrysler team still won almost every major race, but the crowd-favorite underdog Chevrolet was usually right behind in second place. On the shorter tracks, however, it was another story. The huge Chryslers simply couldn't get around without tearing up their tires. The Chevrolets had a much lighter engine and were better balanced, and they could pass the Chryslers on tire change pitstops. At one race this was made strikingly apparent, when Rose showed up with a truckload of softer-compound Firestones for all the Chevrolets. Kiekhaefer promptly stormed up to the officials and demanded they ban the tires because they weren't available to everyone. In response, Rose offered to sell him as many as he needed for his Chryslers … and Kiekhaefer was stumped. He knew his cars would tear them to shreds. Obviously, Chevrolet's advertising concentrated on the shorter tracks in 1955.

Toward the end of 1955, Ford Motor Company had been thinking about what Chevy's advertising was doing to their image, and they set out to remedy the situation. Two factory cars were built for the October 2nd Charlotte race, with Joe Weatherly and Curtis Turner driving. As usual, the Chryslers qualified fastest, but the Fords led most of the race. Eventually, however, both Fords broke their suspensions and Chevrolet came in 1-2-4-7-8-9-10. Ford rapidly became aware of the magnitude of the problem, and hired Pete De Paolo to run another pair of cars. Before the season was over, Fords had won two Grand National races … but they were run by independent Kiekhaefer, with Speedy Thompson and Buck Baker driving, and those people weren't about to cooperate with Ford Motor Company. Ford was going to have to fight its own battle in 1956.

There were other skirmishes going on in stock car racing in 1955. The AAA had a circuit which ran similar cars with similar rules, but it was not as large or strong as NASCAR in that area. Both groups were somewhat jealous with their name drivers, so Marshall Teague ran the Chevrolet show in AAA … for as long as they lasted. 1955 was also the year of the infamous LeMans disaster, in which a Mercedes crashed and killed over 80 spectators. The AAA had been trying to drop race sanctioning for years, and they finally used this as a justification. Their primary responsibility was to motorists, and therefore they didn't care to be liable for a similar occurrence in America. The race drivers and organizers pulled together and reorganized under a new name, United States Auto Club, but all their operations were in turmoil that year, and stock car racing was not their main interest.

Therefore, 1956 opened with Chevrolet and Ford meeting in direct factory-assisted competition on the NASCAR and USAC stock-car circuits. In less than a year, Chevrolet had come from obscurity to become a power in American racing, and now Ford was out to put them back in their place. Although the Fords—and/or their drivers—were fast from the start, it took a while for them to become durable enough to win. In Grand National, Kiekhaefer was taking everything in sight, and everywhere else, Chevrolets were dominating: USAC, Convertibles, and Short Track. The competition was fierce all over the country that year, and big money dominated. There were car switches, driver switches, team switches, and questionable modifications. The pressure was so great that NASCAR finally had to crack down on engine specifications and factory optional equipment, demanding "public availability" of all components months before they could be raced. Enforcement was through fines, suspension, and the loss of all-important Championship points.

Then, in mid-season, the Chevrolet camp got shaken up. Herb Thomas, who was pushing the Chryslers with his Yunick-Chevy, was replaced by Paul Goldsmith, a motorcycle champion with no auto racing experience. Mauri Rose went back to production engineering to apply his experience with heavy-duty components to taxicab and police car components, and Vince Piggins was hired from the Hudson racing team to replace Rose. It wasn't until September at Langhorne that Goldsmith gained enough experience to put a Chevrolet in front of Kiekhaefer or the Fords. That gave Chevrolet a total of only three wins for the season in NASCAR Grand National, but it is hardly a complete picture of the year's stock-car racing activities. That was the first and last complete year of overt factory competition between Chevrolet and Ford, and too many conclusions have been forced out of the statistics.

As with any statistics, you can fairly well juggle the racing results to come up with whatever you want to say, especially because of a few complicating factors in NASCAR and USAC rules. In the first place, neither series runs a *manufacturer's* championship. The whole show is operated around a *driver's* championship, which means that the best drivers often switch cars if another model seems faster. Second, where manufacturers *were* scored, it was based on a 10 to 1 scale for first through tenth place, which means that the greatest number of cars will likely win the greatest number of points. Third, there were three separate series in both USAC and NASCAR, and Grand National was merely the most publicized. NASCAR Convertibles and Short Track, and USAC National Championships, Pacific Coast, and Short Track were just as competitive, but there wasn't the obvious "factory team" aura to attract attention. The complete factual results for 1956 are:

NASCAR	Grand National		Convertibles		Short Track	
	Wins	Points	Wins	Points	Wins	Points
CHEVROLET	3	598	10	1088	25	1024
FORD	14	912	27	801	11	604
CHRYSLER	22	431				

USAC	National Champ.		West Coast		Short Track	
	Wins	Points	Car Owner	Points	Car Owner	Points
CHEVROLET	11	423	Rush	705	Rush	569
FORD	4	245	De Paolo	400	Dane	684

It's apparent that anyone can make what he chooses of the results, and even then, there are two more factors. Which is more important, having the fastest car for part of the race, or a slower car that has the durability to finish? And most of all, the statistics totally disregard the immeasurable contribution of both drivers and teams.

But advertising and claims were flying. Campbell-Ewald had Chevrolet competition successes on full pages in *Road & Track, Popular Mechanics, Life,* and even *Boy's Life, Police Chief, and Law and Order* (promoting the V-8 Chevy as a police car). Ed Cole was authoring a series in *Popular Mechanics* about how Chevrolet Engineering made the car a race winner. And Ford Motor Company was following right along in their attempts to be "number one" in the public eye.

To ensure Chevrolet's future, Cole had Duntov working with Rochester on a top-secret fuel injection system, and when the news broke in late 1956, Ford was only temporarily off-guard. They responded with McCullough superchargers, and the engineering battle was on. NASCAR saw what the escalation could do to their economy-style racing, however, and they began to tighten their limits on "production" equipment. For 1957, the rules allowed only a single four-barrel carburetor on Convertibles and Short Track, and no bolt-on "kits" could be raced. All special equipment had to be factory-assembled and available in quantity. Rule-bending was soon going to grow into an expensive art.

With Ford's entry into the game, Chevrolet decided they needed better control over their product's competition activities. In the fall of 1956, Vince Piggins began assembling a totally new and separate operation in the South, called Southern Engineering Development Company, or SEDCO. Quartered in Atlanta, it was to be staffed by experienced racers and financed by Chevrolet Engineering, and it would campaign team cars with ex-Kiekhaefer drivers Speedy Thompson, Buck Baker, Bob Welborn, Rex White, and Jack Smith. Not only were they going to run all NASCAR races, but they would act as a clearinghouse for *all* Chevrolet stock-car racing activities including USAC.

Behind Chevrolet's record-shattering Pikes Peak climb are important engineering changes

by ED COLE, *Chevrolet Chief Engineer*

Since Chevrolet's record-breaking run up Pikes Peak, people have asked me just what we've done to this new Chevrolet to make it the mountain-climbing champ.

Well, to begin with, our job was to produce a car that would out-perform last year's Chevy which, you'll recall, was the leading winner on the stock car tracks. That was a big order.

Our men started by making refinements in the "Super Turbo-Fire V8" engine. They raised the compression ratio to 9.25 to 1. Horsepower was boosted to 205. You can imagine what these changes did for performance!

Next we went to work on the "Blue-Flame" 6. The compression ratio went up to 8 to 1. Horsepower was increased to 140. The final result of these and other improvements is the most powerful, sweetest running 6 we've ever had in a Chevrolet passenger car!

Drivers who like a full-flow oil filter will be pleased to hear that we've made provision for one on our V8 engines. And *all* engines—both 6- and 8-cylinder—are now equipped with Hydraulic-Valve lifters. This eliminates the need for periodic valve adjustments.

Drop by and drive this record-breaking new Chevrolet at your Chevrolet dealer's. . . . Chevrolet Division of General Motors, Detroit 2, Michigan.

1956 Chevrolet setting new record for Pikes Peak climb

Chevrolet

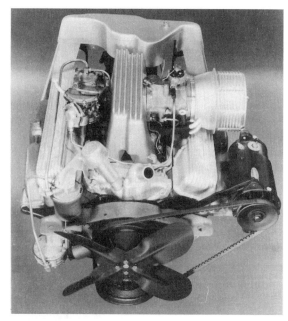

Chevrolet's Ramjet Fuel Injection was developed in 1956 for the coming NASCAR season, and to guarantee top honors at the spring Daytona Beach speed trials. The electrical shielding over the distributor was necessary in Corvettes.

From the beginning, about the only people happy with the arrangement were *some* of the employees. Within months, Piggins went through three managers, finally settling on Jim Rathmann. The rest of the independent Chevrolet drivers wanted an equal opportunity, and Smoky Yunick and Paul Goldsmith flatly walked out to buy and campaign a Ford on their own. Even at Chevrolet there were dissenters who felt that the best way to operate was to simply build and supply the very best equipment and leave competition up to the individuals. Still, there was a tremendous amount of talent under SEDCO, and Ford would have to sweat blood to beat them. The stage was set for 1957.

However, other Chevrolet stock-car activities had been going on in 1955–56. In the summer of 1955, when it was becoming obvious that the V-8 was a performer, and that advertised performance sold cars, Chevrolet went looking for new fields to conquer. At the last AAA-sanctioned Pikes Peak hill climb, an independent builder named Loren Roberts put a Chevy engine in a sprint car chassis and was second up the hill, behind a Lincoln special and ahead of four Unsers. Mauri Rose seized on the idea and got together with Cole, Duntov, and Campbell-Ewald. What could be more sensational than a new Pikes Peak hill-climb record for the upcoming 1956 Chevrolets? There was a prototype available, and with a little body camouflage it could be run before the official release announcement date. This was in the middle of

Pikes Peak, 1956: Because of a disagreement over timing authority, Chevrolet had to back up the previous year's hill-climb record. Three factory cars were entered, and Jerry Unser and Bob Korf brought two of them in first and second.

the AAA-USAC changeover, however, and official record-sanctioning was a problem. So NASCAR was called out to witness the runs, the road was rented, and on September 9, 1955, Duntov took the car up in 17 minutes, 24 seconds—a new record! The feat was blared all across America both in magazines and on television. But there was one minor point that was overlooked: The old record was set by a Ford V-8 roadster twenty years previously ... and AAA had not even *run* a production car class since then.

This, of course, was followed by Ford using NASCAR to authenticate record speed runs on their proving grounds, and the general use of NASCAR records at Daytona Beach for the establishment of "world's records." The U.S. was in an uproar over auto speed records. The problem was that all the trained timing personnel had deserted AAA for USAC, and AAA (who wanted to maintain the authority) had the only FIA-certified timing equipment in America. NASCAR might be capable, but they weren't approved by the FIA. USAC was in poor humor over the matter, so they assembled the necessary timing gear, and reopened an official stock-car class at Pikes Peak. Chevrolet was naturally obligated to do it all over again.

According to the rules, stock cars could only be modified to protect the driver and spectators, which was a very vague stipulation. Therefore, Mauri Rose took three sedans and added all the heavy-duty suspension components that had been developed for NASCAR: springs, shocks, steering and brakes.

Daytona Beach, 1956: Speedweeks was the publicity event of the year. At the top, the flying mile finish line. Center, Betty Skelton, Duntov, and John Fitch in the "factory" Corvettes. At the bottom, Smokey Yunick receives a checker from Paul Whiteman.

Ford was quite aware of the situation, and they set out to block a repeat Chevrolet performance, with two NASCAR Fords from Pete De Paolo's team. But this was just after Rose left the Chevrolet racing group ... and then Duntov was hurt in an accident at the GM Proving Grounds. Piggins, the new operations chief, rounded up three new drivers—Jerry Unser, Bob Korf, and Marshall Teague— and set out for Colorado with the cars. When the dirt had settled, Chevrolet had done it again, Unser was first, Korf second, and Duntov's previous time had been lowered by an "official" one minute, sixteen seconds. Proof enough.

There were other "stunts" performed primarily for advertising in those years. Rose had assembled four Yunick-prepared sedans to run at top speed for 24 hours at Darlington, with eight of the top NASCAR drivers running them in shifts. The results, if not accepted "world's records" were at least good, honest ad copy. In addition, there were numerous wins at performance trials around the U.S. to promote, and there was a lot of rub-off from the Corvette in amateur road racing.

At the same time, the Corvette was becoming more and more professional. Duntov was merely an engineer on the car in 1955, but he was making waves, anyhow. For many years his activities and proposals kept getting him in and out of favor with management, but they always improved the quality and reputation of Corvette. As soon as the V-8 was available, Duntov began developing it for more power, and developing the Corvette chassis to use it. As the chassis was derived from a very non-racy production sedan, there was little that could be done for it. With the steel body removed, the frame was very flexible, and the front suspension geometry was hopeless. The understeer was so great that the car could hardly be steered around a race track. It didn't take long for Duntov to replace the Powerglide with a three-speed manual transmission, but the poor ratios and non-synchro first gear were totally unsatisfactory, and he continued to campaign for the four-speed. But the production brakes, as might be suspected, were the weakest link of all. Through extensive testing at the proving grounds, and by constant liaison with amateur Corvette racers such as Dick Thompson and Dick Guldstrand, the car finally came around. Metallic linings and heavier drums improved the brakes, a steering arm adapter was offered to quicken the ratio, and an anti-roll bar was adopted for the rear suspension, along with a heavier bar at the front. Chevrolet ran ad campaigns showing it in the company of Ferraris, Mercedes, and Jaguars ... and then it began keeping up with their company on race tracks. Before long it wasn't embarrassing for an SCCA member to be seen in a Corvette.

After the first Pikes Peak runs, Duntov and Cole got together over a similar promotion for the Corvette, and they decided to prepare some factory entries for the 1956 Daytona Beach Speedweek. This was the original justification for the famous Duntov camshaft for Chevrolets, and it also marked the beginning of fuel injection development. To guarantee the objective of 150 mph, one of the

Sebring, 1956: Chevrolet entered four production Corvettes against the world's best. At the start, they all pulled away for an instant, but the best they could finish was a ninth by Fitch and Hansgen, behind the Ferraris and Jags.

After Sebring, Harley Earl prepared a stylish "Sebring Racer" (SR-2) for Dick Thompson to run in SCCA amateur races. Although it wasn't highly developed mechanically, it attracted a great deal of attention.

Corvettes was also aerodynamically improved. It had a full-length belly pan, the windshield was removed, and the cockpit enclosed with a flush fiberglass tonneau, a headrest/fin was added, and the grille and headlights were taped over. The only thing that kept the week from being a Chevrolet benefit was that Ford was suddenly reacting to the 1955 stock-car advertising incident. They also showed up with factory cars, dozens of engineers, and a streamlined Thunderbird. Considering all the classes of competition that were run, the event was more or less a draw. Corvette was fastest, at 155 mph, and T'bird won the sand-drags.

With that kind of performance on sand, it was certain that the Corvette could run away from the Thunderbird on an asphalt road course, and so Duntov and Cole set out for Sebring. There was very little time between the events, but straight-line acceleration and aerodynamics had been taken care of at Daytona, handling was being worked on for SCCA amateur racing, and brakes didn't seem to be too great a problem. However, Sebring is one of the worst courses on brakes, and in the ensuing development battle, Duntov and management were at odds, prompting his return to Detroit. In the race, Walt Hansgen and John Fitch drove conservatively to bring one of the three factory Corvettes in ninth overall, in its first professional competition. Not a bad showing, considering that Fangio won in a Ferrari ... over Moss in an Aston-Martin and Hawthorn in a D-Jaguar. Actually, the Corvette was first in its class, and the first true "production" sports car to finish.

Daytona (New Smyrna Beach) 1957: Ford showed up with a modified T'bird to run against the production factory 'Vettes. At that, Paul Goldsmith's Corvette led the Panch-'Bird at one point, but was willing to settle for first in class.

Those cars became known as Sebring-Racer-1, or SR-1's, as Harley Earl capitalized on their limited success with an SR-2. The original SR-2 was built for his son, but when it first appeared at the 1956 Road America June Sprints, it was being raced by Dr. Dick Thompson. It never was a great racing success, however, as it was largely a styling exercise. With an extended nose, headlight bubbles, a vented hood, low racing windscreens, brake scoops in the doors, and an incongruous dorsal fin, it gathered more attention than outright wins. At a final attempt at Nassau in December, it went out with terminal structural failure in the engine.

But after little more than a year in direct factory racing, Chevrolet had gotten hooked. They had the right engine, a new four-speed transmission, advanced technology, and unbounded enthusiasm. On October 1, 1956, Cole gave Duntov authorization to start on the only complete racing car that Chevrolet has ever built and campaigned. He was given one engineer, a handful of draftsmen and technicians, and six months to build and develop a car that would beat the world's best at Sebring 1957. Not only was it to have an entirely new chassis and suspension from the tires up, but it would also have a totally new body, and if time permitted, an all-aluminum engine. The fuel injection was already well on its way, and basic engine durability was being proven in the SR-2.

The SS Corvette chassis was somewhat similar to the Mercedes 300 SL, with a web of small-diameter tubing surrounding everything. Note the latest Firestone 6.70 x 15 Super Sports tires on narrow Halibrand knock-off wheels.

As the SS progressed behind schedule, things started getting a little cramped. The combination of radiator air ducting into the cockpit and the header pipes looping over the drivers' legs, was to make driving rather uncomfortable.

Everyone went back to Daytona in 1957, but with Sebring in mind, it was small potatoes. This year, however, was the racing debut of Chevrolet's fuel injection engines, and they ran away with the speed trials. Three factory Corvettes were there also, including the SR-2, and after the runs they went road racing. Since Daytona wasn't very "sporty" at the time, a race was scheduled at the New Smyrna Beach airfield, fourteen miles south. It might have been a great Chevrolet-Ford showdown, except that the only Thunderbird there was modified to the extent that it couldn't run in production class with the Corvette. In the all-production race, a Mercedes 300 SL was first (in a class all by itself), while Corvettes were one, two, three in C Production. All the fast cars could run together in the feature race, however, and the Corvette-Thunderbird duel was quite a show. Paul Goldsmith's production 'Vette even led for a time, but he dropped back to finish fourth overall, again first in class ahead of the Jags. Immediately after that, the three Corvettes went directly to Vince Piggins's SEDCO in Atlanta. While Duntov was working on two totally new racing Corvettes, SEDCO would work around their stock-car preparation schedule to get the stock 'Vettes ready for Sebring.

Duntov's SS Corvettes were unlike anything ever built in America in 1956. The frame was closely patterned after one of the most advanced European cars, the Mercedes 300 SL. It was an intricate web of small-diameter tubes connecting large-diameter tubular crossmembers at the front and rear suspension attachment points. The "space frame" dropped low at the door section for easier entry, although it was more heavily trussed there. At 180 pounds, the frame may have been a little overdesigned, but the limited time meant that it wasn't possible to allow for structural failures in testing. The front suspension was of conventional geometry, with unequal-length wishbones welded up from steel stampings, and springing by concentric coil-shock units. At the rear, however, things got tricky. A conventional large-diameter deDion tube connected the rear hubs, bending around behind the Halibrand-derived center-section and inboard brakes. The locating linkage was something new for race cars. It had only four trailing links, the top two nearly parallel, and the bottom two converging to a point below and to the rear of the axle tube. These bottom links therefore not only took fore and aft thrust, but they prevented lateral movement and established the roll center. The top links merely prevented rotation of the dead axle, though the stress was minimal because of the inboard brakes and differential, and because the coil-shock units were mounted directly above the hub carriers. Oddly enough, all the suspension mount points were rubber-bushed, an unusual practice for any race car.

For brakes, it seemed wise to stick with the drum system that had been developed for the SR-2, instead of taking a chance on the experimental new discs. The shoes were of a double-leading design, having a very high self-servo action, and they carried cerametallic linings. The drums were something a little different, however, with the finned external portion cast in aluminum around a cast

The first prototype fiberglass body for the SS was tested at the GM Tech Center in mid-winter. Heat was not a problem in Michigan, so the "mule" was shipped to Sebring for development, while work continued on the second car.

The final magnesium SS body with a flip-up plexiglass canopy, as it was displayed at GM Styling. Although the design is aerodynamically unsound by today's standards, it had a sensationally exotic appearance for its day.

iron wearing surface. What was most unusual was the brake actuation plumbing. With a complex arrangement of hydraulic lines, vacuum boosters, and electrical switches, it was possible to change the point of lockup at the rear wheels. The point was controlled by an adjustable mercury gravity switch, which sensed deceleration and prevented brake pressure increase at the rear above a preset value. It was one of the very first anti-lock brake systems, and the potential seemed great.

Because the special aluminum block was not ready in time, a fairly conservative cast iron short-block assembly was used. It was the first year of the new 283 size, and a few blowups in the SR-2 had uncovered most of the weak points. The aluminum heads were ready, although they were run with a compression ratio below 10:1 for insurance. The injector system was modified to rotate the metering body forward, so that ram air could be more easily ducted from the nose, and the 40-inch long header pipes were looped over the footwells. A very straightforward powerplant, but one that was expected to last for twelve hours at Sebring.

Harley Earl had been playing with clay models of a racing Corvette since the last Sebring race, and he had his aerodynamicists studying shapes before Duntov started on the chassis. The wind tunnel studies by Kent Kelly are obvious in the final Corvette SS—from a low drag standpoint—but the shape points out the total disregard for aerodynamic lift which has since become so critical. The first body was built in fiberglass, and it was installed on the first chassis, the "mule," which was taken to Sebring for advanced development. Meanwhile, the fabricators stayed at Chevrolet and finished up the second chassis, which was identical except for a magnesium-alloy body.

The "mule" was to run almost two complete simulated races in mileage, and any failures would be relayed to Detroit for correction on the race version. But even with this system, the SS was running late, and it had to be finished in the van that trucked it to Sebring. Two days before the race it was driven for the first time, and it was apparent that all the innovations were going to be troublemakers.

The duo-servo brakes were pulling left and right, and the pedal pressure was not progressive enough for the drivers to modulate them properly. With a slight increase in pressure, one of the front brakes would lock up and flat-spot a tire before it could be unlocked. Under hard acceleration the rear axle was acting up also. Because of increased power and reduced weight, the SS had to be fitted with a locked differential, and under acceleration it produced violent axle hop. The drivers weren't happy with the new body, either, because the radiator wasn't cooling properly, and with the enclosed exhaust pipes, the cockpit was like a furnace. There was further complication in the driver selection. Because the car was so late, a succession of drivers passed it up, until John Fitch and Piero Taruffi were finally chosen. But they still had very little time in the actual race car for either fine development or practice, especially with all the last-minute problems.

If practice was hectic, the race was a madhouse. In the LeMans start, Corvettes pulled out first, but they were soon passed by the thundering herd of

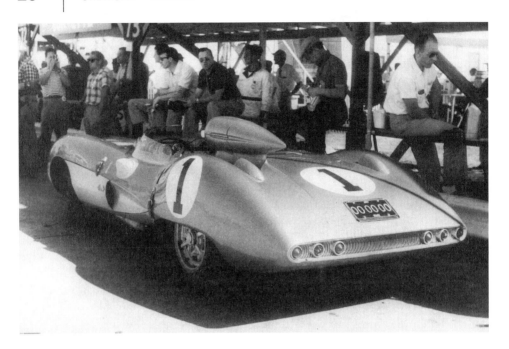

At Sebring, the SS went a little less spectacularly than it appeared. In twenty-three laps it had to stop five times with various difficulties, and eventually it was retired when the rear suspension rubber bushings collapsed.

Ferraris and Maseratis. Then, on lap three, Fitch brought the SS in with a flat-spotted front tire to be changed. Six laps later the engine started cutting out and he barely made it to the pits. The problem was diagnosed as a condenser short, and Fitch went out again. On lap eleven the engine stopped out on the course, but a coil had been tossed in the cockpit, and Fitch was able to change it, which seemed to solve the problem. Lap twenty-one was the scheduled fuel stop, and Taruffi replaced Fitch. But two laps later, one of the rear control arm rubber bushings squeezed out, and the loose axle allowed a tire to wear through the mag body. By this time the SS was far out of the running, and it was retired. Fangio and Behra won in a 4.5-liter Maserati. At least Chevrolet's contingency cars did a little better. The three production Corvettes that went through SEDCO finished 12, 15, and 16.

No one really expected the Corvette to beat world champion drivers in Ferraris, Maseratis, and Jaguars in its first attempt, but this was embarrassing. Cole had announced that Chevrolet might send two SS's to LeMans with Cunningham that summer, although he was aware of growing aversion toward factory racing activities. But after Sebring it was quite apparent that it was going to take a lot of effort to make the cars sufficiently fast and also more durable. The SS had tremendous potential ... after all, it had only been a little over two years since Chevrolet's hottest engine was a 150 horsepower inline-six, and now they were running against the world's fastest sports cars. Chevrolet versus Ferrari. A fantastic accomplishment considering their relative backgrounds, and the publicity benefits couldn't be matched.

On the other hand, a large number of people were unhappy with the American racing situation. Since mid-1956, influential groups such as the Automobile Manufacturers Association (AMA), the National Safety Council, and the Association of State Vehicle Commissioners had been objecting to the promotion of racing performance and horsepower figures. At the same time, they were usually supported by whichever manufacturer seemed to be losing at the moment, whether in engineering, wins, or advertising success. Out in the stock-car circuits, independent competitors were protesting factory involvement by staying home, and starting fields shrank. This, of course, prompted NASCAR to crack down on the factories. First there was the limitation of fuel injection and superchargers to Grand National only, and then limitations on national advertising of NASCAR racing wins. Ford and Chevrolet were both caught on that one, and their drivers had to forfeit points when the equipment they were using was not publicly announced. NASCAR felt that any advertising ought to be far more specific, stating exactly what happened and exactly how it was done ... including any special equipment that was used. Then, in April, NASCAR came back and said no more fuel injection or blowers in *any* stock-car racing. The competition was fairly even between Chevrolet and Ford, in the beginning of 1957, but not between the factories and the independents. The idea was to get everyone back on a more equitable level.

At the same time, the AMA had another approach in mind. Both GM and Ford were feeling each other out on terms for an end to hostilities on the race track. At the February AMA session, a proposal was submitted for a committee to draw up the precise contract that would be voted upon. Naturally, the racing teams had word of what was going on, but they had little to say at the level where such decisions were made. Racing was simply not a major or influential activity within either corporation at that time. Even at the public level, auto racing had not yet developed the national prominence that was to come ... perhaps coming partly as an overreaction to the AMA interference.

Actually, through 1956, relatively little was being done in automotive high-performance by the American manufacturers themselves. True, a few million dollars were being spent in NASCAR and USAC stock cars, but as part of the advertising budgets, it was an inconsequential expenditure. And that was only a couple of race series under two sanctioning bodies. Detroit had still not dis-covered USAC Championship cars and Indianapolis, Formula One, the Euro-pean Manufacturers Championship, or drag racing. The SCCA was still a minor amateur organization of no real publicity value, although Corvettes were beginning to overrun their races in the hands of hundreds of low-budget amateurs. Only Duntov's assaults at Sebring showed any organization or poten-tial, and to the true sports-car *aficionado,* that appeared as a fiasco. The idea of a real *racing* car being produced by Chevrolet or Ford was ridiculous.

In June, the AMA met again, while Chevrolet and Ford and NASCAR held their breath. NASCAR had suddenly decided that factory participation wasn't all bad—that they ought to stay involved after all ... though at a more regulated level. But the new resolution went before the board of directors of the AMA, and it was voted in unanimously. And this wasn't an outside regula-tory body imposing its will on helpless manufacturers. The directors consisted of fifteen top executives from all the automotive corporations. However, the decision might be better understood when you realize that that included men from Studebaker-Packard, Kaiser, American Motors, International Harvester, Mack Trucks, White Motor, and Diamond T. What did they have to lose?

No one was surprised by the official announcement on June 7, 1957, but everyone who had been involved on the inside took very careful note of the final wording:

"Whereas, the Automobile Manufacturers Association believes that the automobile manufacturers should encourage owners and drivers to evaluate passenger cars in terms of useful power and ability to provide safe, reliable, and comfortable transportation, rather than in terms of capacity for speed.

"Now, therefore, this board unanimously *recommends* to the member companies engaged in the manufacture and sale of passenger cars and sta-tion wagons that they:

"Not participate or engage in any public contest, competitive event or *test of passenger cars* involving or suggesting racing or speed, including acceleration tests, or encourage or furnish financial, engineering, manufacturing, advertising, or public relations assistance, or supply "pace cars" or "official cars," in connection with any such contest, event, or test, directly or indirectly.

"Nor participate or engage in, or encourage or assist employees, dealers or others to engage in the advertising or publicizing of (a) any race or speed contest, test or competitive event involving or suggesting speed, whether public or private, involving passenger cars or the results thereof; or (b) the actual or comparative capabilities of passenger cars for speed, or the specific engine size, torque, horsepower or ability to accelerate or perform in any context that suggests speed." (The italics are mine.)

There are few corporate policy decisions that have had the total impact on auto racing that this resolution has. It was a good, carefully worded, ironclad document, with no loopholes ... except for the word "recommends." And if it had been an enforced contract between the manufacturers, no one would have even been able to loan cars out to the motoring press, since they inevitably note acceleration and top speed. But no one paid much attention ... particularity the press. *Road & Track* was primarily road race and import oriented, and *Motor Trend* carried a single derisive column. Every manufacturer was absolutely free to do exactly what it chose, anyhow, because the resolution had all the implied power—and unenforceability—of a United Nations censure. However, the top executives at GM and Ford had agreed, and they immediately began to disassemble their racing operations.

Duntov was on vacation at the time, but he knew what was going on. He wasn't too shocked to return and find out that he had no competition program left. It was fairly well certain by then that they weren't going to LeMans and there wasn't much being done on the two SS Corvettes. They were cleaned up and sent to storage, and Duntov went back to development of the production Corvette.

The Southern Engineering operation was a little more difficult to wrap up, because of the distance and the fact that none of the personnel were Chevrolet employees who could be transferred to another operation. Piggins got authorization to give away all the racing equipment instead of having to scrap it, and so it was divided up and piled around race cars, all of which were donated to the drivers. Everyone was paid off and SEDCO simply disappeared. The resident manager, Jim Rathmann, made out fairly well, as he eventually took over a major Chevrolet dealership and a Firestone distributorship. Vince Piggins stayed with "Product Performance" at Chevrolet, although this involved little more than economy runs and the Pure Oil Trials for many years. And his boss, Walt MacKenzie, went to Product Information to deal with the press ... and convince them that Chevrolets were still the "hottest ones" even though the factory couldn't race them.

It hardly needed to be said to anyone who closely followed stock-car racing in the ensuing years. Bob Welborn, Jack Smith, Speedy Thompson, Rex White, Buck Baker, and Fireball Roberts kept up their own Chevrolets after that, and in 1958 they won most of the major NASCAR races. Everyone conceded that Chevrolet had the advantage in its basic package, the lightweight and high-revving V-8, and also in a couple of other clever moves.

In the first place, NASCAR had demanded a minimum of 1500 units of any components used in racing. But Chevrolet seemed to feel that if that many were required, they ought to become a profitable sideline in themselves, and production eventually exceeded that figure simply because the demand was there. Second, very few of the special parts developed and sold were "peculiar to racing" (as the "inside" agreement phrased it) and subject to cancellation. There were high-performance camshafts, carburetors, and pistons, but everything else had always been referred to as heavy-duty parts, "engineered for maximum durability and safety under extreme conditions." The list included radiators, brake shoes, axles, differentials, wheels, hubs, steering linkages, transmissions, drive shafts, wheel bearings, and springs. Their existence could be justified for use on police cars alone, not to mention off-road use, use on taxicabs, and in trailer towing.

They weren't necessary on the everyday sedan, but they were available for those who needed them, for whatever reason. Chevrolet couldn't *keep* them from anyone who wanted to race. Everyone had equal access to all the pieces, too, since the list was distributed to every Chevrolet dealer from coast to coast.

Equally important, was a very educational little booklet prepared by MacKenzie and Piggins a few months before the AMA resolution. It was called the *"1957 Chevrolet Competition Guide,"* and in twenty-three pages of type and photos it explained just exactly how to modify the Chevrolet for racing. It was very explicit, as well it could be since Chevrolet wasn't at all shy about racing involvement at the time. Specifications were even given for racing suspension alignment and tire pressures, and at the end, the guide offered advice on joining the proper sanctioning organizations—with addresses provided.

To anyone who has discovered auto racing since that fateful day of June 7, 1957, it seems incredible that Chevrolet *ever* had a direct involvement in the sport.

2

The Public Carries On

For a number of years following 1957, there was not much doubt in anyone's mind as to Chevrolet's attitude toward racing. They still made the Corvette, and Duntov was as active as he could be, but Chevrolet was *out*. In just a few years, however, the potential of the new V-8 had been demonstrated, and the enthusiastic public had caught on. Because of its small size and light weight, the little 283 could easily replace just about any other engine. And because Duntov had shown that it was possible to run it to high rpm and get a surprising amount of power, it became the road-racer delight. The smallblock Chevy has probably been transplanted into more different chassis than any other engine ... Ford products and Chrysler products, and imports from MG to Mercedes-Benz. Because it was so inexpensive and available, all the low-budget backyard builders were using it, but because of its performance, the professionals were, also. Of course, factory help or not, the speed equipment industry always jumps into the market next to anything that looks good, and all the necessary racing components were soon available. If racing has benefited from Chevrolet supplying the raw material, Chevrolet ought to be thankful for all the support their products got from the independent and professional teams who used them. This chapter is about all those people with whom Chevrolet really was never involved. Those who carried the ball on their own during the lean years—and did a tremendous job of it.

At first, everyone began using the overhead-valve Cadillac, Olds, and Buick engines in their specials because they were the first available. There were the Allard-Cadillacs, and then the Balchowski-Buick "Old Yallers," which astounded (and repelled) all the purists in West Coast road racing. But the most practical operation seemed to be transplanting an American V-8 into an established European sports-car chassis, because most American builders knew little of the subtleties of handling. When the ohv Chevrolet finally came out in 1955, people started putting it in everything. The availability of parts for imported engines may have been an influence, but in addition to that, the Chevy usually had less weight and more power than the smaller displacement engine it replaced. For street use, it was traded with 4-cylinder MG's, 6-cylinder Jags, and even 12-cylinder Ferraris, and if anyone *ever* did the opposite—trade a Chevy V-8 for a European engine—they haven't made it common knowledge.

As builders started replacing the engines in race cars, however, they began to learn about handling. The change in weight, distribution, and power demanded it. One of the earliest successful such operations was the Sadler-Chevrolet, built by Bill Sadler in Ontario, Canada. As early as 1956, Sadler was installing the 283 engine in his special sports cars and doing quite well with them on road courses. The increase in power over his previous TR-2 engine, however, meant that major revisions were necessary in the suspension and driveline, and so he began building his cars around the engine. Experiments with suspension geometry and roll centers were proving very educational, to the point where his first Chevrolet-inspired car had a home-built transmission-differential unit at the rear, combined with independent rear suspension. Considering this was in 1957, it was an extremely advanced design for North America, even compared to Duntov's Sebring SS Corvette with its deDion rear axle. Reventlow was only just beginning to think about building his Scarabs. The next year, Sadler met up with the Scarabs, and although he was able to lead them occasionally, numbers and dollars were against him. Sadler's racer was built from junkyard parts, and even if it didn't fail, it was still two to one.

That was the Mark II which was finally sold to Bob Said, who campaigned it with great speed and few successes. With a market appearing for his creations, Sadler started his Mark III with limited production in mind. His first cars were built on a simple large-diameter tube ladder-frame, which was both heavy and flexible, so for the Mark III he began using a tube space frame. Because of their rarity, he had to give up the ENV rear-mounted gearbox for a more common Corvette four-speed mounted to the engine. Although this was in 1959, Sadler preceded Chevrolet by a few years in opening the 283 up to 327 cubic inches, and he replaced the stock fuel injection with Hilborn injectors.

This general layout was common for sports-race cars of the day, however. What was really unusual about the Sadlers was the suspension refinement. Bill had spent a year in England working for John Tojeiro, and he picked up a good education in suspension design. He didn't have all the answers yet, by any means, but he was probably more advanced than any other independent in America. He began using such terminology as "roll steer," "camber change curves," and "roll center height," and the other racers started listening. He was still using swing axles at the rear, and double wishbones at the front, but everything was more easily adjustable so that he could experiment with toe-change and camber-change curves. Again Bob Said campaigned the Mark III, and again he had difficulty finishing races.

The Sadler Mark III at Cumberland, 1958. Bill Sadler was one of the first independent constructors on this continent to build and race a refined sports racer around the Chevrolet engine and four-speed transmission.

But the new European mid-engine race cars were starting to influence Sadler, and he started off on a totally new design. First he tried squeezing the Chevy into a Formula Junior, although there was no room for either a transmission or clutch, and the experience from that inspired him to build the first rear-engine Chevrolet single-seater. Because this one was to be raced, it had a clutch, but there wasn't a suitable transaxle available, so he decided to try and broaden the engine output curve and run high gear only. Using many of his standard suspension components, the car was thrown together in time for the 1960 Watkins Glen Formula Libre race, where Peter Ryan ran it as high as fifth behind such greats as Moss, Brabham, Bonnier, and Gendebien, before blowing his engine. Still, Sadler had stolen the show from Duntov, who didn't expose his own mid-engine Chevrolet CERV-I until a few months later. On the other hand, Duntov's car was long enough to include a four-speed transmission, it had a stronger aluminum engine, and it was far more attractive.

That winter, Canadian champion Grant Clark asked Sadler to build him an unbeatable sports car for the 1961 season, and they began the two-seater Mark V. By now Bill knew that the engine location was correct, but they needed more gear ratios. The engine had proved to be quite flexible, though, so two gears were deemed adequate. To adapt a transmission with the absolute minimum weight, Sadler merely extended the Halibrand quick-change differential

The Mark V, with body removed, reveals one of the very first mid-engine Chevrolet sports-car layouts. The engine was opened to 360 cubic inches, and it must have been quite a challenge to drive with the limited available tires.

Sadler's home-built two-speed transaxle was based on a Halibrand quick-change center section, with an extended case holding the slider forks and reverse gear eccentric. Note the modern suspension geometry and inboard disc brakes.

housing to hold an extra set of gears, and machined Ford synchronizers to fit. It was utterly simple—but it was unproven. The rest of the car was merely the best components from the previous design, only widened for the extra seat. It had inboard rear brakes and the rear suspension was similar to the new Lotus, with the axle serving as the upper link. Two cars were assembled, one for Sadler and one for Clark, both identical except that Sadler's engine had been increased to 360 cubic inches. The first real test for everything was the 1961 Mosport Players 200, and as might be expected, the newest component was the troublemaker. The transmission was basically strong enough, but little details such as the shift linkage were coming apart. Still, Grant Clark put his Sadler Mark V in third place behind Moss and Gendebien while Sadler limped in with only high gear usable.

That was the end of Sadler race cars. A month later, he announced that he was returning to the electronics profession at Westinghouse, and he was going to finish his engineering degree. Even though he finally obtained an M.S. degree he never went back to car building, and today he is employed in classified U.S. Government projects. Bill Sadler built some amazing race cars, which were continually more advanced than Hall's or Penske's, and perhaps even Chevrolet's research vehicles. But he was also one of the first notable examples of the conflict between innovation and reliability.

The Sadler Mark V at Mosport, 1961. Two of these were the last cars Sadler built before retiring from the sport. They were highly advanced for their day, but not tested and developed enough to have race-winning reliability.

The Chevrolet-powered Scarabs were a legend in their own time. Every car that was built by Reventlow Automobiles (eight in total) was an engineering showpiece, but most were a disaster in timing. Only the first three cars, the front-engine Chevrolet sports cars, were an unqualified success, and they won races for years after Reventlow sold them. It had started in August 1957, when Reventlow and Bruce Kessler were looking for cars to drive the next season, and they decided they could build an all-American car that was as good as the best European cars. Duntov had demonstrated the capability of the Chevrolet engine at Sebring, but ever since the AMA racing ban that followed, a number of the best racing talents had been at loose ends.

Reventlow finally put it all together: Dick Troutman, Tom Barnes, Phil Remington, Warren Olson, Chuck Daigh, Jim Travers and Frank Coon (Traco), Ken Miles, Emil Deidt—and the Chevrolet engine and transmission. For a given set of racing rules it was an unbeatable combination. The rules wouldn't stay static, however, and by the time the first car was running in January 1958, European racing was limited to 3-liters. Work was begun on an Offy-powered Scarab, but the car was simply too big for that engine.

With all the experience behind it, the very first car was a masterpiece as it rolled out the door. It was of fairly conventional layout for that period, with front-engine, front independent suspension, deDion rear axle and a tubular space

Scarab 1958: The original hand-formed aluminum body as it first appeared. After cooling tests and a few races, the grille was closed down to about half this size, and it was painted in the familiar blue and white scallops.

frame, but the execution was its strong point. Ken Miles made the basic frame drawings, and it was constructed by the master chassis builders, Troutman-Barnes. The front suspension was of parallel, unequal length wishbones mounting a Ford knuckle, and the rear was a deDion tube located by trailing radius rods and a roller-guide. The differential was a standard Halibrand quick-change, but it mounted some very unusual inboard brakes. All four brakes were drums, perhaps the last, most advanced ever used on a competitive race car. The drums were custom-cast in aluminum with deep radial fins, and metal-sprayed on the wearing surface. A shroud was built up over the fins to form centrifugal fans at the rear, while the wheels served the same purpose in front. Because of the extreme width, 4.0 inches in front and 3.5 inches in the rear, custom shoes and linings had to be built.

Although over the years, the engines came in many sizes, the first 283 blocks were opened up to 302 and 340 cubic inches. They were also totally modified to the highest standards, including Hilborn injection, Racer Brown cam, Vertex magneto, and complete head work and headers. It was hardly necessary, though, because the car/driver/engine combination was so strong that it seldom had to run at the limit. In testing and practice at Willow Springs, Riverside, and Phoenix in the spring of 1958, it demolished course records at the hands of Daigh, Kessler, Reventlow, and Richie Ginther.

The Scarab rear end was rather exotic for American sports cars. A deDion tube was located by four trailing arms and a roller-guide at the right. Huge fins on the brake drums acted as air pumps with the enclosing shroud.

In its first race, at Palm Springs, the Scarab went out with a cracked cylinder wall, but it was so potent while it ran, that the engines were conserved somewhat after that. Reventlow and Daigh campaigned two of the cars sporadically throughout the year, while car number three was being fitted with the 3-liter engine. It was a sensational show, if only half successful, in that the two Scarabs were nearly always fastest until one of them broke. At that, since it was a team effort, Scarab won practically every race entered under Reventlow's sponsorship. That wasn't good enough for Reventlow, however, because the competition wasn't of world-beating quality. He considered the sports cars technically obsolete, and under those conditions, winning wasn't important.

At the beginning of the 1959 season, all three of the sports cars were moved out so that work could be continued on the new Formula 1 cars. The

Chuck Daigh in one of the two right-hand drive race cars at Laguna Seca in November 1958. Daigh, Reventlow, Ginther, and Kessler campaigned these cars while the original was being fitted with a 3-liter four for International events.

two road-racing cars were sold to the Peter Hand Brewery Company and Nickey Chevrolet to be raced by Jim Jeffords, Harry Heuer, and Augie Pabst. The original test car, the prototype, had the "four" removed, and was rebuilt with a slightly more docile Chevrolet engine for Reventlow to drive on the street. Mufflers were installed and carburetors and a distributor replaced the fuel injection and magneto. The exterior was refinished in concourse condition, and to make it a little more practical and legal, it was fitted with a glass wind-shield, wipers, bumpers, and upholstery.

Under the sponsorship of the "Meister-Brauer" racing team, the two racing Scarabs were just as successful, and for years they continued to win road races all across the United States. Many detail changes were made as minor components gave up, but the basic design was still competitive in SCCA amateur racing through 1962. Perhaps Reventlow should have stayed with the sports cars, since the succeeding effort to build an American Formula 1 car was continually frustrated. When rules changes didn't scratch a project, lack of development or lagging technology did. Finally, after five years of fighting, they had to give up as a money-losing company. In April 1962, the doors closed behind the last Scarab, the 3-liter, rear-engine Buick which Mecom was to race to further glory.

In this same period, there was a strong effort from a British race car builder—using the Chevrolet engine. In 1957, the name Lister was almost

Harry Heuer and Augie Pabst in the Scarabs at El Paso, 1960. After Reventlow sold the two race cars, they were raced for a number of years by the Meister-Brauer Team until replaced by a pair of front-engine Chaparrals.

Reventlow kept the development Scarab and restored it for street use. It was fitted with mufflers, wipers, bumpers, and upholstery. The engine was also detuned somewhat, but it was still one of the fastest cars in Beverly Hills.

synonymous with Jaguar. Brian Lister was expanding his ornamental iron-works into building race cars, starting with MGTC powerplants and working through Bristols to the D-Jaguar engine. But the same 3-liter 1958 FIA decision that had caught Reventlow was disturbing Lister, because the 3.8-liter Jag was barely adequate as it was. Briggs Cunningham was racing the Lister-Jag in the U.S., with Walt Hansgen driving, and he had experience with American V-8's in his own race cars. So he commissioned Lister to build him a car with the Chevy V-8 for American racing.

The Lister chassis was still of the current standard layout, but it was stronger than necessary for Jag power. The frame was made up of a pair of large-diameter tubular rails, with raised crossmembers for the front and rear suspension. Up front the suspension consisted of simple and not-too-efficient parallel, equal-length wishbones, and in the rear it had the deDion, which was the inspiration for Reventlow's cars. It naturally used many Jaguar pieces, such as the sprung differ-ential and disc brakes, but it was somewhat lighter than the great D-type. With its monstrous tail and droopy nose, the Lister was a wild-looking machine, but not too sophisticated compared to the competition it was to meet. On the other hand, it was exceedingly durable, and frequently outlasted everything else. But most important, it was far more available than other American cars it raced against, such as the Scarab, and spare parts existed.

A typically brutal-looking Lister-Corvette at VIR, in 1958, with Fred Windridge driving. This was the first semi-production Chevrolet-powered sports racer, and it became quite popular among the really bold amateur drivers.

Duntov had been making his engines easily available since Sebring, and one soon found its way to England. The ladder-tube frame made installation far easier than it was in the semi-space frame D-Jag, although the Chevy was somewhat wider than the original six. In fact, the result seemed so natural that many of the original Lister-Jags in this country were eventually converted.

Another limited-production Chevrolet sports car that was conceived in the fruitful 1957–58–59 years began in Southern California—with a little help from Ireland. Bill Devin had been building fiberglass sports-car bodies for years, and he was involved in a few complete cars for racing, such as a front-wheel-drive Panhard and a Porsche special. But when an Irish sports-car builder asked for a body to install on his Jaguar-engined tube chassis, Devin decided to keep in touch. The finished product was so well-detailed that Devin began contemplating marketing entire vehicles in the United States, instead of simply bodies. The Jaguar engine wasn't quite to Devin's preference, however, so he requested a chassis that could take the American standard 283 Chevrolet.

Because it was based on Jaguar components, the Irish-built chassis was very similar to the Lister, with the Salisbury differential and inboard rear disc brakes, large-diameter steel tube frame, and parallel, equal-length front A-frames. It was considerably cheaper, however, in that it was available without

Bill Devin's first production sports car used this ladder-tube frame imported from Ireland to take the Chevrolet engine and transmission and Devin body. Running gear and suspension was somewhat similar to the Lister's.

the expensive aluminum body and D-Jag engine. The first chassis to arrive in California was quite different from the prototype. To make more room for the V-8, and to get the seats between the frame tubes, the frame was widened between the front and rear crossmembers. The original frame wasn't any too stiff, anyhow, so additional crossmembers were welded in at the proper location to mount the engine and transmission. Also, the upper tube structure was revised to more closely fit the Devin body. Actually, the body was modified specifically for this chassis, to allow more room for passengers and luggage, and it also had integral mounting brackets in the necessary locations.

The original Devin SS was fitted with a relatively stock engine. The 283 Chevrolet was equipped with all high-performance equipment, except that the astronomical fuel injection was replaced with dual four-barrels to hold costs down. Even the stock cast iron headers and a stock Corvette radiator were used. At that, in full street trim—upholstery, windshield, wipers, heavy-duty wire wheels, and mufflers—it was still only slightly heavier than the Lister. Devin's original purpose was to take advantage of low-cost Irish labor in producing the car for under $6,000, and considering the appearance of the first cars, it would have been quite a bargain. But months of development and perfection of details meant that each car ended up being practically custom-built, and they had to be sold at closer to $10,000. However, that still beat the used-car price of $17,000 on a year-old Scarab.

The finished Devin SS in street trim was an exceedingly well-detailed limited-production sports car, but at just under $10,000 it was difficult to find a large market or to stay in business, in spite of economical European labor.

The Devin SS was built primarily as a street sports car, with all the necessary comfort refinements, but Devin couldn't deny the value of free racing publicity. One of the first cars went to Pete Woods, a former D-Jag racer, to run in local SCCA road races. Operating on his own, and racing with all the street hardware, Woods won the regional C-Modified championship in Southern California.

Over a period of years, Devin turned out a total of fifteen of the Chevy-powered SS's, but with all the detail hand work he felt was necessary, production could never reach the volume that was needed to be profitable. It is quite possible that he was too much of a perfectionist to be a successful businessman. Later, he began building complete Porsche- and Corvair-powered sports cars with a similar body, and he showed a new coupe design at the New York Auto Show in 1964, but time and financing were running out. All the orders he received on the coupe had to be refunded and Devin Enterprises was out of business.

Yet still another car builder in Denver had gotten the same idea at about the same time. Bob Carnes started building the first Bocar in his garage in the spring of 1958. He had built and raced various other conversions in the past, but this was his first all-out complete home-built. Although it was not a particularly good-handling road-racing car, it was light and powerful, and attractive enough to find a buyer when Carnes decided to improve it in another model. Finally, after making an educational number of mistakes and corrections in his first three complete vehicles, he decided to finalize the design, and he went into limited production on his XP-4.

The XP-4 was of classic—if oversimplified—design for American V-8-powered sports cars. Fiberglass body, tube space frame, live rear axle, and, of course, the 283 Chevrolet and four-speed gearbox. Because of his experience with Porsches and Jaguars, Carnes used some European components in the suspension and brakes, but not without considerable difficulty. The brakes caused so much trouble that he eventually went to the Corvette heavy-duty cerametallics. At that, his reputation was so strong in Colorado hill-climbs and road racing, that the first five XP-4's were built and sold almost immediately. Before the first full year of Bocar operations was over, Carnes began production on the next version, the more refined XP-5.

The Bocar body was designed from low-drag aircraft principles, neglecting the then unrealized problems of aerodynamic lift. Although the shape was wind-tunnel tested, the lift was so great on the front that when a wheel came off during a track test, the brake drum didn't contact the ground until its speed dropped below 90 mph. Even so, the body and frame were far more advanced than the suspension. Whereas most specially built sports racers of 1959 had independent rear suspension, all Bocars used a standard Chevrolet live rear axle, located by four trailing links, the lower two of which were Porsche rear torsion bar arms. In addition, there was an upper A-frame mounted high in the center, which was to prevent lateral movement. By all logical analysis, it should also

Bob Carnes's Bocars at the factory in Denver. On the right is the production XP-5 as it was sold for street use, and at the left is an XP-6 with coupe top which was set up for road races and hill-climbs such as Pikes Peak.

The space-frame Bocar chassis was certainly well-triangulated, but the suspension was out of date. Note the driver's seating position next to the engine. On later models the front axle was moved forward to clear a supercharger.

have prevented any roll whatsoever, but perhaps through bending of components, it merely acted as an anti-roll bar. The front suspension was right off a Porsche, and it was one of the most understeering designs available, if the car *did* lean in a corner. But it was a simple, light car, it had good weight distribution, low drag, and the Chevrolet engine and transmission. All five were sold at the list price of $8,700.

The XP-6 was a rather unusual one-off. Bob Carnes was in racing to *win,* and what his cars lacked in finesse, he planned to make up for in power. In the rarified air of Denver, there is no quicker route to power than supercharging, and so he decided to adapt a GMC 4-71 Roots-type blower to the 283 engine. To avoid bulging the hood and ruining the body lines, it was driven off the nose of the engine, and the pressure plumbing was ducted up to the standard Rochester fuel injection housing. Of course, this meant that more space was needed in the engine room, which Carnes solved by stretching an XP-5 body and chassis over a foot in the cowl area. It looked rather odd, with a 104-inch wheelbase, and it must have been a chore to get around the Pikes Peak switchbacks it was intended for, but with all that power it was certainly an improvement over the previous models. Part of the improvement could have also been due to the abandonment of the Porsche front suspension. The torsion bars were retained, but the upper arm was replaced by double ball-jointed trailing links, and a solid tubular front axle was used to link the front knuckles. Lateral location was by a Panhard rod.

The 7.00 x 16 racing tires of 1960 were simply not capable of handling 500 horsepower on road-racing courses, however, and Carnes's next run of XP-7's was built without blowers. Apparently, the long wheelbase and solid front axle were significant aids to handling, as they were continued on all subsequent models. Otherwise, the XP-7 was identical to the XP-5, although the 100-pound weight gain had a slight effect on performance.

For the Stiletto and XP-9 chassis, Carnes kept the same dimensions, but in returning to the nose-driven blower, needed more space again. The Porsche lateral torsion bars were placed longitudinally in the chassis, next to the engine instead of in front of it. At the same time, the list price of a complete running Bocar had risen to $11,000 with the blown engine. As usually happens, costs were rising and demand was dropping correspondingly. With such a small production run, one or two lost customers was a large percentage of lost sales. As a last ditch effort, the all new Stiletto body was built on an XP-9 chassis. It was wider and longer (primarily in front overhang) and sensationally styled. Carnes raced it around the country in SCCA events with little success, and the business began to suffer. In 1961, when things looked darkest, a fire destroyed the entire Bocar factory. After the insurance was settled, one of Carnes's loyal Denver customers bought out the rights and what equipment remained, and tried to reestablish the design as the Gazelle. Capitalization did not materialize, and neither the Bocar nor the Gazelle was heard from again.

The last Bocar, a "Stiletto" body on an XP-9 chassis, was raced by Carnes everywhere from Pikes Peak to Daytona in 1960, before a fire at the factory destroyed most of the fiberglass molds and put him out of business.

Jim Hall testing the prototype Chaparral 1 at Riverside in 1961, with master builders Dick Troutman and Tom Barnes doing the adjusting. With the help of Hall's engineering, it was a great advancement over their previous Scarabs.

Reventlow was still trying to get his Formula 1 cars in competitive condition when another millionaire began to follow his lead. Jim Hall and his brothers were running the oil business their father had left them, and Jim also got involved in a sports-car dealership with Carroll Shelby. Although it never was a great success, that is where Jim first began racing (at 19), where he met Hap Sharp, and where he became inspired to return to college to get a degree in mechanical engineering. Hall could always afford the best, but he worked his way up slowly, until the 1960 U.S. GP at Riverside, where he became visible by running as high as third place with the world's best Grand Prix drivers. That is also where he began negotiating with Troutman-Barnes. The incomparable sports-car-building pair had left Reventlow to re-form their own independent operations, and they were anxious for a project. Jim Hall was frustrated with the unavailability of the best European race cars—and the parts with which to repair them. Hall ordered two cars to be built under his engineering direction.

It was an ideal combination; Hall's actual engineering ability, and the years of practical experience behind Troutman-Barnes. The years they had spent building, testing, and developing the three Scarab sports cars was an extremely valuable education for this next design. In the three years between the two projects, enough ideas had come up—and across the ocean—that it wasn't hard

Hall's original cast iron Chevys were built by Art Oehrli, who, like many engine builders, once worked for Traco. This photo illustrates the utter simplicity of the 1500-pound car, before advanced technology overcame racing.

to one-up the Scarabs. The fact that their chassis hadn't broken, meant they were too heavy, and compared to the Europeans, they were also too big. The prototype Chaparral 1 had a four-inch shorter wheelbase, and it was two inches narrower and fifteen inches shorter overall. In its first configuration it weighed 1500 pounds dry—almost 300 pounds lighter than the Scarab! The weight was reduced in many areas, through components that were not only made lighter, but better. The deDion rear axle was replaced with the latest design of independent rear suspension with the obvious influence of Chapman. The standard Halibrand center-section had new side plates which also incorporated the mounting brackets, and to save the weight of unneeded knock-off hubs, simple bolt-on Halibrand mag wheels were cast. Because of the lighter weight, less braking was required, which meant Girling disc brake calipers could be used. The body was simply four beautifully shaped panels of aluminum—a nose section, a tail section, and two doors, with the side-mounted fuel tanks serving as the rocker panels. Moving the tanks to this location meant that no heavy structure was necessary behind the rear wheels. Art Oehrli, who had worked at Traco, built up the engine, which was a 318 cubic inch version of the 283 Chevy. It was fairly conservative, but with this car they were willing to give up a few horsepower for reliability. The finished Chaparral 1 was something new in American sports cars—it was a masterpiece of craftsmanship, functional design, and simplicity.

The car was first tested at Riverside in June 1961, and it was so right as it was, that Hall immediately took it to Laguna Seca and picked up a second to a Birdcage Maserati, in spite of a failure in the valve train. Meanwhile, Troutman-Barnes began work on the second car for Hap Sharp, and they also started accumulating extra components for a production run. The original idea was for the group of them to build and market the cars, with Hall's financing and Troutman-Barnes's facilities. But Hall and Sharp got so involved with racing that they lost interest in trying to profit from the design. Also, there might have been a bit of reluctance to make such a potent racer available to their competitors.

So Troutman-Barnes proceeded on its own as a builder-seller. This was going on 1962, however, and the demand for Chevy-powered road-racing specials had been fairly well satiated by all the earlier cars such as Sadler, Devin, Bocar, Lister, and Scarab. It made no difference that the Chaparral 1 was by far the best yet—at a price around $15,000 each, there weren't many customers waiting in line. One car went to England, where it was run primarily in hillclimbs. The last two of a total production run of five Chaparral 1's finally went to the Meister-Brauer racing team for Pabst and Heuer, replacing the two old Scarabs. The Chaparrals could take the same engine, and yet were much smaller and lighter. Hall and Sharp ran their cars for just over two years, with moderate success and tremendous recognition, but by September 1963, the front engine design was finally proved obsolete.

One last holdout appeared about that time, but this was based more on economy than all-out performance. Bill Thomas had been around Chevrolet products for a number of years, first managing a team of Corvettes, and then handling special-effects cars for Chevrolet advertising through Bill Stroppe. While there, he met Don Edmunds, and because Stroppe was more sold on Ford and Mercury performance activities, the two of them left to handle the Chevrolet work on their own. That sort of work got a little slow, however, and so Thomas and Edmunds went their own way. They decided to get back into high performance cars, to show what they could do.

Their first project was a '62 Chevrolet, a stocker, which was built specifically for Dan Gurney to drive in the first Riverside stock-car race. It was rather unusual in those years to see a Chevrolet up among the Pontiacs and Fords, but Gurney qualified fifth without even practicing. In the first 100-mile heat, Gurney won easily, as Goldsmith, Ward, and Foyt dropped out. In the second heat, Goldsmith stayed together to finish just ahead of Gurney, who therefore took first overall. But then, *after* the race, the tech inspectors noticed that some stiffening panels and the wheel wells had been modified or removed, and Gurney was disqualified. That was enough USAC for Thomas, who decided to stick with sports cars in SCCA.

Hall and Hap Sharp ran two of the Chaparral 1's for years, while Troutman-Barnes built three more for other customers. But eventually front-engines became obsolete, and Chaparral Cars began planning the mid-engine chassis.

The Bill Thomas Cheeta was an economy street version of the old Scarab-Chaparral school, but it was also competitive in amateur road racing. This is the engine room of one of the three aluminum-bodied competition versions.

The Cheeta was never really intended to be a race car. Like most other Chevy-specials, its primary purpose was to make money. But to make money, it had to be produced as economically as possible, which meant few specially machined or welded parts. Thomas was in close with Chevrolet Engineering, so he was quite aware of the new 1963 Stingray independent rear suspension. By knowing the right people, he was able to get all the new components almost as soon as the car itself was available, and Edmunds began building a frame around the engine, driveline, and suspension. Practically every piece in the drive train, from the radiator back to the rear hubs was right out of the Corvette. One notable exception, however, was the driveshaft. There wasn't any. To get the engine as far back as possible, they simply coupled the transmission output shaft universal joint to the one on the frame-mounted differential.

At the front, 1962 Chevrolet knuckle assemblies were located 90 inches from the rear hubs, and a frame was sketched up to connect everything together.

The front suspension was finished with conventional tubular A-frames, with a large number of optional mounting holes for experimentation. At the rear, geometry was standard Stingray, but the heavy stamped trailing arms were replaced with fabricated tube arms, and the transverse leaf spring was replaced with Monroe coil/shock units. This was a few years before disc brakes were readily available, so the Cheeta used the heavy-duty Chevrolet drums, with sintered-iron linings. Most of the rest of the components were hand-made, but in conventional design for race cars of the day.

The first body was hand-formed in aluminum, to match a simple wooden buck built over the frame, and a tubular sub-structure was formed to support it. From that, molds were taken so that the production bodies could be rapidly reproduced in fiberglass for the street model. While that was going on, though, two more bodies were built in aluminum for a trio of racing versions. Jerry Titus tested the first car in the fall of 1963, and was highly impressed with its performance-per-dollar ratio. With a weight of 1500 pounds, and the recent 327 fuel-injected engine, it certainly had tremendous acceleration, and the brakes were adequate for a car of twice the weight. The handling was never widely acclaimed, however, and it was obvious that Titus's skill was making up for a lot. A local Chevrolet dealer picked up the sponsorship, and Titus raced the car briefly, but never with any outstanding success. After all, when they were in the same neighborhood, the Cheeta had to race against Hall's Chaparral. Jerry Grant also drove one of the cars, until he wrapped it up at Daytona. Cheeta number two was never raced, because it was sold to Chevrolet Engineering at about the time Duntov was building his first lightweight Stingrays. It was extensively tested, and did quite well on the skidpad, but it was concluded that the lack of torsional rigidity in the frame was responsible for the erratic handling.

Edmunds left the company to get into the more profitable USAC game, but production eventually reached a total of sixteen cars. The price was from $7,500 to $12,000, depending on equipment and state of competitiveness, but the average car went for about $9,500. Many of those cars are still running around Southern California, some on the street, some on the strip, and at least one still on road courses. By reverting to the manufacture and marketing of components only, primarily drag parts, Thomas was able to keep operating for a number of years. But finally, in 1969, the economy caught up with him, and he quit to go into the real-estate business.

As the Cheeta disappeared, another race-car builder in Chicago rode in on the rear-engine wave. Although Bob McKee has never built an all-conquering road-race car, he is probably the most prolific of all American constructors. There has never been anything sensational about his V-8-powered sports cars and Formula cars, and yet he continues to build and sell them, and he continues to make a profit. That fact ought to say more about his product than all the press clippings on the "stars" of the game.

A well-detailed Cheeta was a beautiful machine, although it had a number of critical drawbacks in either everyday transportation or control on a race track. A few of the fiberglass-bodied cars are still seen today.

Bob McKee's all-American four-speed transaxle utilizing the Borg-Warner T-10 transmission. It never replaced the Hewland, but it established McKee in the sports-car-building business which produced a number of Chevy-powered racers.

From 1955 to 1964, McKee worked on stock cars, Indy cars, dragsters, and sports cars. His first venture into sports cars was to adapt an aluminum Buick engine to a Cooper chassis for Roger Ward's first attempt at road racing. Since the available transaxles weren't satisfactory to McKee, he built his own unit mostly out of stock production American components. The basis was the common Borg-Warner T-10 four-speed gear case, fitted at the front with a McKee differential casting, and Halibrand quick-change gears on the rear. The differential took a Ford ring and pinion, but it also could accept a ZF limited-slip assembly. It was really an ingenious solution. The gear case was mounted upside down so that the input shaft could pass under the differential, thereby lowering the engine, and the output went upstairs through the quick-change gears, and back through the gear case nested between the transmission gears. The only new castings required were the differential housing, two identical side cover plates, and the quick-change gear housing. A number of new drive shafts and axle shafts were needed, but aside from that, it was all off-the-shelf hardware, including bearings and shift mechanism. At a price below $2,000, it was a bargain, and it became relatively popular in the American-engine/European-chassis craze. It was eventually used in a number of Cooper-Chevrolets, Lotus-Chevrolets, the Shelby King Cobra, and, of course, all of McKee's sports racers.

One of McKee's well-known cars, the Mark VI, driven by Mak Kronn at Laguna Seca in 1966. Although they never won any significant races, they could hardly be called unsuccessful, and the company has survived where others failed.

Soon after McKee built the Ward/Buick/Cooper transaxle, Dick Doane came to him for a specially built car to replace the Chevrolet lightweight Stingray coupe which he had sold to John Mecom. (More about that later.) McKee responded enthusiastically, and the result was the first Chevette, a name that Chevrolet probably regrets not registering. Except for the transaxle, there wasn't anything really spectacular about the car, as Hall had brought his Chaparral 2 out almost a year earlier. The Chevette had a tubular space frame much like that of the Cooper Monaco, and all the suspension arms were adjustable for the buyer to tailor the handling to his own preference. Front knuckles were Chevelle, and the rear hub carriers were Stingray. The body was rolled out of aluminum by Bill Leahy of the Meister-Brauer Team, and as each car was somewhat custom-built to order, very few McKee cars were quite the same. Since the first McKee Chevette was built for Chevrolet dealer Doane, Chevrolet components were used wherever possible. The first engine was a highly modified 363-inch cast iron "smallblock," using a fuel-injection unit like the one on his superlight Stingray. Doane did tolerably well with it in local amateur road racing, but again, it was not a radically different car.

On the other hand, unlike Chaparrals, McKee's cars were available for anyone to buy, and at $10,500 to $15,000 minus engine, there was a waiting market. Almost immediately he had orders for two more Chevettes. The second car was bought by Jerry Hansen, who ran it for two seasons, and number three was promptly crashed at Laguna Seca by Ed Leslie.

For the next two McKee cars, the name Chevette had to be dropped. They were quite similar, but the buyers had different tastes in engines. Number four had a 427 Ford, known as the LMD Special, and number five was hemi-Plymouth powered. Cars six through eight were designated McKee Mark VI, and there were significant changes. More of the production components were replaced with lighter fabricated parts, and the bodies were fiberglass instead of aluminum. Two of the cars were raced with Oldsmobile engines, but the third one, for Mak Kronn, got a Traco Chevy which pushed him to a fourth at Las Vegas and a second at Watkins Glen in the 1966 USRRC, and a win at the Road America June Sprints. Of the three updated Mark VII McKees, again two were Olds and one, taken by Bob Nagel, was a Chevy.

The next McKee-built cars were undesignated, because they were to be named the Salathe Mach I. An industrial designer for Alcoa named John Salathe decided to design and market a mid-engine Corvette-powered street/sports car since Chevrolet wasn't. He took the drawings to Bob McKee, who built two prototype chassis using a sheet aluminum backbone structure. By the time they were bodied, upholstered, and running, they were neither refined nor particularly attractive, and they went the way of all other "limited-production" specials.

Since then, McKee has built a number of exotic race cars of all kinds: the three Howmet Turbine cars, the driveline for the Adams Indy-Turbine, and the Armco 4WD-Olds. But almost every year he gets orders for Chevy-powered USAC, Formula A, or road-racing cars, and he has survived. Even Bob McKee is getting wise now, however, since his Mark 15, 16, 17, and 19 are all *electric* car prototypes. Whenever a tradeoff was necessary, McKee could always sacrifice recognition for profits, and now it looks like racing is not a very marketable venture any more. As he says, "These are less than vintage years for road racing."

What happened? Where did all the specials builders go wrong? Sadler, Devin, Bocar, Scarab, Salathe, Chaparral, Troutman-Barnes, Cheeta ... just to consider those who specialized in Chevrolet-powered sports cars. When Chevrolet Management declared that they were not going to build race cars in 1957 it looked like a tremendous market was wide open to the individual high-performance car constructor. There was such a rash of attempts right after that, that it appeared that Chevrolet must have been promoting them. Actually, however, nothing more than a few special engines and a few early four-speed transmissions (which were destined for scrap, anyhow) ever left the Engineering Center. All else was handled strictly through ordinary business channels, and paid for with real dollars. Finally, American production components were suitable for racing, and the public carried on as best it could.

With at least a decade of hindsight, it is not hard to see why so few survived. Even at the time, it was difficult to understand why some of them began. If you discount pure altruism, the only motives could be (1) to justify their racing activities (2) to satisfy a creative ego, or (3) to make a profit. The first one is understandable enough, if the involved persons were honest enough to at least admit it to themselves ... although for tax reasons they may not have admitted it openly. But those activities were certainly destined for termination, since the principal instigator could not be expected to maintain an interest in auto racing for a very long time, especially not as a driver.

Even weaker than that, was the company built around a person's need to establish himself as a famous—genius—automotive designer, engineer, manufacturer, marketer, or what have you. Those were doomed from the start, because they were based on the unlikely assumption that *their* taste was *everyone's* taste. Or that *they* finally had the right formula, and hundreds or even thousands of people wanted what they had ... and they were willing to pay for it. In a case such as that, there is no logic, no reasoning, and all you can do is sit back and watch the money flow until the truth becomes obvious, or until even the most unlimited supply runs dry.

The odds are best for those in whom the profit motive is above all else, but even then there are an incredible number of possible reasons for failure. Is the business well-capitalized? Will the market remain stable? Are *both* the engineering and management faultless? How close to perfection must the product be developed? Is the market's taste understood? What is the proper advertising? Can it endure until the volume is apparent? Will government safety or ecology standards end it all? It takes unlimited talent and determination to overcome all these obstacles, and a person who could do it could easily be the president of General Motors instead.

Even Ford Motor Company stopped producing the Cobra, and they are experiencing continual frustration in importing and marketing the special Ford-powered Pantera. Right now it looks as though that project may cost them a great deal more than it could possibly be worth.

Although a few independents survived, none of them really expected a pot of gold at the end of the rainbow. Some suspected it was there—out of reach—at Chevrolet Engineering, and that Hall, Penske, and McLaren had full access to it. To them it was obvious that they couldn't compete with that sort of collusion, and after 1963–65, most of them gave up to the common available European race cars and chassis.

3

Chevy Begins to Reappear

General Motors never consciously broke the AMA decision not to participate in "speed events." Even Chevrolet never overtly decided to go racing. But in an organization as big as General Motors, powerful individuals can conceal a large number of nebulous activities. Especially if those activities are privately admired by anyone who happens to stumble across them. Therefore, the reason Chevrolet began looking a little suspicious was not that a racing organization was formed, but because individuals—high-, middle-, and low-placed—were interested in racing, for any number of personal reasons. You will find the same interest in any corporation, but at Chevrolet, the people had the means to get involved.

As more and more upper-echelon people realized what was going on down deep inside the company, justification appeared as it was needed. The continuation of any activity was always based on the relative value of man-hours versus demonstrable results. And because of the comparatively low costs—compared to what Ford, Ferrari, Porsche, Lotus, and others were investing in competition—it didn't take much to convince the people with the purse strings that they were getting a lot for their dollars. As far as the corporation hierarchy was concerned … a few people had made a relatively arbitrary, inconsequential decision, and since they felt it had no great influence on the corporation one way or another, it simply was not worth internal policing. There were other problems far greater than that of a few inside people who were racing fanatics.

One of the most prominent enthusiasts was Bill Mitchell, who became head of GM Styling in December 1958. Mitchell had always been sketching advanced designs for the Corvette, some of which were based on his impression of a fish called the stingray. When he reached the top of Styling, he acquired both the influence and personal finances necessary to build his own sports car. Of course, General Motors was always receptive to exotic, new styling exercises with which to promote the product, and there was no reason why a body should not be built on an obsolete racing chassis. The chassis

Bill Mitchell's original Stingray, a new fiberglass body on Duntov's Sebring SS Corvette test chassis. The aerodynamics were poor, and it was still not totally debugged, but it generated sensational publicity wherever Mitchell ran it.

Mitchell had in mind was the first tube-framed Corvette SS which Duntov built for Sebring in 1957—the "mule." Duntov had stored both the mule and the finished SS very carefully when the AMA shut his work off, and now, over a year later, there seemed to be no future for either car. Mitchell was quite welcome to use one for experimental Corvette body design.

The mule was actually the better of the two chassis, because it had been the development car, and so very little was ever done to it after the Sebring race. When Mitchell got the car, he merely stripped off the well-used original fiberglass SS body to make room for his new design. The Stingray shape had already been wind-tunnel tested, but this was before there was any real comprehension of the problems of high-speed driving. There was no other data on sports cars to compare the drag and lift to, nor was there a background of experience to indicate how to reduce either one. In spite of the "logical" theory of an inverted airfoil shape holding the car down, the model still seemed to be rather light in the front. More concerned with appearance, and unaware of the severity of the problem, the skin was molded up as it was. The first panels were laid up in .125-inch fiberglass, because the frame was not designed to support this particular shape, making the mounting points too far apart. When that body shell proved its strength, however, the same styling molds were used to produce a skin of only half that thickness. To maintain the same rigidity, the lighter skin was reinforced with ribs molded around strips of balsa, and yet it still weighed 75 to 100 pounds less than the first one.

Because the "ducktail" and "spoiler" had not been invented yet, the driver had to compensate for aerodynamic lift as best he could. Nose lift was countered somewhat by raising the rear and lowering the front, as predicted by the wind-tunnel tests, but it still turned out to be a challenge to control at high speeds. The car was raked forward at Elkhart Lake, and it was noted that not only did it corner faster, but it was much faster down the straight. This was the first proof (to GM engineers) of that old aircraft theory that lift contributes to drag.

While the car was being rebuilt at GM Styling, Mitchell was fortunate to have the assistance of an engineer who had been on the original Sebring team. When Duntov's crew was broken up, Dean Bedford left Chevrolet to work for Peter Kyropolous at Styling. Therefore, when the car showed up, rebodied, at his new location, Bedford was an obvious and willing participant. The operation wasn't quite the size of the original effort, however, as it was no longer condoned by the corporation. The car was let out of the GM gates in running condition, but that does not mean it was in debugged *racing* condition, and Mitchell's sponsorship could only be stretched so far. There was enough money for Bedford and the mechanic, Ken Escheback, to get the car to the track, but there was no prize money or outside sponsorship to bolster the program. Both of them had to keep up at their regular jobs at GM Styling. When the Stingray was first run, at Marlboro in April 1959, with Dick Thompson driving, a large number of development problems became obvious. Duntov was there for its maiden flight, but when the best the car could do was a fourth behind two Porsches and a Lister-Jag, he conceded that it needed more work than he had time for.

In addition to the aerodynamic lift problems with the new body, there were a number of mechanical alterations necessary. The basic chassis was quite strong enough, and the suspension and driveline were still advanced for their day, but small detail improvements can use up a lot of time and dollars. The car was too heavy—every race car is too heavy if it doesn't break—and in its second season the body and brackets were lightened. To lighten the front end and improve cooling, an aluminum radiator was installed after these became available on the production Corvette. The springs and shocks turned out to be too soft for Thompson's preference, so they were stiffened to reduce roll and eliminate bottoming. At the same time, of course, the anti-roll bars had to be switched around. Two of the problems that plagued the SS at Sebring, suspension bushing failure and differential bearing wear, were countered by replacing these components at regular intervals, because there was no time for a redesign. Apparently, the cause of retirement at Sebring was only one of many durability problems that would have occurred eventually. Even if each problem had been taken care of on the spot and the car limped to the finish, it never could have run 24 hours at LeMans without an extensive durability development program.

The brakes never were satisfactory, either in durability or balance. Throughout its last two seasons, the car served as sort of a test bed for Delco-Moraine in the improvement of linings and brake fluid. Finally, a sintered-iron lining was settled on, which had to be welded to the shoes. The dual-leading-shoe design was still prone to lockup on the Stingray, but as an option on the stock Corvette of 1960, the new linings were almost satisfactory for amateur racing.

The Kelsey-Hayes vacuum-boosted anti-lock rear brake system was a noble experiment, but even two years after its introduction at Sebring it was still not refined enough for competition. The first race for the Stingray was run in the rain, where anti-lock should be at its best advantage, and yet Thompson could not get the right proportioning ratio and he spent most of the race learning how to cope with them. There was another worry in that the automatic anti-lock actuator was vacuum-operated, and as Bedford explains the system, a sudden loss of vacuum would have fully locked up the rear wheels. Finally, the entire system was pulled out and replaced with a standard production vacuum-boosted system.

The original Stingray may not have been an unbeatable race car, but it was a sensational crowd-pleaser wherever it went. Because it was a one-off, it had to run in C-Modified—the fastest class in SCCA road racing of that day—against the best European sports cars. That meant that usually a single American car was pitted against Maseratis, Ferraris, Listers, D-Jags, etc., and Thompson could do no wrong. Throughout 1959, they usually ran second to Walt Hansgen in either a Lister-Jag or a Maserati, but the car was improved by degrees, and in the 1960 season, Thompson and Mitchell's Stingray were National Champions in C-Modified.

Toward the end of the 1960 season the excitement started to wear off. Bedford had plans for improving the Stingray during the winter, which would have cured most of the difficulties. It really needed an anti-roll bar at the rear, and the nose should have been dropped more, and it was time to adopt disc brakes. But Mitchell was under pressure from corporate management. What he did with his own money on his own time still reflected on his position with GM. It was bad enough that he *looked* guilty by association, but there was a question of legal liability because it was actually GM's car. It had worn out its promotional value, anyhow, and so Mitchell brought it back to the Styling garages. If nothing else, it must have been quite a relief to his pocketbook. From then on, Mitchell continued to build exotic "sports cars," but never anything that was not practical for street use. In fact, the Stingray was later modified so that he could drive it on the street. The exhaust was quieted, and a radiator fan was added, and finally, Dunlop disc brakes were installed. The original engine, a 283 with the Sebring fuel injection, was the most faultless part of the car. But it was rather loose, and the compression ratio was a little high for everyday use, so a specially-built 377 was installed under the aluminum heads. The car may not be *strictly* street legal, but Mitchell says that the local police keep an eye out for him and

Elkhart Lake, 1960: Dr. Dick Thompson temporarily leading Augie Pabst's winning Scarab. Thompson raced the Stingray through 1959 and 1960, before it was returned to GM Styling, where Mitchell converted it to street use.

his expensive creations. Who would *dare* get into an accident with an irreplaceable antique such as the original Stingray. The original Sebring SS Corvette was restored and donated to the Indianapolis museum when it began getting in the way at the Chevrolet warehouse. But the Stingray—when not being driven—shares a special fireproof garage with a few other Mitchell creations.

It would be interesting to see how either car would perform today with all the latest bolt-on advancements. Add a plow and rear spoiler, mount the latest Can-Am tires, install an all-aluminum engine. There would still be the disadvantage of the front-engine, but it might be surprising to see just how much has been gained from tires and aerodynamics alone.

Both cars were extremely significant for their time. The Sebring SS was Chevrolet's only "factory team" assault into all-out professional road racing, and the impulsive, cursory attempt helped bring the curtain down on that sort of activity. On the other hand, the Stingray was the first venture into a new era of "reserved interest," and it served as sort of a test case as to the GM interpretation of the AMA decision.

Meanwhile, back at Chevrolet, engineering research was continuing on a grand scale. Schilling had replaced Olley as head of R&D, and in February 1959, he brought in Duntov and an engineer named Frank Winchell. There was a new vehicle under design, called the "Q car," which was to have a conventional front engine, but with a rear-mounted transaxle and independent suspension. Winchell had come from the transmission group, where he was responsible for the Corvair transaxle, so his purpose was obvious, but Duntov's major interest was still Corvette, and all he could see was the application of the transaxle to a mid-engine Corvette. Before long he was visiting with Mitchell over at Styling, and they came up with a layout mounting the 283 V-8 behind the driver and ahead of the "Q car" transaxle. Mitchell even went so far as to create full-size clay models of the proposed Corvette. The "Q" was dropped, however, and without mass-production justification for the transmission, a mid-engine Corvette was impossible.

That didn't stop Duntov, though, as he still wanted to work with a mid-engine layout. The best rationalization he could come up with was a research vehicle for testing tires, independent rear suspensions, and vehicle dynamics in general. There were a number of spare parts left over from the SS program, so it didn't take much to put the car together. The engine and four-speed were moved rearward to mate directly to the Halibrand quick-change differential from the SS, and the driver was moved forward, in line with the engine. When it came to getting the driver's feet, the pedals, and a crossmember structure between the front wheels, the wheelbase had grown to 96 inches, four inches more than the SS. Of course, later transaxle designs which mounted the differential between the engine and transmission shortened that back down to about 90 inches.

The internals of Duntov's CERV-I. Its all-aluminum engine was overshadowed by the general appearance. With the transmission between the engine and differential, the driver had to be squeezed up against the front suspension.

Practically all of the front suspension was directly from the SS—control arms, steering, spindles, even the Halibrand knock-off wheels. But new progressively-wound springs were tried, and the tread was widened by four inches. At the rear, Duntov gave up on the deDion tube axle to try fully independent suspension, using the drive axles as the upper links. After all, this *was* a suspension test vehicle, and in fact, the geometry was very similar to that of the production Corvette independent rear suspension which was to show up almost three years later. Outside of that, very little else was needed to construct the new car. A tubular space frame resembling the SS frame in construction and tube size was built around the components, and a simple fiberglass shell added over that. The fuel containers were flexible rubber bladders in the sides, which was perhaps the first automotive application of military aircraft fuel cells. That was one innovation that fortunately was never put to functional evaluation.

One of the most far-reaching aspects of the car, however, was practically ignored. It had an aluminum-block 283 cubic inch engine. Aluminum heads had been run at Sebring in 1957, but this was the first Chevrolet vehicle to run a driveline with absolutely no cast iron components. Every casting, from the water pump to the differential, was a lightweight alloy. There were not even iron liners in the cylinders, because this was one of the very first experiments with the high-silicon alloy that is now used in the Vega engine. Obviously, the external appearance of the car was so sensational, that the announcement of an all-aluminum engine in it was of small consequence. It really didn't make much difference in the vehicle, anyhow, because all the overweight components borrowed from the SS kept the total weight over 1500 pounds.

When the car was exposed to the press during tire tests at Riverside in the winter of 1960, it had quite an impact on those who were aware of the SS and the Stingray. To hold down speculation as to its ultimate purpose, Duntov constantly referred to it as the CERV, an acronym for Chevrolet Engineering Research Vehicle. But the fact that it was suitable to be raced in the SCCA's Formula Libre, and the chassis was within USAC's dimensions for Indy cars, whetted everyone's imagination. It didn't help a bit when the car was shown at such places as Riverside, Sebring, Daytona, Continental Divide Raceway, and Pikes Peak. But Duntov knew better. Perhaps he had something other than pure research in mind when the car was under construction, but by the time it was running, Mitchell's corporate experience with the Stingray had demonstrated exactly what the policy was on racing activities. And Mitchell had far more influence than Duntov. At one time there was a scheme whereby Firestone would borrow the car for tire tests, and test their tires up Pikes Peak in the summer of 1961. In advance trials, however, it appeared that the car was not up to the current record, and so the possibility of dire corporate repercussions scratched the attempt. But as for its affirmed purpose, the CERV was a success. It demonstrated beyond a doubt that the vehicle dynamics of a rear-engine car were manageable at the limit of adhesion. A lot had been learned

Duntov demonstrating the CERV at Riverside in the winter of 1960. Because the vehicle dynamics of rear-engine cars was just being researched, it was fitted with an odd mixture of tires on the front and rear.

A private practice session at Pikes Peak in 1961. Duntov was going to loan the car out for a record attempt, but erroneous times indicated that it was too slow, and corporate influence caused the program to be cancelled.

Riverside, 1962: The first battle between the new production Stingray and the new Shelby Cobra. The Corvette was obviously outclassed, as it was far heavier, but that prompted Duntov to start on the superlight Grand Sports.

since the pre-war Auto-Union race cars established the axiom that "rear-engine cars oversteer."

That was not the end of the CERV, though. It was a research tool, and it remained in sporadic use for over ten years. Duntov kept updating it with the latest engines available and many other components under development. Finally, with a 327 aluminum engine with Weber sidedraft carbs, a new, more slender body shell, and the latest racing tires, the car was timed at 206 mph around the 4.5-mile banked circle at the GM Proving Grounds. Perhaps that proved nothing about production cars at highway speeds, but ... like Everest ... it was there. The car was available, the track was available, and it cost nothing to run. It won't happen again, though, because the CERV was subsequently donated to the Briggs Cunningham Museum.

After building the CERV, Duntov had little time to spare for competition activities, anyhow. The most radical Corvette revision of all was in the works—the production 1963 Stingray. It had its own all-new frame and suspension, a totally new body design, and it was a major project to detail and debug. By the summer of '62 it was about ready to go to the showrooms—but so was a new Ford project called the Cobra. Ford had recently made an official break from the AMA non-race decision (though they were never persecuted in any way for it), and one of their many blooming competition activities was a road-racing

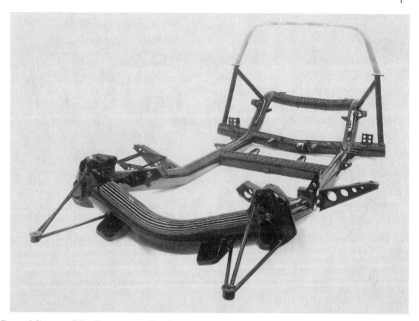

The Grand Sport (GS) Corvette tube frame with integral roll bar. The outriggers supported the radiator, while other mounts (from the front) are: front suspension, engine, clutch, body, transmission and seat mounts, and rear suspension pickups.

team run by Carroll Shelby. Duntov was more than a little curious as to how the two cars compared—after all, Chevrolet could not afford to have their advanced new sports car humiliated by an upstart California hybrid.

Duntov had good information that the Cobra was going to have its first racing exposure at Riverside in October, and he made Stingray racing debut plans accordingly. Before the Stingray had even been officially announced, Mickey Thompson received one that had been well-used as a brake test vehicle at the GM Proving Grounds. It had a pre-production body which was hand-built, and was far heavier than the assembly-line versions, but the car was a fairly accurate representation. Supposedly, the Cobra was also, which would be one of the very rare occurrences of two showroom-stock cars having an honest showdown. And it was a disaster. For as long as it lasted, the Cobra (with Billy Krause driving) ran off from all the Corvettes, including Doug Hooper in Thompson's new Stingray. Statistically, it could have been anticipated, as the Stingray was 50 percent heavier with only 25 percent more displacement— and the Cobra was due to get an even larger engine. But that was no consolation to Duntov. He immediately got with Bunkie Knudsen, the current General Manager at Chevrolet, and they decided on the strategy—a lighter Stingray.

Corvette had a strong reputation at the time. There were good amateur drivers racing them with notable success all across the country. All they needed

The dressed chassis ready for its body. Although the front suspension was of conventional geometry, it was obviously lighter than the production suspension. This engine was merely installed for mockup, as the racing versions had Weber carbs.

A rear view shows chassis identification "No. 1," the alloy differential castings, cutoff frame, and relocated fuel tank. This was the last high-performance vehicle that was designed around skinny racing tires and wheels.

A standard Chevrolet chassis "stroking machine" used for determining the stress capability in the GS tube frame. Pneumatic cylinders pound the suspension up and down, while an air motor torques the driveline.

was the basic raw material, and Chevrolet would not have to get involved with factory support. The FIA had a minimum limit of 100 identical cars to qualify as production, and Chevrolet could easily build and sell that number of any-thing, at practically any price. It couldn't be an obvious *race* car, but a light-weight version of the production Corvette seemed to be within the letter of the AMA rule. And so Duntov and his first lieutenant, Walt Zetye, immediately set out to build a hundred Stingrays as light as possible, as rapidly as possible.

It was quite a project. To begin with, the entire frame was thrown out and redesigned. There wasn't time to build tube space-frames to fit inside that many Stingray bodies, so a simple, large-diameter tube "ladder-frame" was constructed. The longitudinal tubes ran directly from the front suspension attachment points to a kickup which mounted the differential assembly, and everything else was subjugated to the frame. All component mounting points (for engine, differential, suspension, body, and controls) were kept in the same location, but they were far lighter than stock, and there were no sacrifices to comfort, convenience, or durability. The frame ended at the suspension points because there were no bumpers and no need for structure other than radiator and spare tire supports. Suspension geometry was nearly stock, but all compo-nents were fabricated by hand or extensively lightened. To anyone who has seen a production Stingray chassis, this one was a work of art. When finished,

A special hand-laid-up, lightweight fiberglass Corvette body for the GS. Not only were all the panels much thinner, but many components, such as the disappearing headlights, were replaced with integral structures.

the entire frame, suspension, and driveline were mounted on a "stroking machine" to determine whether lightness had been overdone to the point of weakness. This is a standard procedure for all production prototypes—rapidly cycling typical stresses into the chassis—but in the case of a race car, it requires racing loads and yet fewer cycles.

The steel sub-frame that supports the body is a rather complex structure, so it was merely trimmed and drilled to within a pound of its function. The body, however, was specially molded to the last panel. Instead of the thick "random fiber" components produced in matched molds, it was hand-laid-up from the stronger woven fiberglass cloth. And at that, many superfluous pieces were left out if they merely added to comfort or convenience. The doors were literally empty of hardware, as the plexiglass windows were raised by a Velcro strap, and even the stock-appearing dash was gutted. At the same time, all the interior upholstery was replaced by panels barely strong enough to support their own weight—but it *looked* like a production interior. Even the lightweight bucket seats were custom built in the Chevrolet shops.

When it was finished, the first Grand Sport (or GS-I) Corvette weighed 1900 pounds. This may not seem too light for a racing car, but it was a 37 percent reduction from the production sports car! And ... with mufflers and a

The first production GS Corvette rolling off the assembly line. It could have been great commercial success, but after a total run of five units out of a planned one hundred, production was shut down for political reasons.

little detuning, it would still make a fairly practical coupe for street use. It was assembled in time to take along on a test trip to Florida in December 1962. Mickey Thompson had picked up another production Stingray and was renting the Sebring track to practice for the race in March. He was promoting his own speed equipment for Chevrolet engines, and yet he needed Chevrolet's help, so he and Duntov shared the track.

Duntov's primary interest was in developing a raceable brake for both the stock Stingray and his Grand Sport, but it was also a chance to see how competitive the cars were. Dick Thompson and Masten Gregory were there with Duntov, and Doug Hooper and Bill Krause were driving Thompson's cars. The GS-I was by far the star of the show, but none of the cars was satisfactory in brake durability. The Corvette drums with cerametallic linings were not ideal, as they had a tendency to pull or lock up when overheated. But the production cars were too heavy for the available Kelsey-Hayes, Lockheed, or Girling discs under test. Even the GS-I was marginal as it was with the Girling system.

A little too much information leaked out about the Sebring testing, however, and GM management announced in January that Chevrolet was definitely *not* going to build 100 lightweight Corvettes. The five that were built or under construction at that time were to be scrapped or sold or used as test vehicles,

Daytona 1963: The start of the race for "GT" cars on the banked oval. A 421 Pontiac Tempest "ringer" took the pole, and the race, while Mickey Thompson's special 427 Corvettes dropped out in the rain due to handling problems.

One of Thompson's Corvettes on the banks ahead of Goldsmith's Tempest in the rain. This was the first public appearance of the mysterious new 427 Chevy, and chassis technology wasn't up to the extra weight.

Daytona 1963: The "slightly illegal" new 427 Chevrolet engine in NASCAR. Here Johnny Rutherford in Smokey Yunick's familiar No. 13 leads G.C. Spencer's 427 Chevy, a Pontiac, and eventual winner Tiny Lund in a Ford.

but Duntov had to be very careful what happened, because the corporate eye was on him. But the situation immediately got worse. With Ford's return to overt racing, and Duntov's "obvious" racing program going on inside, the Chevrolet Engine Group had shipped out a number of new engines that had just been developed. These were of an all-new 427 design to replace the 348-409-427 "truck" engines. Not only was the new 427 lighter, it had a sensationally different head design. With individual rocker pivots as on the smallblock, the valves could be inclined laterally with respect to the camshaft, allowing a more hemispherically shaped combustion chamber. With the valve covers removed, valve stems and pushrods angled in every direction, causing the mysterious unnamed engine to be referred to as the "porcupine."

Mickey Thompson had acquired two of the engines, and he purchased two more Stingrays to put them in. The cars were set up like stock-car sedans, with roll cages, and superspeedway tires, to run at Daytona in a special preliminary race to the Continental. Unlike the Continental, the "Challenge Cup" was run only on the banked oval, and it was to compare the performance of sports-racing cars to NASCAR sedans on the same circuit. As such, the rules were rather loose, and the race included Ferraris, Porsches, production Corvettes, Thompson's Corvettes, a Pontiac Tempest, and a Maserati-Ford, which crashed in practice. The 427 Stingrays should have walked away, but all that new weight in the nose was more than could be balanced out with the limited time and current technology. The race was run in the rain, and Thompson's cars simply did not handle right. Doug Hooper lost his car frequently, and Krause finished third, six laps down. The winner was Paul Goldsmith in a "ringer," a Ray Nichels 421 Pontiac stocker in a Tempest body, and A.J. Foyt was second in a production Stingray. Corvettes did even worse the next day in the road race, with Dick Thompson in a production Stingray third behind two Ferraris, and nine-tenths of the rest dropping out in the first half—including the two porcupine engines.

A number of the engines also found their way into NASCAR. They were not exactly the same 427 engine that was being marketed in the showrooms, but Bill France allowed them to be weaseled into the Daytona 500 to create a little excitement. And they did indeed. Suddenly, the obscure Chevrolet sedans were the fastest things on the track. This time they were driven by Junior Johnson, Rex White, and a new driver for Smokey Yunick, Johnny Rutherford. And again they failed to finish. By then, however, the publicity was entirely too great, and all the "porcupines" were recalled, leaving those who cared, to run the more legal 427 truck-derived engine in NASCAR.

Sebring came and went, and there was no sign of the Grand Sport Corvettes. They didn't show up for their stated goal, and Duntov was "clean" again. Actually, he no longer had much to work with, as he had already sold two of the three running cars. Dick Doane, a Chevrolet dealer, bought one, and Grady Davis, an executive with Gulf Oil Research, bought the other for Dr. Dick Thompson to race. In April 1963, (exactly four years after the Mitchell Stingray first appeared at the same track) Thompson quietly appeared at a Marlboro National race with the GS-I, for its first official competition. It was especially inauspicious because Thompson could not keep the car together, and when it did run, it was far from competitive in its class. As it turned out, it did take a class win in its first race, but only because it was the only car in C-Modified to finish—and last overall, at that.

Davis and Thompson kept at it, however, and the car began picking up: fifth at Cumberland, fourth at Bridgehampton and VIR, third at Elkhart, and then finally a win at Watkins Glen near the end of the season. The problem was that the car had to compete in C-Modified, like Mitchell's original Stingray race car, and that was not what it was built for—it was a Grand Touring (GT) coupe. It was also closing out the era of the front-engine race car, as the most common winning car then was the Cooper, particularly Penske's Zerex-Cooper.

At the same time, Duntov was keeping his "development" GS-I running, and trying all sorts of new engines and suspensions on it. A mere stock-design aluminum-block engine was not good enough for the original GS-I program, so he had initiated a dual-overhead-cam conversion for it. The engine was a little late, however. The first one built (of three finally assembled) was not dynoed until after the GS program had been canceled and two of the cars

Nassau 1963: The Chevrolet "factory team" garage. From the right are Foyt's Scarab/Chevy, Pabst's Lola/Chevy, Penske's Cooper/Chevy, and the three Corvettes. Hidden behind the Corvettes are two front-engined Chaparrals.

Start of the main feature at Nassau, with eight of the first ten cars recognizable as Chevrolet specials. Although Penske was fastest, Foyt stayed together for the finish, and Dick Thompson was first in the GT class.

were gone. It was quite an engine, with 550 horsepower, and Duntov ran it in his coupe for a short time.

It was obvious that Dick Thompson's car needed something to make it competitive in C-Modified, but the release of such an exotic engine would be a dead giveaway. Duntov was in the production Corvette engineering area by then, but back in R&D, Winchell and Jim Musser were still working on wheels, tires, and suspensions, and so the GS-I was loaned to them for development. Roger Penske was called in as a consultant, and the three of them began running the car at a local road course. Originally the car was built on 6-inch wide wheels, but eventually they grew to ten inches at the rear. New Goodyear 8.20 x 15 stock car tires were tried, which looked a little awkward, but there was no doubting their performance. As Penske recalls, cornering capability on the skidpad rose from 0.9 to 1.1 g's. The GS-I coupes were becoming potent sports racers … which meant that by now they ought to be terrors as prototype sports cars.

This was toward the end of 1963, and the next FIA Manufacturer's race was at Nassau. John Mecom was running a race team that consisted of the first Lola Coupe, with a Chevy engine, the last rear-engine Scarab, with a Chevy engine, and a Ferrari. He was also backing Penske's Zerex Special in American amateur racing. Dick Doan and Grady Davis still had the two Grand Sports, and Jim Hall had recently been sold Duntov's development car. Of course, he

By the time the GS Corvettes got to Nassau, tire widths had nearly doubled, necessitating the crude fender flares. New hood scoops were necessary to clear the Webers, and air scoops were tacked on the rear, but lift was never cured.

was also currently running his front-engine Chaparral 1. When this accumulation of four Chevy-powered sports racers, and three lightweight Corvettes, and their professional drivers and crews, all showed up for the boat ride to Nassau, practically everyone else went into shock. Carroll Shelby, who had expected a runaway with his Cobras, almost fell off the pier. In Nassau, everyone with a Chevrolet engine naturally tended to congregate in the same area, and so it "obviously" was a Chevrolet factory effort. Chevrolet engineering was not totally disinterested, however. Duntov was there to watch, although he might have well had two broken arms and laryngitis as far as being any help was concerned.

On the other hand, there was *one* slight lapse in company policy when the differentials in the Stingrays began burning up. Apparently, the increased traction due to the monstrous rear tires and the local track condition was too much for the Corvette differential gears, but a frantic call to Detroit resulted in a diagnosis and possible cure. Instead of the "green," or stock-off-the-shelf gears, they should run sets that had been gradually broken in. To "shotgun" the problem, differential oil coolers should also be mounted on the rear deck. The pieces were quickly gathered up in Detroit, and a company engineer took a sudden vacation to Nassau with very heavy luggage.

All in all, it was a very successful week for Chevrolet engines. Augie Pabst won a couple of races in the Lola/Chevy, A.J. Foyt won a couple in the

The quarter-scale wind-tunnel model that was used as a basis for the CERV-II body. Enough nose shapes were tried that there was no aero lift there, but a number of "fixes" had to be tried on the rear of the final vehicle.

A rear view of Duntov's four-wheel-drive CERV-II after installation of the 427 engine. The transaxle ought to be recognizable as a "Chaparral" automatic, except for extra ears at the top of the case to mount the upper suspension.

Scarab/Chevy, and Dick Thompson won his class in one of the Grand Sport Corvettes. He and John Cannon in another GS-I could have done even better if the aerodynamics had been worked on a little bit, as the nose-up attitude was causing so much front-end lift that air pressure was blowing the hoods off.

When Duntov got back to Detroit, he was so enthusiastic about how well Chevrolet products were doing in the hands of the semi-pro independents, that he made a major proposal to Knudsen. He wanted to first work out the aerodynamic lift problem, and then sell the remaining two GS-I Corvettes. One could go to Mecom, who had been so impressed with the cars in Nassau that he bought Doan's GS-I on the spot. The other would be offered to Grady Davis as a backup to the one he had. And Hall would run his single car as time permitted given his other projects. Simultaneously, Duntov would begin development on an all-new car, with LeMans finally in sight. They couldn't lose.

The CERV-II was *really* a "Chevrolet Engineering Research Vehicle." Duntov had an outright win at LeMans in mind, and his experience from Sebring in '57 to Nassau '63, convinced him that a Chevrolet engine could do it if the chassis was right. While development continued on larger displacement and new heads for the basic aluminum smallblock, he began putting together the most radical and/ or advanced vehicle yet to come from Chevrolet. A projected 550 horsepower from the engine was far more than could be utilized with racing tires of the period, so Duntov concluded that four-wheel-drive (4WD) was mandatory.

Two of the major problems with 4WD, however, are added weight and front/rear torque split. To try and counter both with one system, Duntov came up with the original idea of separate transmissions and torque converters for each end of the engine. Engineering Staff and R&D were working on high-performance converters and lightweight two-speed transaxles, and it looked like a pair of them would be lighter than one large transmission, plus clutch, transfer case, and driveshaft. At the rear, he merely adapted the automatic transaxle which was soon to become public on the Chaparral, while at the front it was necessary to cantilever the converter out in front of the differential to keep all the parts in the same working relationship. For the torque split that Duntov thought was proper, he called upon the converter engineers to design the front and rear with different torque ratios at the same rpm. Since all four tires were the same diameter, at any speed the converters would be carrying a different share of the load until both had reached "lockup" somewhere around 4500 rpm.

Recent experience with the lightweight Corvettes had shown the value of much rubber on the road, and Duntov was aware of the new wide tires Firestone was developing for Indianapolis after the revolution begun by Mickey Thompson in 1963. Firestone made a set available that winter, and the chassis and suspension were designed around the radical new driveline and tires. The suspension was fairly conventional, with double A-frames at the front, and reversed A-arms

Just behind the radiator is the separate front torque converter cantilevered out ahead of the differential. The front drive axles are partially obscured by the rack and pinion and by the massive sheet-steel chassis.

Duntov on the banked "check road" at the GM Tech Center. The CERV-II was not as quick as a comparable two-wheel-drive Chaparral, and so it was relegated to research in tires, engines, converters, and four-wheel drive.

with trailing links at the rear. The only special consideration was added anti-lift and reduced kingpin offset at the front, to accommodate torque reactions there. The prototype chassis was sheet steel unit construction back to the roll bar, where the engine and a tubular sub-structure carried the loads. The rear suspension links were pivoted directly off the transmission case, a design that wouldn't be incorporated in the Chaparral for another six years.

Wind-tunnel studies had been performed on an interesting racer/sports-car shape called the XP-817, and the results fairly well-defined the shape of CERV-II. Both a roadster and a coupe were tested in models, with the coupe intended for LeMans, and the first roadster to be built for testing and development. Although it was a low-drag design, wind tunnel engineers soon discovered that it wasn't too stable at the speeds it could attain, and various appendages were tacked on the rear deck until it felt better.

The first car, the prototype, was the last one of the planned series of race cars. Fortunately, it had been designated a "research" vehicle, and as such it could be kept alive and could be further developed as long as it was never known outside the company. But Duntov's current surge of competition interest was running into corporate resistance again.

In January 1964, a semi-official press release stated that Chevrolet had not been—and was not going to be—associated with the John Mecom Racing Team in any way. And one more time Duntov was shot down. One of the things that made him so valuable to Chevrolet—his flamboyant image—made him so visible that non-adherence to the company line was highly embarrassing. But there were other people within Chevrolet who were beginning to look at automotive competition with a different viewpoint. And those people were not only highly anonymous—at the moment—but they were safely concealed in the walled and locked chambers of Chevrolet Research and Development.

If there ever was a human model for Al Capp's character of "General Bullmoose," it could possibly have been a man named Frank Winchell, who started his GM career at Chevrolet Engineering. Frank knew little and cared less about racing, or about the glamour and "important people" who were behind it at the time. However, he had a consuming interest to learn, and he was a fanatical competitor in his own sphere. For financial reasons, he never completed his engineering degree—and yet he rapidly rose the hard way, to become an engineering vice president of GM A good example of his impact is his hatred for the phrase, "That can't be done." Upon hearing that, there would be an inner explosion like a mine blast, and he might grab an engineer by the lapels to bellow, "What you mean is that *you* can't do it. So, by God, I'll find someone who *can!*" And he usually did. You might not have appreciated his technique, especially if on the receiving end, but everyone certainly had to respect him for his accomplishments.

S.E. Knudsen, presently chairman of the board, White Motor Corp.; was general manager of Chevrolet Division/GMC.

J. Musser, now president of White Motor Corp.; his last position at Chevrolet was as chief engineer on Vega.

F.J. Winchell, currently vice president of engineering, General Motors Corporation.

Late in 1959, Winchell became the head of Chevrolet R&D, and he soon brought in Jim Musser, an impressive young engineer from Engineering Staff. If Winchell was the king in his relatively closed domain, Musser was his eager young lion. On the surface, Musser has an image similar to Jim Hall's in that they are both talented mechanical engineers, but Musser made up for his lack of racing experience with better organizational talents and by being a more aggressive manager. They were also similar in that Winchell had a close—almost fatherly—relationship with both of them. He seemed to admire them for the few abilities that he might have been lacking—whether the cool, calculated, driving technique, or the deliberate, composed management, or their combination of engineering knowledge. In return, they could have accomplished little without his personal power and influence. With everything going for him, Musser rose so rapidly that he was credited with the establishment of the *"vertical* training program"—from research engineer in 1960, to head of R&D in 1966, and over to assistant chief engineer in charge of all vehicle components later the same year. In 1968 the Vega project was started, and Musser became the chief design engineer.

For the years he was in charge of R&D, from 1959 to 1966, Winchell had a great advantage over other department heads such as Bill Mitchell and Duntov. He had his own locked shop, separate from all other engineering activities, and it was almost totally self-sufficient. In addition, even if they were invited, few

The Corvair Monza GT (or XP-777-1) as it was displayed at race tracks. It was primarily a show car, but it was Chevrolet's first experience in monocoque chassis, and it was the "icebreaker" between Jim Hall and Chevrolet.

other managers were comfortable in Frank's world, and one of his superiors made it a point to visit only when Frank was out of the building.

There was one problem, however. He could not build a test track inside his shop. And so eventually every one of his projects had to be taken out onto the corporate tracks, whether the mile-long "check road" at the Tech Center or the 1000-acre GM Proving Grounds. The public could be kept out, but other departments or other divisions could see what he had ... at least the external configuration. Then, too, over-the-fence shots with 500-mm lenses occasionally turned up in public, and some were hard to explain. Especially the vehicles that looked suspiciously like race cars. There might be some sort of test vehicle that had a mid-ship V-8, fat tires, a low driving position, perhaps not even a body shell, and running with open exhausts. That's *sensational—who* would ever believe that it was purely for experimentation and would never leave the test track, much less show up at a *race* track?

It did happen that way, though. Bill Mitchell and his chief "special projects" stylist, Larry Shinoda, were always designing exotic sports-car bodies in clay. Mitchell was still strongly racing oriented, and he frequently took his exotic new creations to Watkins Glen or the Road America June Sprints to test public reaction (and to stay involved). Shortly before the '62 Road America Race, he decided that he wanted to take a sports car based on the Corvair, and he knew that Winchell was also working on various configurations with the Corvair driveline package mounted ahead of the rear axle. So Mitchell and Winchell got together, and Musser was given the job of engineering the chassis, project number XP-777. Within a month, Musser sent a steel monocoque chassis to Styling, where Shinoda had a fiberglass body waiting. One day before the race, the car was completed and it left for Elkhart Lake—as the Corvair Monza GT. This time not only Mitchell went, but also Winchell, Musser, and four technicians. It was a good excuse for a test trip on two other well-disguised experimental Corvair sports cars. (One was built beneath an Alfa coupe body.)

For an amateur race, there were a number of drivers there who were—or were to become—very well-known in racing. In the large production (i.e., *Corvette*) race, Don Yenko and Grady Davis were beaten by Dr. Dick Thompson. In Formula Jr., Tim Mayer (brother of McLarens' Teddy Mayer) finished a number of positions ahead of Hap Sharp and Augie Pabst. Even Chuck Cantwell was there, picking up a fifth in his MGA. In the feature Sprint, Jim Hall and Harry Heuer were in front-engined Chaparrals, and Roger Penske and Hap Sharp had Cooper Monacos. At the start, Hall, Penske, and Heuer traded places until Roger started moving away, setting a new lap record in the process. At one-third distance, however, Penske's distributor cap broke, putting him out, and Hall, Heuer, and Sharp finished in that order. Hall and one of his Troutman-Barnes Chaparrals had beaten the "Europeans"—with his Chevrolet engine.

The Chaparral 1 with a new nose and tail being laid up with the "inverted airfoil" underside. Although it was raced with this body, the heavy front engine concealed lift problems which were to appear later.

The men from Chevrolet R&D were very impressed. When Hall saw the Monza GT, he, too, was impressed, and he described the mid-engine V-8 fiberglass chassis that he was building at home in Midland. A few months later, Hall was in Detroit, after also winning the Elkhart Lake "500" in the same car, and he stopped in at the GM Tech Center for a visit. Shortly after that, he invited Winchell down to his shops to look at the new chassis. It did not have a body yet, but it was still obvious that it was as good as anything Chevrolet was building. Slowly, a strong professional relationship was forming.

Chevrolet's interest lay dormant for a while, though. Hall was planning a coupe body for his chassis so that he could run it in the manufacturers series as a prototype. In the spring of '63, however, the FIA revised their rules, making the new Chaparral uncompetitive as a coupe. So Hall cut the roof off, and set out to make the car suitable for American road racing.

When the car was first tested, it was run without the body, and yet it was immediately faster than the Chaparral 1. With the sleek new body, Hall really expected it to fly—and it did. It literally would not stay on the track. To assist in design, Bill Mitchell had volunteered some aerodynamicists on his staff at Styling to work with Hall. The theory of the moment was to raise the nose and curve the underside, to create half a venturi. Bernoulli's principle then assured a low-pressure area beneath the car, holding it down. But it didn't work like that. After much experimentation and discouragement, Hall called Winchell and asked for some advice from Chevrolet. With only a week remaining before the first race at Riverside in October, the car was instrumented and run at the GM Proving Grounds. Right away, the height indicators showed that the front suspension was going into full rebound at 120 mph. In other words, the nose was trying to lift the front wheels off the ground. The shape didn't make much sense to Winchell, anyhow, so he had sheet aluminum riveted under the

The Corvair Monza SS (or XP-777-2). This version of the Monza GT was highly developed through track testing by a number of race drivers, before it was rebuilt and polished into concourse condition for the show circuit.

The Astro I (or XP-777-3) was the refined version of the Corvair sports car chassis program. After it served its technical purposes, Larry Shinoda used it as a bed for one of his most advanced and functional body designs.

nose in the shape of a plow. On the first test run, Hall stopped halfway down the straightaway. The aerodynamic downforce was so great that the front fenders were forced down on the tires, rubbing them through the thin fiberglass. After a little trimming, the proper plow depth was determined, a new nose was laid up in R&D, and the car left for California. At the Riverside G.P., the new Chaparral 2 debuted by qualifying on the pole, and it led the race until an electrical fire retired it.

In the meantime, through 1963, Chevrolet R&D was well-occupied. With the XP-777 chassis tied up in the Monza GT show car, Winchell had Musser make another, only this time with a conventional rear-engine position. The word was out about Ford's Mustang project and Chevrolet wanted to be ready with a Corvair-based sports car. After considerable chassis development, Mitchell fitted the second car with a roadster body—eventually known as the Monza SS—and it was track tested by a number of well-known drivers. It was through their acquaintance with Mitchell that Penske, Cunningham and Hansgen set the lap record at Waterford, a local road course. Then, a third car showed up at Riverside for testing, and through Mickey Thompson, Bill Krause came close to Penske's Zerex Special lap record. Of course, by that time the Corvair engine was out to three liters, and 180 horsepower with fuel injection. The third chassis was even more highly refined, with all coil springs replacing the torsion bars, and four-wheel disc brakes. Eventually XP-777 number three was recovered from storage to become the chassis under Shinoda's stiletto-like Astro I show car.

The Suspension Test Vehicle. At the right is the radiator and open suspension, in the center is the square monocoque cockpit, and partly obscured by the author is the Chevy V-8 and rear suspension adjustment.

The proposed production Corvette II that never was. At least it was never production. However, there may be more than a passing resemblance to other Chevrolet-powered vehicles that appeared shortly after it was canceled.

One of the most important lessons from the XP-777 cars was that no one knew anything about competition suspensions or vehicle dynamics at the limit of performance—where a race car ought to be. That's when the Suspension Test Vehicle (STV) was born. The STV may be the most amorphous car ever built. To evaluate and establish various suspension geometry configurations, it was designed with up to a dozen different mounting holes for each control arm. Therefore, all suspension parameters were totally and rapidly adjustable: roll center height, camber-change curves, anti-dive, anti-squat, roll steer, and caster. In addition, it was fenderless, to allow any width or diameter of wheel or tire. The fact that it was powered by a mid-engine 327 V-8 was not irrelevant. Enough power was needed to drive the larger tires.

Chevrolet kept well aware of Hall's progress on his Chaparral 2 all this time. As it neared completion, Winchell's thinking on a production rear-engine sports car began to change. The Corvair engine would be overstressed, and Hall had a very clean design with the V-8. But there were other more subtle considerations. Winchell also wanted to demonstrate how much he was learning from the XP-777s and the STV—*and*—he probably felt a necessity to one-up Duntov's GS-I Corvettes. So he appropriated the designation GS-II and began to build a car around it.

At the time, the intention really was to design a lightweight mid-engine sports car that could be profitably marketed. Therefore, the chassis of the GS-IIa was constructed of light-gauge sheet steel, and spot-welded together as it would be in production. The basic layout was very similar to Hall's Chaparral 2, but it was not so much because of racing considerations, as it was an opportunity to experiment with a new V-8 progression of the Corvair sports-car prototype. Perhaps a monocoque chassis with huge rocker boxes to climb over is not too practical for everyday use, but it *had* been accepted by those who could afford a Mercedes 300 SL. To keep the cost, weight, and complexity down, the GS-IIa was built around an all-aluminum 327, and a single-speed automatic transmission—but that's another story, covered in another chapter. Anyhow, the STV was ungainly-looking enough that it *might* be accepted as a research vehicle, whereas the IIa was blatantly a radical new high-performance sports car ... who knows... perhaps even a *race* car. It was only a research project at that point, though, and nowhere near the prototype or pre-production stage. If it was seen around GM—and anything that extreme would be seen—the other divisions or even other manufacturers would be in hot pursuit. A place was needed where the car could be run with absolute security, and since winter 1963 was coming on, a place where the climate was a little more favorable. Perhaps ... somewhere in the desolation of west Texas ...

Sebring 1963: The new Chaparral 1 body with FIA-required windshield and minimum door opening. The Chaparral 2 was under construction, but it had to be converted from a coupe to a roadster because of rule changes.

4

The Chaparral Relationship

For the Chaparral team, 1963 was only a mediocre year. Jim Hall and Hap Sharp were still campaigning one of their Troutman-Barnes-built front-engine Chaparrals and a number of other backup cars. In the first race of the year, at Sebring, the Chaparral went through a major hassle to get through the FIA tech inspection. To get an FIA door on it, it ended up looking like it was made out of cardboard. Then the engine broke while Hall was leading the race. Hall won the very first USRRC race at Daytona in a Cooper, which Sharp subsequently destroyed in a spectacular flip at Elkhart Lake. But by September, it was obvious that the front-engine car, even with its Chevrolet V-8, was no longer competitive with all the European mid-engine designs. On the other hand, when the mid-engine Chaparral 2 first ran at Riverside and Laguna Seca in the fall, hardly anyone paid it any attention, even though Hall was third at Laguna and was running away in first at Riverside when an electrical fire put him out.

Chaparral Cars was still showing a lot of promise. Hall was a graduate engineer from Cal Tech, and obviously knowledgeable in race-car design. He and Sharp were also talented drivers, with sixteen years of road-racing experience behind them. The four race cars they were running all had GM V-8 engines, and were highly competitive—if not too reliable—in spite of the fact that they were home-builts competing against professionally built European race cars. As if that weren't enough, their facilities were ideal for race-car construction and testing. They had three large shop buildings, an engine dynamometer room, and an adjacent two-mile test track with a wide variety of turns and a 250-foot diameter asphalt skidpad.

The location of these facilities, however, was rather incongruous with their purpose. Midland, Texas, is a modern oil-boom business community of about sixty thousand people—half of which disappear every weekend to find diversion in faraway places. There is no reason for the town other than the oil industry. The surrounding countryside is so inhospitable that the only thing that keeps it from being known as a desert is meager, scattered cotton fields. If

Riverside and Laguna Seca 1963: The first appearances of the Chaparral 2 went practically unnoticed, in spite of a third-place finish at Laguna. At Riverside, Hall was leading when the ignition system shorted out and he had to be towed in. A few people went so far as to claim that the ridiculous "plow" on the front of his car was positively ugly.

isolation is a drawback to such a specialized activity as racing development, the seclusion was ideal for security. Even out on the wide-open test track, any observers could be seen miles away ... far further than they could make out any details of what they were seeing or hearing. Because the location was six miles outside Midland—and the next settlement on the highway was fifty miles further—it was highly unlikely for visitors to "be in the neighborhood and drop in," and few were invited.

The place was just what Winchell needed to test his research vehicles, especially in the winter when Detroit tracks were snowed in. Experienced professional drivers were also needed to test cars at the limits of adhesion, but having race drivers on the payroll would not only be hard to justify to Chevrolet accounting, they were practically impossible to communicate with in engineering terminology. Consulting engineers were another story, and both Jim Hall and Roger Penske were driver/engineers who talked a common language with Chevrolet. Tractive effort curves, transient stability, roll axis, dynamic response—those were terms that had to be understood by both sides.

Possibly most important was the fact that Chaparral Cars didn't *need* outside help to function. It is conceivable that by not working with Chevrolet, they could have taken a more conventional approach to racing, and eventually have won more races. It's just that at that stage, each party had something that the other was interested in. Chevrolet had lots of valuable knowledge and components, which was a large investment that they couldn't afford to entrust to someone who might switch allegiance overnight and sell out to the highest bidder. "Those who have—get." "The big get bigger."

In January 1964, Winchell made it legal. For the proper remuneration, Chevrolet would be allowed to use the Chaparral shops and test track. In addition, Hall, Sharp, and Penske would receive a mileage rate for testing the R&D vehicles. The facilities were still available for rental to anyone, or any manufacturer, who was interested, but Chevrolet's contract assured them first priority and security of their acquired knowledge. Racing activities, winning, or potential advertising were far from anyone's mind at Chevrolet at the time. If Winchell had been in a product promotion department, he might have thought of using the situation in advertising, but to an engineer, that was not a consideration. Winchell was in charge of R&D, and free to conduct his research and development practically any way he chose. Jim Musser was given command of the Chaparral liaison project.

Before the month was out, Musser left for Midland with both the STV and the GS-IIa. This was two days after he moved into a new home and his fourth child was born, and the trip was to last six weeks. It began the reputation of test sessions in Midland as being somewhat like "discipline trips" ... like a political vacation to Siberia. Each day was made up of twelve hours worth of frantic build and test—and twelve hours worth of ennui, except for an occasional get-together at Hall's apartment for drinks and bench racing.

The original GS-IIb test chassis with Weber carbureted aluminum 327 and automatic transaxle. This is the machine that loaned its driveline to the Chaparral 2, and was the prototype for the Chaparral 2C that was raced.

Chaparral was pretty busy with its own racing activities at the time. While Musser and Tom Goad and the R&D technicians were taking data on their two research vehicles, the mechanics were preparing the three Chaparral 2s for a full season of fifteen American road races. The first mid-engine car had been built around an aluminum Olds V-8 and a Cooper transaxle. Because of their growing association with Chevrolet, however, it was finally fitted with a Corvair transaxle, and the second car was assembled with a cast iron 327 Chevy engine and a Colotti four-speed gear box. At the second race of the season, in Pensacola, Hall won with the Chevy/Colotti. Sharp's car retired with a broken transaxle, however, and it was sent back to Midland. Since Hall's car was noticeably faster and stronger, both were to be run with the Chevy/Colotti combination.

That was April, and the Chevrolet team happened to be back in Midland at the time, running aerodynamic tests on the GS-IIa. The GS was still running with the aluminum V-8 and single-speed automatic, sooo … Out of curiosity, more than anything else, it was decided to try the combination in a Chaparral at a few road races. On May 3, 1964, the Chaparral/Chevrolet aluminum 327/automatic showed up at Laguna Seca, and with Hall driving, won its first race. The car was so much faster, that Hall easily won the pole, and although he played it easy by occasionally running as low as third, he eventually lapped the third-place car. What was so surprising about that, was that it was Roger Penske, already a champion driver, filling in for Sharp for the first time in the other Chaparral.

The aluminum engine's torque curve and the transmission torque converter were matched to each other, so they were handled as a package. Winchell arranged for them to be sent to Hall with the understanding that he would try them and return them, without taking anything apart if it failed. It was sort of: "Here Jim, try out these parts we're working on. If you like them—fine—race with them. Just don't tell anyone where you got them." Hall had to follow the line, but he had nothing to lose and a possibility of something great to gain. And he *was*, in fact, helping Chevrolet develop a possible production driveline for the lightweight sports car. He was dealing with valuable Chevrolet proprietary information.

Aerodynamics Chronology

Up to that point, the interrelationship was purely a balanced exchange of ideas and knowledge. Hall was trading his racing experience for assistance with his aerodynamic problems. Not that he couldn't have eventually solved them on his own, because he is a good aerodynamicist and an accomplished pilot, but Chevrolet had more engineering heads and specialized instrumentation. The initial aerodynamic failure—the venturi idea—was primarily due to the current lack of correlation between actual high-speed ground vehicles and simulation in a wind tunnel. Aerodynamic experimentation continued in wind tunnels after that, but from then on the results were more thoughtfully considered before application to a full-size vehicle. Eventually it led to better model and road-simulation techniques, better data correlation with the actual vehicles, and a better understanding of what happens to the air in that area between the road and the underside of a car.

It didn't take anyone very long to discover that no one really knew much about automotive aerodynamics. A little research had been done on air drag over the years, but the subject of air *lift* had been completely ignored. Some land-speed record cars had been fitted with "dive planes" to keep them on the ground, although they were probably intuitively designed and were never analyzed, tested, or objectively reported on.

Once the problem of excessive nose lift on the Chaparral was countered, then the engineers began contemplating how an inverse effect—downforce—could be created and utilized to increase high-speed cornering traction. Which immediately got them back into the very area they were trying to research—vehicle stability. The problem was not so much how to get aerodynamic downforce, as it was how to distribute it between the front and rear tires, and how to minimize the effect on air drag. The first "snowplow" was so effective that it created massive oversteer. But to settle that, it was chopped off instead of countered with downforce at the rear. Then, when a spoiler was tried at the rear, the car understeered badly. It became a balancing act, trying to get the front and rear downforce to the point where the car handled the same in high-speed corners as it did in tight corners.

Through the instrumentation, it soon became obvious that the front spoiler actually reduced air drag, whereas the giant rear spoiler greatly increased it as expected. No matter what the shape of the nose, whether with a vertical flat plate, or the more stylish "whiskers," if airflow under the car was prevented, air drag was reduced. The rear deck was more of a problem—there it was either downforce or low drag. As the nose got more effective, the tail rose to the point where it was impossible to see over, and something needed to be done to maintain a competitive top speed. As a pilot, Hall was intimately familiar with movable control surfaces, so it was natural for him to devise a method of eliminating the rear spoiler when it was not needed. Because all Chaparrals had automatic transmissions by that time, there was room for a third pedal, with which to pivot the spoiler flap. This meant that the drag could be significantly reduced in long straightaways. That was another step that his competition was never able to copy successfully. What no one realized was that the spoiler was usually trimmed only at high speed when the car was in high gear, and no shifting was being done, anyhow. So a four-pedal system would have worked just as well.

Eventually the aerodynamic downforce at high speeds became so great that another development problem arose. If the suspension springs were soft enough for good handling at low speeds, the combination of cornering forces and air loads in high-speed corners caused the chassis to bottom sharply on the

The Chaparral 2C at Riverside with its "flipper" rear spoiler. Natural air pressure tended to hold it in the vertical position, while the attached link was connected to a pedal so that it could be trimmed horizontal at high speeds.

suspension. This not only upset stability at that point, it was causing failures in the pieces that contacted each other. This time, the solution just sort of materialized out of a Chevrolet bull session. Various ideas were kicked around, such as hydraulic load levelers, or mounting the body on the suspension, or variable-rate springs. Each had its own problems: excessive weight, durability, or suspension dynamics; but there was one idea that was "clean." Why not simply mount the flap to the suspension? Then, to reduce the interaction with body aerodynamics, why not mount a large flap high above the body? Then, why not a *wing?* The resulting idea was novel enough to warrant a patent, and yet no one on the *ad hoc* committee was certain just whose idea it was—so the patent was issued to Jim Hall *and* Frank Winchell *and* Jim Musser *and* Jerry Mrlik (who inherited the Chaparral project when Musser was promoted). The same sort of vague parentage was true for many of the Chaparral/Chevrolet innovations. So many people were involved that it was impossible to give total credit to one person. Of course, as the "front man," Hall was most often lauded for the successful ideas, in spite of his careful but obscure, "*We* did this ..." He could even work in the occasional first-person singular "I," because he was such an integral and important part of every committee decision.

As the recently acquired "department aerodynamicist," even I soon got involved. Selection of the first wing shape was based on NACA Airfoil Data

---

3,455,594
AERODYNAMIC SPOILER FOR AUTOMOTIVE VEHICLES

James E. Hall, Midland, Tex., and Jerry R. Mrlik and James G. Musser, Birmingham, and Frank J. Winchell, Bloomfield Hills, Mich.; said Mrlik assignor to General Motors Corporation, Detroit, Mich., a corporation of Delaware

Filed Mar. 22, 1967, Ser. No. 625,234
Int. Cl. B62c *1/00, 1/06;* F16d *57/00*
U.S. Cl. 296—1   **4 Claims**

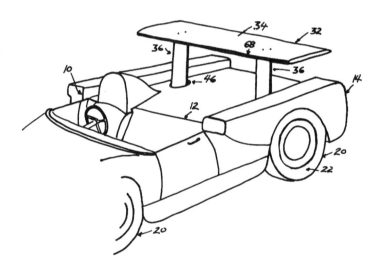

An aerodyamic spoiler member operative to experience substantial aerodynamic anti-lift forces in a relatively moving airstream is mounted on the vehicle by support columns directly attached to the unsprung mass of the vehicle by connection to the two rear wheel support hubs, whereby aerodynamic anti-lift forces on the spoiler may be applied to the ground-engaging wheels for improved traction and maneuverability of the vehicle without loading the sprung chassis mass and deflecting the chassis suspension.

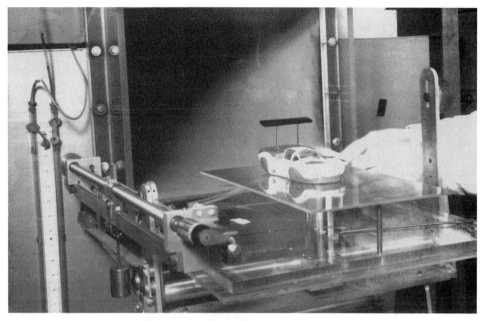

The Chaparral 2D in 1/25 scale in a wind tunnel to study the effects of a wing on body air pressures. Pressure taps and a multi-tube manometer read out the differences when running with or without the wing.

for the best combination of low drag when "trimmed" and high negative lift when "spoiled." Although I had run a wing on a 1/25 scale Chaparral in the wind tunnel, we needed to be *sure* of the performance, to check out predictions of lift and drag forces before the final lightweight wing was constructed. The first wing was carved out of a solid slab of pine, and in April 1966, I was startling visitors at the Tech Center with a Stingray coupe carrying a monstrous wing mounted on struts two feet above the rear window. Because of interference effects and the limited width, it was not quite up to expectations, but it was good enough for Joe Kurleto to proceed on his superlightweight foam-filled monocoque fiberglass racing wing.

Functionally, the new winged Chaparral 2E was a success from the beginning, but its durability left a little to be desired. The first wing struts never even made it to the first race—they failed on the trailer en route to Bridgehampton. It had been proved that they were strong enough to take the air loads, so a particular vibration on the trailer had to be the problem. On the second day of practice, the struts broke on Phil Hill's car. When the raw end of the strut cut a tire, causing the car to crash, Hill borrowed Hall's car (which had already won the pole). Within five laps the very same thing happened to Hall's car. Hall's car was damaged so badly that it had to be withdrawn, but they were able to get Hill's car running in time to start the race, although he had to start

Bridgehampton, 1966: The Chaparral 2E's showed up with their monstrous wings and began a season of frustration. Due to unanticipated vibrations, the struts broke, causing crashes, and when they were fixed, the upper pivots broke.

back in the pack. By welding in heavy reinforcements, they were sure the struts would last. However, while fighting Gurney for the lead the actuating mechanism failed, and the wing was stuck in its natural, high-drag position. Hill had to be content with a fourth, between Bruce McLaren and Mark Donohue in his first Can-Am race.

That kind of failure simply could not be tolerated. If nothing else, failure of the wing was extremely hazardous to the driver, as the loss in rear traction was instantaneous in a corner. On Monday morning, new brackets were designed to take rubber insulators, and they were sketched up and machined out of solid blocks of aluminum. By Wednesday, they were being mounted on the Chaparrals at Mosport and on a Chevrolet van in Detroit, which had been fitted with a loaded wing concealed in the back. They *had* to be proved before the cars ran again.

General Motors' Proving Grounds has a test road known as the Belgian Blocks. As rumor has it, the road was made by pouring concrete over a freshly plowed path, and then driving dump trucks through the wet mess, randomly dumping paving blocks out the back to settle as they fell. Since one mile on *that* is equivalent to a hundred miles of normal use, one-to-one with racing mileage was expected of the wing. After a day and a half of bounding around the track at 30 mph—the limit of control—the wing and struts were pronounced durable. But other areas had been neglected in the panic, and the engines failed in the race that weekend.

Safety was a constant worry among the engineers at Chevrolet, and in such critical areas we were inclined to leave the final design, construction, and maintenance up to Chaparral unless they specifically asked for help. For the rest of the era of wings, Kurleto continued to make lighter and stronger and more efficient wings, but the mounting and actuation was left up to Chaparral. And there were more failures. Although they were supposed to be fail-safe, at Riverside both wing pivots broke, and at Nassau, Sharp's wing went into the lift position and wafted his car broadside into a tree. These failures, and many more among other builders who had even less understanding of the forces involved, were eventually responsible for the FIA decision to ban strut-mounted wings. But Hall saw it coming, and he was preparing the next aerodynamic coup.

The Chaparral 2H was a very fast race car. It had all the right components and it was well-constructed and detailed. It was highly developed and well-driven. However, it was not at all competitive with the current McLaren, and therefore, by Chaparral standards it was a failure. Looking back, it is easy to see the technical reasons for its failure, although the personal or political reasons for its construction are a little vague.

The Chaparral team and the Chevrolet team were actually so isolated from each other, that whenever there was a technical problem each side would have a tendency to say, "If it wasn't for their mistakes ..." Finally, Hall decided to try and regain some autonomy in the aerodynamics and chassis, perhaps to remind everyone that *his* original fiberglass chassis Chaparral 2 had been the most successful of all. However, if the entire team never got credit for all the accomplishments, each individual always felt a slight amount of responsibility for each failure. The 2H was a complete Chaparral design, and highly advanced in many ways, but it also had many reasons for being a fiasco—and aerodynamics was not a small one. Therefore, if I cannot speak for others in the group, I can at least admit my own negative contribution to the 2H. In the summer of 1966, after preliminary road and wind-tunnel tests, I had sent drawings of a similar car to Hall, explaining why the low-drag design looked good—and then forgot about the whole thing. In the summer of 1967, Hall's chief engineer, Paul Lamar, quit, and he hired Mike Pocobello, the current Chaparral project engineer at Chevrolet. Pocobello was to help Hall engineer his new car, about which Chevrolet was kept relatively uninformed.

By February of 1968, when Don Cox went to Midland on a test trip and returned with a report on the new car, aerodynamic thinking had undergone considerable revision. Previously, downforce had been considered a worth-while addition to a low-drag shape. However, that was before my studies of the relative value of parameter variations (quantifying the tradeoff between vari-ous contradicting design effects) such as downforce versus drag. Also, Jim Bennington had been mathematically studying the effect of vehicle width ver-sus race-track width and vehicle path, proving the assumption that the wider the car is, the better. No one realized that Chaparral ought to be kept informed of all this new knowledge—until we heard about the new 2H. Both downforce and width had been sacrificed for the ultimate low-drag shape. By that time it was too late to change, so everyone at both ends had to do all they could to try and disprove the theories in practice. Hall and Pocobello devised a complex tail flap with an interconnected hydraulic suspension leveling system, to regain some air pressure down at the rear. The engine group was trying to develop the necessary low-profile induction system and trying to cram a given length of exhaust header pipes into the limited chassis width. I was gathering the latest test data on duct design for the rear-mounted radiator. And Hall was lapping his track with the windows taped up on his 2F coupe, to simulate the limited visibility in the 2H "roadstoupe."

The car was heavy, unstable, and discomfiting for the driver, but it was slightly faster than the old 2G around Rattlesnake Raceway—and dynamite in a straight line. It almost looked like it might make it. Then disaster struck. One week before the season opener at Elkhart Lake, the rear suspension dem-onstrated a vibration frequency that repeatedly broke the strongest reinforce-ments. Hall had to show up empty-handed at the long-awaited press preview, and then try to resurrect his previous year's car for the 1968 season.

Keeping the 2G running was such a chore that work practically stopped on the 2H. Chevrolet loaned Chaparral all their electronic and aerodynamic instru-mentation, but even when the precise problem was defined, there was little that

Edmonton 1969: The low-drag Chaparral 2H appeared more than a year late, and it still wasn't debugged. It was intended to be a pure coupe, with no obstructions ahead of the rear flap, but it had too many basic problems.

Laguna Seca 1969: By the time the 2H arrived on the West Coast, a grandaddy wing had been mounted. But its effect was never resolved because of other mechanical problems, and it was removed at Riverside for stability reasons.

could be done. After the 2G was destroyed at Las Vegas, work resumed on the new car, and new people were brought in. Among them was John Surtees to race the car once it was ready, and to race a backup McLaren M12 until then. When the 2H finally appeared in the fourth Can-Am of the series at Edmonton, it still was not ready. In its first three races, Surtees was never able to get the car above a fourth place finish. During the next two races, the 2H went back to Midland, while the McLaren car covered for it again. When the 2H showed up at Laguna Seca, it had been fitted with a single, monstrous wing—almost three by six feet—mounted high above the cockpit.

The disadvantage of such a wing is its high air drag and the effect it has on the center of gravity. However, through the use of aluminum and foam sandwich panels, the weight was negligibly greater than that of McLaren's wing, and at that, the winged car was faster around the Midland track in testing. Another influence was the fact that Laguna is the slowest track in the series, where downforce should be far more important than drag. It didn't work out that way, though. A persistent electrical short (downforce was causing the battery box to contact the track on bumps) prevented a complete, good qualifying lap, and Surtees had to start in tenth position. The engine failed on the pace lap because an incorrect converter spacer overloaded the crankshaft. Even without the wing, Surtees was not able to qualify the 2H better than fourteenth at Riverside, and when the engine failed on the fourth lap, he decided he was through experimenting with aerodynamics, and left the team.

Transmission Chronology

The history behind the Chaparral automatic transmission is no more exotic or fascinating than aerodynamics was, but there is more real and imagined mystery because it could be physically concealed from the public. Even if anyone had anticipated how long the "secret" would be perpetuated, they could not have taken better advantage of the inherent sensationalism. Jim Musser later recalled their amazement at the first races:

"We were all new to big-time racing, and maybe a little in awe of those guys. At that time it was a gentleman's sport—not an engineer's—and the old-time railbirds could stand there and tell you which car was going by, just by the sound. They might even be able to tell the *number* of the car. So we couldn't believe it when the single-speed automatic won its first race and no one said a word! No one heard it ... no one even missed the clutch pedal. It was about the third race when the late Dave MacDonald got in a dice with Hall—and realized that Hall never took his hands off the steering wheel!! Then people really started paying attention and asking questions."

Previous attempts had been made to mate a torque converter to a production manual transmission, but the synchronizers could not handle it. So the first Chevrolet prototype sports-car single-speed transaxles were built from scratch,

Riverside 1964: The Chaparral 2 in its first configuration with the iron Chevy and Colotti transaxle. The 6.50 x 15 tires were marginal for the 327 engine. Hall is flanked by two of his best mechanics, Carl Schmitt and Franz Weis.

with a dog clutch engagement for the gears. Jerry Mrlik was the mastermind behind the first automatics, and by the time Chaparral got its first unit, it was almost fool-proof. The single-speed ran in the first six races without the slightest problem. With high gear only, however, the Chaparral was suffering some in the slower corners.

The reasoning behind a single-speed was logical at the time it was conceived. Installing an aluminum 327 engine in a 1600-pound race car (with driver and fuel), which had tiny production Dunlops, was unheard of. The torque of that engine promised to induce wheelspin up to 60 mph. Therefore, a torque converter could be designed to pass only the required torque up to that speed, and no shifting would be necessary. But by the time the first automatic was running, several things had changed. They learned that the aluminum engine was not as powerful as the cast iron version. Also, the car was

The basic two-speed automatic gear case. The upper cylindrical area holds the driven spur gears on the differential pinion, and the lower cylindrical area holds the input shaft and drive gears, with the shifter slider between.

heavier than intended. But most significant, the tire companies were starting to wake up, and Firestone appeared with a derivation of their Indy tire, which had far more traction. Suddenly, one ratio was not good enough.

The experience from that first effort was very productive, though. It gave Hall and Sharp experience in left-foot braking and the better control that resulted, and it also gave the engineers practice in tailoring the converters. The expensive piece—tooling for the converter/gearcase/differential housing casting—had been written off on the production sports-car project. And to fit in an extra gearset merely meant extending the rear gear housing cover. The beginning of shifting, however, was the beginning of problems. The Chaparral automatics required as much care in manual shifting as any other non-synchro transmission. If the engine was not started with a gear engaged, the "garage shift" impact was a terrible jolt to the hardware. To keep the dog clutches from disengaging while running in gear, they were designed so that the transmission could *not* be shifted under power. It always required that the throttle be momentarily lifted to get out of any gear, although the next gear that even came close was grabbed instantaneously. This meant that shift timing was critical, to avoid mismatch between the engine and gearbox rpm and the resultant ... "whunk" ... which lurched the car. Mrlik or Kurleto personally inspected every gearbox as it returned to Chevrolet, and it got to where they could tell who the driver had been by the condition of the clutch dogs. Of all the drivers who have raced with the automatic—Phil Hill, Bonnier, Stewart, Elford, Sharp, Penske, etc.—Hall always caused the least damage, but of course he had the most experience and the most knowledge of what was happening inside the box. At one time, an electronically-timed engine-kill button was wired to the shifter, for wide-open-throttle automatic shifts, but it still was not much better than the best drivers, and an input shaft failure raised enough doubt that it was never raced.

The first two-speed showed up at Mid-Ohio in August 1964, with no fanfare, and won with Sharp driving. At his next race at Riverside, however, he managed to break the first transaxle. By making too many grid starts, the converter was overheated and had to be replaced. Then, in the race, he accidentally shifted into reverse and bent the linkage, which prompted a redesign. Throughout the 1965 season, a few more miscellaneous bugs cropped up, such as fatigue cracks or failures in the case, pinion shaft, and oil pump pickup. And the shift linkage failed again, although the torque converter made it possible to continue in high gear. Fortunately, most of the total failures occurred in testing or practice, and Chaparral had its most successful year ever, winning 16 out of 21 American road races.

With this conquest in mind, Chaparral decided to go to Europe and try out in the Manufacturer's Championship. No one at Chevrolet was particularly interested, because it was felt that anything that was to be learned or developed was better done closer to home. But it looked exciting and challenging enough

Sebring 1966: the first Chaparral coupe, the 2D, marked the beginning of continual minor problems in the transaxle. Closed bodywork prevented adequate cooling air to the converter, and high temperatures began cooking the seals.

at the time so that no one really objected, and it was actually Hall's operation, anyhow—they were his cars and where he raced them was his business. Besides, Henry Ford was spending millions on the same assault, and the only time they had come in direct competition (at Sebring the previous year), the lightweight Chaparral roadster had severely whipped his GT 40 coupe. To run with the manufacturers, however, meant that Chaparral had to build a coupe, and equip it with certain required production amenities such as a luggage area and spare tire. With this, the weight went up, and with that, a three-speed transmission would be required.

It seemed like a small enough project for Chevrolet. After all, the one- and two-speeds had been extraordinarily successful. There had been a total run of twelve cases of the first basic design, and although Mrlik had been called out to apply his experience to production transmission problems, Kurleto was anxious to further refine the transmission in a three-speed design. The case was strengthened where cracks had appeared, and the rear gear housing was extended to enclose the three spur-gear sets.

In the first two 1966 races at Daytona and Sebring, the chassis failed before anything else could, so it was not until the car was taken to Nurburgring (which it won) and LeMans (where the battery failed) that transmission problems began to occur. Jumping out of gear was not a critical problem, but it was quickly worked out. Back home in the Can-Am, the only other problem that year was an exploded shifter ring in the dog clutch. That was the only problem other than the previously mentioned wing failures, and a chronic elusive fuel starvation, which cost the series. When Chaparral went back to Europe in 1967, everyone was so worried about the old transmission standing up to the new 427 engine, that they missed the forest for the trees. As minor, aggravating problems such as seal and bearing and universal joint boot failures occurred, they were painstakingly eliminated. What no one recognized was that the enclosed European coupe body work was not allowing enough airflow around the transmission. The automatic's worst enemy—wasted heat—was simply cooking it. Again, when it was raced in the lightweight roadster in the Can-Am through both 1967 and 1968, it performed faultlessly.

Because the automatic transmission was always so dependable, plenty of time was available for experimentation with other ideas. By extending the gear case cover again, Kurleto was able to fit a *fourth* gearset. Computer analysis and track verification indicated that it was of questionable benefit, however, because of the converter range, and it was never raced. The biggest converter drawback was slippage at theoretical "lockup," no matter how close the rotor/ stator tolerances were held. The combination of lost rpm and lost torque added up to an intolerable amount of lost horsepower when it was most needed. To counter that, Gates designed a totally manual clutch to replace the converter, and Kurleto came up with a converter with a mechanical locking device that automatically engaged at a certain rpm. Other than that, there was little more to be learned about transmissions from racing. On a strength/weight/performance basis, it had practically reached the ultimate level of development. Chevrolet R&D decided that the cost was no longer justified by the feedback, and Chaparral could either maintain the automatics on their own, or switch to Hewland.

Chassis Chronology

The progression and development of race-car chassis and suspensions between Chaparral and Chevrolet is also a story in itself. But first, perhaps, it is necessary to straighten out the confusion in nomenclature between the two camps, since both used similar designations except as distinguished by Arabic versus Roman numbers:

Chevrolet	Chaparral	Appearance Date	and Description
	1	6/11/61	Front Engine, Tube Frame
G.S.I		12/15/62	'63 Lightweight Corvette Coupe
STV			Open-Wheel Test Vehicle
	2A	10/13/63	Mid-Engine, Fiberglass Chassis
G.S. IIa			Steel Chassis
G.S. IIb	2B		Aluminum Test Chassis
G.S. IIc	2C	10/10/65	Aluminum Race Chassis
	2D	2/6/66	Coupe Version of 2A
G.S. IIe	2E	9/16/66	Winged Version of 2C
G.S. III			Open Wheel Race Chassis
	2F	2/4/67	Winged Coupe Version of 2D
G.S. IV			Fiberglass Chassis
G.S.. IIg	2G	9/1/68	Advancement of 2E
	2H	7/27/69	Fiberglass Chassis Streamliner
G.S. V	2J	7/12/70	Aluminum Chassis "Sucker"

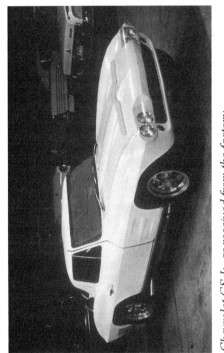

Chevrolet GS-I: as received from the factory.

Chevrolet GS-IIb: test chassis with original body.

Chaparral C1: with Sebring bodywork.

Chaparral 2: with 1965 Sebring bodywork.

Chaparral 2D: with tail and roof scoop added for Europe.

Chevrolet GS-III: Under the skin—a 5-year-old Indy chassis.

Chaparral 2C: with the "flipper" tail.

Chaparral 2E: The 2C with all-new external skins.

Chaparral 2G: A 2E with fender flares and taller induction.

Chaparral 2J: as run in its last 3 races.

Chaparral 2F: A 2D with all-new external skins and wings.

Chaparral 2H: with the "Laguna wing."

At the time at which Chaparral and Chevrolet started exchanging hardware, the 2A and the GS-IIa were operational. Musser's car, however, was somewhat cruder than Hall's, with its production prototype spot-welded steel tub. The Chaparral fiberglass chassis was an extremely advanced design by anyone's standards. It was made up of eleven pieces, which were hand-laid-up in separate molds, and when cured, they were riveted and bonded into one extremely rigid unit. Because it was a first attempt in this direction, some panels were likely heavier than necessary, and the large overlapped bonding surfaces required excess material. Still, the entire tub, with all engine and suspension brackets bonded in, weighed only 150 pounds, compared to 240 pounds in the GS-IIa. Refusing to be outdone, the team at Chevrolet decided to use its experience to produce an all-aluminum GS chassis.

The suspension components on the STV and GS-IIa were too heavy, also, as the cars were intended for rough testing instead of racing. On the other hand, the Chaparral 2 components were largely Lotus items, and were too fragile for a V-8-powered race car. Right away, Hall broke one of the Lotus convoluted-disc wheels, and Frank Boehm was given the task of engineering a better wheel. Partly because Chevrolet had done so much work in investigating the value of rim widths, and partly because the new racing tires were so hard to mount, and partly because more clearance was needed for brake calipers, Boehm eliminated the standard "drop-center" rim with a split-rim that could be rapidly changed in width. From an engineering and strength standpoint, a solid-disc wheel was best, but when mounted on a car that had no engine braking due to the automatic, the lack of cooling airflow became an immediate problem. By the first race of the 1965 season, Boehm had designed, built, tested, and supplied the familiar "Chaparral" split-rim, cast-spoke wheel, which was still in use six years later on the 2J.

Along the same line, Chevrolet R&D was also interested in learning how to design other components that were currently available only on European sports cars. Aside from the engine/transaxle package, the first Chevrolet part that Chaparral tried on its cars was a rack-and-pinion steering assembly. After that, it was not long before the entire suspension system—control arms, springs, knuckles, and shocks—were designed and built by R&D for Chaparral's evaluation … and safety. Of course, Chevrolet's pieces occasionally broke, also, but due to the then unrecognized occurrence of the chassis bottoming on the suspension, not due to basic underdesign.

Therefore, when Musser began the first aluminum monocoque chassis, he had a good idea of the proper suspension components and geometry. When the GS-IIb was first operational, it was merely used for testing. At 70 pounds, the complete tub was only half as heavy as Hall's, but because of the light-gauge aluminum, and inexperience in bonding the panels with epoxy, no one trusted it for competition. It did show what could be done, however, and the lessons

The GS-IIb with an aluminum monocoque tub that weighed 70 pounds. The solid wheels were run briefly on the Chaparral, but didn't allow brake cooling. Jim Musser is taping on instrumentation, with C. Petersen standing by.

The Chaparral 2C was a reinforced-chassis version of the GS-IIb, but it still worried drivers because of its noisy chassis panels. Considering it was a hundred pounds lighter than the 2A, however, most drivers tolerated it.

were used to produce a pair of GS-IIc's (or Chaparral 2C's). Although the "C" was a hundred pounds lighter than the plastic-chassis car, none of the drivers was too fond of it. Because it incorporated a large amount of anti-dive and anti-squat in the suspension, it rode very stiffly, and Sharp began referring to it as the "eyeball jiggler," or EBJ, due to the effect on his vision at speed. Also, it worried the drivers because of the noise it made. It was not until the tub was twisted in the lab to measure torsional stiffness that the engineers really appreciated this, as heavily loaded panels warped and popped like giant "mechanical crickets." The chassis stiffness tests verified that the 2C was as rigid as the 2, although the fatigue resistance was an unknown, and while the mechanics worried about repairability, the drivers were concerned about crash-ability.

When Hall crashed at Mosport in 1964 and Laguna Seca in 1965, the fiberglass chassis were hardly cracked. At Mosport, he went off the road, leapt a twenty-foot ditch, and the car came to an abrupt stop upside down. Six months later, both the chassis and Hall's broken arm had been repaired, and with Sharp assisting, they won Sebring. When the 2C made its first appearance at Kent in October 1965, it easily won, but with considerable apprehension on Hall's part. Through the next season, the 2C (and the later 2E) aluminum chassis held up well, although off-road excursions due to other problems pointed up areas where they needed reinforcement. After a season of Can-Am development with Hall and Phil Hill, the 2C was considered acceptable, and Sharp took it to Nassau. Crash-testing it due to the previously mentioned wing failure proved that it had another advantage—in energy absorption. The car T-boned a tree on the driver's side, and after neatly crushing the rocker box and enclosed foam-filled fuel bladder, came to rest within an inch of Sharp's hip. Merely sore—but shaken— Sharp was able to channel his competitive interests toward polo from then on.

There wasn't much that Chevrolet R&D could do—or *wanted* to do—with the aluminum chassis at that point. Because we had the patterns and dies, another duplicate was bonded up and shipped off to Midland in exchange for the bent tub. But Chaparral knew how to make minor repairs and report the results. R&D was going ahead on new, if not better, high-performance investigations. Musser was convinced that his men knew enough about vehicle dynamics to build a car for Indianapolis racing, especially if the chassis were loaned to someone who wanted to run there with a stock-block Chevy engine. If it turned out that it was a different game, and all-new problems were discovered—well, problem-solving was the challenge that R&D thrived on. It didn't seem like much of an effort, anyhow, as all the suspension components and driveline were on hand from the GS-II. So a "Dynamics Evaluation Vehicle" project was modified slightly, to fit USAC specifications, and Frank Boehm was assigned to produce the new vehicle. It just barely got up on its wheels before there was a new man upstairs in the executive suite at GM, and he wanted to tour all the facilities and see just what was happening. To avoid any embarrassment, it was felt wise to ship the rather odd-looking chassis off to someone else for completion, and Smokey Yunick ended up with the hardware. When Musser left the department, no one else wanted to remember the project. But Smokey wasn't doing anything with it, and when Jim Hall expressed an interest in the SCCA Formula A series in early 1968, he inherited the chassis … and there it stayed. It had been built around his dimensions, anyhow.

After considerable experience with aluminum chassis in R&D, a number of engineers began to feel that Hall had the right idea in his fiberglass Chaparral 2. Also, in the five-year interim, many new aerospace materials had been made available, such as super-strength directional-weave fiberglass cloths and more rigid epoxy resins. The most exciting development was a pre-impregnated combination of the two, which could be laid up more cleanly and was cured in an oven instead of by catalyst. Kurleto was convinced that this was the answer to the weight problem in Hall's chassis and the fragility problem in R&D's, particularly when coupled with an all-new structural design based on previous findings. A year later, the GS-IV was a complete tub, and it was crated up and sent to the warehouse. It was the stiffest and lightest vehicle frame that had been built—but it was built around the 327 engine, and in the meantime, the 427 engine took over. Because of the carefully engineered structure and integral design, a major revision in all the molds would have been necessary, and the cost of the car was already well over budget.

Donnybrooke, 1971: Beneath this skin is a chassis designed by Chevrolet in 1966 to experiment with at Indianapolis. Chaparral inherited the project, and when it closed down, Franz Weis resurrected the car for F-A racing.

The aborted GS-IV did contribute a great deal to Hall's next car, however. Considering the cost of time involved in designing and mold-making and layup, the cost of any fiberglass-reinforced plastic material was relatively insignificant, and Hall wanted the ultimate in his 2H. From a structural standpoint he almost got it, although that fact was overshadowed by other drawbacks which kept it from being a winner. The 2H had one of the most purely monocoque racing chassis ever built—from the engine forward, at least. Practically every panel forward of the roll bar, whether hidden or external skin, was stressed in torsion or beaming of the car. Anything that could possibly contribute to strength was made integral, and therefore lighter: fuel containers, bellypan, roll bar, fenders, nose, roof, seats, dash, and all brackets. The only removable pieces were the doors and windscreen, and small access panels for all fluid containers. To accomplish this, Pocobello used a new technique—building the car from the outside in. First the external shape was decided on, and then after a female mold was taken off the full-size clay model, a skin was laid up inside, and the entire structure was built up inside that. This was the reason that the shape was practically impossible to change from the beginning, regardless of anyone's later misgivings.

The rear skin could be easily changed, because there was no structure back there. The engine was rigidly bolted to the roll bar, and the only other reinforcement was a pair of diagonal braces back to the transmission. There wasn't room for any other structure, because the car was so narrow that the rear tires came very close to the cylinder heads. This meant that there was also little space for any sort of rear suspension.

Ever since Chevrolet R&D began studying the suspension dynamics of high-performance cars, there had been no major changes in the linkage or geometry. Now it appeared that the only option from a space standpoint was an all-new deDion rear axle. No one at Chevrolet or Chaparral was particularly worried, because all the years of analysis and experience with independent suspension had provided a great bank of knowledge in that general field. The exotic new linkage, however, produced exotic new problems. Coupling the two rear wheels through a semi-rigid axle brought out complex dynamic forces and motions that were never encountered before. The basic geometry was ideal, but due to the high loads and short links, the compliance, or unintentional flexing, was allowing gyroscopic forces to develop an unanticipated resonance. Analysis instrumentation, simulation hardware, and engineers converged on the problem and found both the specific cause and a cure, but that set the rest of the vehicle's development back by months. All in all, the car was a classic example of asking for too much, too new, too soon. But if the specific reasons for the 2H's failure were lack of downforce, lack of width, and lack of suspension space, the basic reason was the subjugation of aerodynamic downforce to air drag—or, perhaps—the skepticism toward performance prediction by computer simulation.

The rear assembly of the Chaparral 2H. In the center is the articulated deDion axle located by leading links, and at the right, diagonal braces can be seen next to the engine. Quite a change from the simple Chaparral 1.

Even the violent ends of both the Chaparral 2G and 2H were valuable lessons in themselves. Though both cars were running at the same time, the 2G was raced in 1968, and crashed at the end, while the 2H ended the 1969 season. The *cause* of Hall's disastrous crash in the 2G at Las Vegas is well-known. It impacted the rear of a slowing, disabled car, rode over its tires and was catapulted into the air. Coming down, it flipped end-over-end, breaking the car into two pieces at the dash. The *reason* for the impact is known only to Hall, if he could remember the details, and he is not sure he wants to try. Don Cox summarized the racing season with a list of fatigue cracks and failures attributed to three years of hard use in the structure, wheels, spindles, axles, and transmission—but none could be blamed for the final destruction.

The 2H was wiped out a year later when it broadsided a concrete wall at Texas International Speedway. The only similarity between the two accidents was the total loss of the chassis. In the case of the 2H, though, it was because a single, mighty blow had cracked the entire unit structure. Whether the impact absorption of the chassis was responsible for the driver's safety in the second case cannot be concluded, but if there had been enough time, it might have influenced the material selection on the next car, the 2J.

"Sucker" Chronology

Even creative professional people have a tendency to denigrate someone else's imaginative efforts by disclaiming their originality. "I thought of that years ago," or "The idea was first explored in the thirties." But whoever thinks about something, or *talks* about it, is rapidly forgotten next to the person who *does* it. In fact, the idea of vacuum-traction for automobiles was patented in 1925, and although a few people made half-hearted attempts to build one, it was not until the winter of 1968, that the Chevrolet high-performance group made a concentrated assault. Everyone else's good intentions were of no more value than those of an anonymous young admirer of Chaparral. He had sent Jim Hall a crayon sketch of a race car held down by horizontal fans sucking the air out from below it. Few of the dreamers had any idea how much development was required to make such a system work.

By luring Pocobello down to Midland to help design and build the all-Chaparral 2H, Hall had taken the burden of chassis component development off R&D. By using the computer performance prediction of various possible approaches then, it didn't take long for us to discover that vacuum-traction was the most profitable area of investigation. A few months worth of basic research into fans and sealing methods demonstrated that the idea was feasible, and I tested a crude device on the old Suspension Test Vehicle in November 1968. The device was so crude, however, that it was hardly promotable, so Don Gates bought a plastic model of the 2G and modeled the system on it in clay. Taking it before Charlie Simmons, the new head of R&D, Gates explained that nickel-and-dime projects had taken all the enthusiasm out of his group, and they needed such a radical new project to raise morale. Simmons agreed, and gave Gates all the draftsmen, technicians, and budget he needed to have it ready during the next racing season—in case Hall still had problems with his 2H.

Gates continued work on the fan-and-skirt system, while Don Cox, Ernie DeFusco, and Joe Marasco were given the job of engineering the actual racing chassis. The prototype had fans that were belt-driven off the engine, but because the vacuum requirements were greatest at low engine rpm's, an auxiliary constant-rpm engine was used instead. An alternate plan to use a Salsbury variable-ratio snowmobile belt drive off the transmission was set aside as too complex, but as it turned out, that might have proved more dependable. The final skirt seal never created any problems, because of the amount of experimentation and number of designs that Gates tried.

In the chassis department, Cox was as straightforward in design as possible. The amount of downforce and the subsequent cornering, braking, and acceleration forces, meant that the chassis and suspension components had to be almost twice as strong as any previous race car. Because of his experience in stress testing all the previous race-car tubs, Cox was the best man for the job, although it was still an area of many unknowns. The extremely high air pressure loads on many panels meant that aluminum honeycomb was the best material to avoid buckling. Because it is practically impossible to curve, however, all those flat panels gave the 2J its characteristic box shape.

In its final running configuration, it weighed almost 600 pounds more than the McLaren, but was probably the strongest, stiffest race-car chassis that has ever been built. Not only was the basic vehicle much heavier, the auxiliary engine weighed over 100 pounds with its own electric starter, and then there was the mounting structure, the skirts and actuators, the dual axial-flow fans, plus all the extra oil-mixed fuel for the two-stroke engine. The fans were practically ideal for the job right off the manufacturer's shelf, because they were designed to cool a military tank engine as efficiently as possible. They were not designed to clean the grit off race tracks however, and each one of the alloy blades had to be fitted with its own steel leading-edge shield.

As the car took shape in Chevrolet R&D, it began to attract a lot of attention. So much so, that it began to become rather embarrassing to have around. It was not that it was recognized as a great engineering breakthrough that had to be protected, but more a case of being so ridiculously sensational that everyone was talking about it. For example, the first time the auxiliary-motor fan-drive system was fired up on the Suspension Test Vehicle, it literally smoked out the engineering lab. The combination of clouds of dust and the smoky exhaust from a pair of two-stroke engines sent people for the doors—and brought Plant Security on the run.

But at the same time, a number of other problems were occurring in Midland. Surtees was testing the 2H, and it looked like a number of revisions were necessary. As a coupe, the visibility was intolerable, so the seat was tilted forward and the top opened. But Surtees was somewhat shorter than Hall, and he still found it difficult to see out the top. The weight was enough greater than the 2G, that it was felt that perhaps it was time for a four-speed transmission. The rear suspension broke. The nose was lifting and the rear had no downforce. One of Hall's mechanic/drivers went off the high-speed turn at 150 mph and tore up the underside.

By May, Chaparral decided that the 2H had too far to go, and Hall bought a McLaren for Surtees, in which to begin the Can-Am series. When the 2H did show up at Edmonton and it finished a poor fourth, Hall and Pocobello had a falling out, and Mike returned to GM. The same week, Hall visited Chevrolet to test drive the vacuum-traction STV, and he talked to Gates about going to Midland to help debug his 2H. Because Gates was also the project engineer on the 2J, it was decided that there was nothing more Chevrolet wanted to do with it, and it was sent along also. When the 2J left in September, it was no more than a tub and crates of components, although all the systems had been proven on other vehicles. There was only a few months left in the season by that time, so Gates concentrated on trying to get some sort of accomplishment out of the car that was running. It was not until Tom Dutton, a driver/engineer whom Hall had recently hired, shattered the 2H chassis against a wall in the last Can-Am that work could resume on the "sucker car."

Before the 2J was assembled, however, Chaparral picked up the Camaro Trans-Am project when Penske defected to American Motors, and Hall's meager enthusiasm for "someone else's" Can-Am car faded even more. Dutton was a Can-Am fanatic, and anxious to absolve himself of the accident, so he stayed with the 2J, along with Gates. Practically everyone else viewed the project either with distrust or malice. Even when the car made its first runs, and broke the track record at Rattlesnake Raceway with Dutton driving, the mechanics still referred to it as the "skidpad racer," and refused to put any faith in it.

There was another problem that had everyone wondering—was it legal? At the end of the 1969 season, the FIA reiterated its ban on "wings," and further expanded it to include any "movable aerodynamic devices." Jim Kaser, director of professional racing for the SCCA, was invited down to Midland to examine the car and judge whether it was within the spirit of the rules. After all, a carburetor butterfly valve is a "movable aerodynamic device." Kaser was not the FIA, so he could not know what was in its mind, but he did know what would draw spectators into his races—so it looked legal to him. Development of the 2J continued leisurely.

The 2J ran for the first time in November 1969, and as could be expected, it, too, was far from perfected. In its original configuration, there was a separate fan and drive motor in the rocker panels on both sides of the engine, and the skirt-enclosed low-pressure area was only the length of the rocker panels. However, regardless of how much basic understeer was incorporated with the fans off, when they were turned on, the car oversteered uncontrollably. Apparently, the center of downward pressure was too far forward. And in addition, the brakes were not powerful enough to utilize all the traction in braking—the wheels literally could no longer be locked up. But in spite of all the problems, it was still tolerably fast without downforce, and with the fans working it was as fast as any other car ever run at Midland. John Timanus, the SCCA Technical Inspector, stopped in to examine the car as to legality and safety, and was suitably impressed. With Dutton driving, they demonstrated the conspicuous vacuum gauge warning device and the relatively slow rate of pressure loss when any part of the system failed. With the entire engine room acting as a vacuum reservoir, even shutting off both fans in a corner allowed sufficient reaction time before traction was totally lost. In addition, due to the noticeably greater steering effort required with downforce, when pressure was lost the first indication was a lightness at the steering wheel.

To overcome the stability problem, the downforce area was quickly extended to include the rear-wheel area by enclosing everything with plywood sheets, and the dual-fan systems were moved to the far rear and mounted above

The Chaparral 2J "sucker car" in revision No. 2. At this time the rear wheels were enclosed, and the two fans and engines were mounted above the transaxle. The guides for the side skirts can be seen around the door opening.

The Chaparral 2J in its final form. The suspension-actuated cable running across the tire controls skirt height through the bell crank. The two fan engines were replaced by a single two-cylinder engine with electric starter.

Lime Rock 1970: Chaparral's Trans-Am program interrupted work on the 2J when a lack of experience in the series, and just plain bad luck, drew all their time. It made little difference, anyhow, with only one win for the year.

the transaxle. This also nearly doubled the low-pressure area. With this arrangement, and both fans on full blast, and the skirts nearly touching the ground, Dutton was able to circle the skidpad at a fantastic 1.7 g's lateral! This was a major jump from the previous best of 1.3 g's, and was without the normal high-speed air pressure downforce on the body. At that, Dutton went out on the road course and knocked nearly two seconds off Hall's previous best time of just under one minute.

The car ran pretty well—but it looked terrible. With all the plywood and jury-rigged pieces, it was far too heavy. The further use of honeycomb panels would help, and with both fans next to each other, a single two-cylinder engine could be used to run them. And the entire car needed a complete rebuild and cleanup. There was plenty of time left, however, with the first 1970 Can-Am race four months away, so Gates and Dutton diverted their energies to the Trans-Am Camaros, which appeared first in the season's schedule. In their "spare" time, they disassembled the 2J, and it sat around in pieces.

The first Trans-Am race created another setback, when the Camaros demonstrated an obvious lack of competitiveness. Also, one of the cars was nearly wiped out when an axle broke, and it ran off-course into a tree. Then there was a plague of problems with thrown belts, exploding vibration dampers, and oil pressure loss. Once the cars were on the road, they seldom went back to the

The Chaparral 2J in Midland just before leaving for its first race. The flat sides were necessary because of the sliding Lexan skirts inside and because the body was made up of unbendable honeycomb panels.

shops in Midland to interfere with work on the Can-Am project, but at the same time, most of the mechanics had gone with them.

With meager support, the 2J simply was not ready for the first Can-Am—nor had a driver even been decided on. Before the second race, a durability test had broken the transmission mount, and the water-pump belt broke, blowing a water hose and scalding Dutton. Finally, Chaparral vice president Cam Argetsinger, as former director of Watkins Glen, insisted that the 2J show up there, ready or not. Hall was not up to driving it yet, but the same public relations group representing Chaparral was working with Jackie Stewart, and so he was negotiated for the inaugural 2J race. But the car was not ready. In practice, pieces of asphalt were drawn through the fan system and broke the drive belts, on the starting grid the ignition failed on one cylinder of the auxiliary engine, and finally, the increased braking requirements boiled the brake fluid.

Hall was disgusted. He refused to put any more of his own money into the project, and because of its poor showing at the Glen, sponsorship was unlikely. He recalled the crew to Midland and began shutting the place down. The draftsmen and machinists were laid off and the 2J was disassembled and packed in crates to be sent to the warehouse. Only the Camaros were to continue.

But then there was a sudden change in fortune. Lexan, a General Electric plastic, along with Silicone lubricants and sealants, was used extensively in the 2J. General Electric engineering was well aware of that, and when Gates explained the financial situation to them, they contacted the advertising department. The result was that GE dropped out of the sky to put up enough money to run three more races. Stewart was still too expensive, however, and the 2J was so strong that it did not need a World Champion to win. Vic Elford had recently won the Watkins Glen Trans-Am in a Hall Camaro, so he got the 2J ride.

The Road Atlanta Can-Am was a memorable experience for Team McLaren. For the first time in three years, they did not have the fastest car on the track. Not only that, but they made no secret of pulling out all the stops to make up the difference. In the earliest practice, Elford was easily three seconds faster than Hulme, and Teddy Mayer practically went into shock. They mounted the stickiest tires they had, and Hulme went out to push his car harder than ever done before, clipping more and more off the corners and dangerously approaching the critical limit of control. He still never got within a second of the 2J.

In the race, however, the 2J never led a single lap. There was 400 miles of testing on the fan system without a rebuild, and early in the race an ignition wire fatigued and the fan motor began missing. This established the fact that the snowmobile engine would not run forever putting out a constant 55 horsepower at 5500 rpm—under those conditions of vibration. From there, the 2J went on to verify the assumption that no all-new race car can be a success

Watkins Glen, 1970: Jim Hall, Teddy Mayer, and Don Gates having a good laugh over the 2J before it ran. Mayer's expression changed considerably at Road Atlanta when the McLarens couldn't get within a second of the 2J in qualifying.

A gathering of significant people around the 2J before practice at Watkins Glen, including Hall, Gates, Tom Dutton, Franz Weis, Troy Rogers, Stirling Moss, and in the cockpit, World Champion Jackie Stewart.

without extensive durability testing. All Team McLaren needed to do was sit back and wait for something else to fail—at Laguna Seca it was a connecting rod, and at Riverside it was a crankshaft.

But at the last race, a number of people decided that the next season was going to be a Chaparral benefit, and a meeting was called to fairly and objectively discuss the legality of the 2J. As fairly as you can discuss anything without the defendant being present (because anyone from Chaparral was pointedly not invited). The primary attendees were Jim Kaser, Teddy Mayer, Eric Broadley, Carl Haas, most of the Can-Am drivers, and even such non-participants as Robin Herd and Roger Penske. The theoretical points of dissension were safety and cost of development to other competitors, although both were emotionally—rather than objectively—argued. The only proponents present, oddly enough, were Herd, who was about to begin building the first March Can-Am car, and Penske. Penske's logic perhaps included the fact that one of his engineers, Don Cox, had been involved with the system at Chevrolet, and he could nearly duplicate it. Kaser could not make the absolute decision, anyhow, because the FIA has final jurisdiction for all international races, and the matter rested. In retaliation, Chaparral Cars held a press conference and made a statement that read, in part:

"There seems to be a misunderstanding or misconception regarding both the cost of installing a ground effects system and its application to cars other than Can-Am cars. A system identical to the one on the 2J can be installed on any existing Can-Am chassis by Chaparral Cars at a cost of between $3,000 and $4,000.

"Another possible area of contention has been one of safety. For example, what will happen if the fan system stops in the middle of a turn? We know from actual experience that what happens is that the loss of downforce is sufficiently gradual to allow for the driver to compensate for this loss.

"The original concept of the Can-Am series was to provide one race series with an absolute minimum of rules to promote engineering innovations. Jim Hall's Chaparral is the only entrant that has attempted to fulfill this concept to any degree."

But the Chaparral 2J, or any other fan-powered vacuum-traction vehicle, was never raced again. The last time it ran was at the Chaparral test track in Midland, where Jim Hall used it to set the final absolute track record there. In spite of the fact that it was slightly slower than either the 2G or 2H in the straights, it was five to eight miles per hour faster in every corner, and two seconds quicker overall.

The 2J may have been a failure as far as racing statistics and history goes, but it still was one of the greatest successes in racing in another more important aspect of the sport. To General Electric, it was one of the best advertising investments ever made. In only three races, and at a cost in the "low five-figures," over *two hundred million* impressions (person-event-exposures) were made ... of the last General Electric-Chevrolet-Jim Hall-Chaparral 2J.

Laguna Seca, 1962: Penske wins the Pacific Grand Prix in his controversial "single-seater" Cooper sports car. The passenger seat is hidden under the cowling to his left, although the driver is nearly centered in the chassis.

Cumberland, 1963: With a little goading, Penske opened up the cockpit somewhat the next season for better passenger access, but it didn't slow him down any. Here he won an amateur race over Augie Pabst in a Cooper-Buick.

5

Penske/Donohue Team

Although Roger Penske and Mark Donohue account for only one chapter in the Chevrolet story, Chevrolet is also only one chapter in their story. Long before Roger got involved with the engineers and executives at the factory, he was building a successful name on his own. Starting in Porsches in 1959, he won SCCA Championships in 1960 and 1961 and also a special award from Competition Press as the North American Champion in *all* road races, including SCCA, USAC, and FIA. (At the same time, the New York Times gave Mark Donohue the "Most Improved Driver" award.) In 1962, Roger was driving for Cunningham, while assembling his famous Zerex Special, with which he astounded the most professional drivers from Europe. And again he outperformed every North American driver for the Competition Press award, and he was also acclaimed Sports Car Driver of the year by the New York Times, the Los Angeles Times, and Sports Illustrated. He also won $34,350 in five races.

With such a record, it's not surprising that he had met Bill Mitchell at one of the races. Then, when Mitchell and Frank Winchell were testing the XP-777 chassis (Corvair Monza GT), it was only natural to invite Roger for his professional opinion. The work was being done at a tiny road course north of Detroit, called Waterford. When Roger got there, Winchell was driving and Jim Musser was doing the mechanical work. Neither of them was into racing, so Penske filled them in on some of the basics—it needed quicker steering, wider wheels, and more tire pressure. He saw what they were doing, and he knew what Hall had, so he suggested they get together, little suspecting that he and Hall would eventually be competing—both in races, and for engineering assistance from Chevrolet.

In return for his services, Penske not only was paid a consultation fee, he was given an all-aluminum 283 Chevrolet engine. This was of the series that Ed Cole meant for production, Duntov meant for the SS Corvette, and Mickey Thompson was going to try at Indianapolis. Penske had recently begun driving a Ferrari GTO for John Mecom's racing team, and because Mecom was inter-

The Penske/Mecom Cooper/Chevrolet never was as much of a success as the Zerex-Cooper. At this stage, Troutman-Barnes had just installed the Traco-built aluminum Chevrolet engine.

ested in practically every form of road racing, he financed the purchase of a new Cooper chassis to take the aluminum Chevy. Because of their reputation with the Scarabs and Chaparrals, Traco and Troutman-Barnes were a natural selection for the engine build and installation, and work began in early 1963.

As soon as Traco got the parts—which actually consisted of little more than a machined block and heads—they proceeded to work their formula on them. Because of the cylinder wall problem, the bore stayed at 3.88 inches, but the displacement was increased by stroking with a late-model crankshaft. Other than that, it got the standard Traco-Chevrolet treatment, only with a relatively conservative cam and compression ratio, and six two-barrel carburetors. It then took a three-block ride down the street to Troutman-Barnes, for installation in the Cooper.

By March the car was running, and with the 350-pound V-8, it was actually a little lighter than it had been with a Climax engine. It was tested at Riverside shortly after that, but the inevitable problems began cropping up, and Penske was too busy driving for Mecom and as a sales engineer for Alcoa to develop it. As it was, he was practically unbeatable with his GTO or the old Zerex-Cooper in the Mecom stable. They tried the Chevy at a few tracks, but it wasn't cooling satisfactorily and the carburetors weren't good enough for a road course. Because they really didn't have any development facilities, Roger took the car to Detroit, and the Chevy R&D crew took a look at it. They ran thermo-couples all over on different radiators and ducts, and finally got it to cool—not incidentally learning tricks for their own rear-engine projects. Roger then went to sidedraft Webers, and that really brought it to life.

For the memorable 1963 Nassau race week, Mecom took the Cooper-Chevy for Roger, along with the Scarab-Chevy for A.J. Foyt, and the Zerex for Augie Pabst. In the Nassau Trophy race, the Mecom-Penske-Cooper-Chevy was a sensation, setting fastest lap of the week, and lowering the old record by eleven seconds. Roger easily led the race for twenty-seven laps—until a water leak, a lost rear body shell, and an overheated engine put him out. Foyt won in the backup Scarab.

But it was shortly after "Chevrolet week" in Nassau that Chevrolet made an official announcement that they were definitely not close to Mecom. After all, he had more than simply Chevy-powered cars, and he was even about to come out with the Dodge-powered Hussein sports racer. Almost simultaneously, Chevrolet R&D was embarking on the rear-engine research project with Chap-arral at Midland, Texas, and Winchell wanted Penske and his Cooper to be available. He was still full-time with Alcoa, but he had invaluable knowledge of the vehicle dynamics of high-performance rear-engine cars, and Winchell was willing to pay for it. The ideal situation, from Chevrolet's viewpoint, would have been a business made up of Hall, Penske, and Sharp (later: Hall, Penske, and Donohue), that could be contracted with for each development program. But Hall wasn't interested in that, as he figured he would be giving up more than he would be gaining, and so Roger merely remained a close associate.

Because Penske was then free of Mecom, he began teaming up with Hall and Sharp in the Chaparrals. Actually, however, his first race in 1964 was with Hall in one of the Grand Sport Corvettes at Sebring. Roger led the opening laps, and between them they kept up fairly nicely behind three Ferrari GTO's for the first half of the race. Finally, an axle broke, and although Penske went out and replaced it with one from a pit car, they could never work their way up again. His next race was at Laguna Seca, where he drove the number two Chaparral, which was still using the Colotti transaxle, and he finished third. Hall won, in the debut of the automatic transmission. At Mosport, Roger drove the automatic, and finished ninth because of a broken sparkplug wire, while Hall didn't finish the other Chaparral. Roger continued to alternate with Sharp in the backup car, and he ran second to Hall in races at Watkins Glen and Meadowdale. For the Road America 500, all three of them drove the new (third) Chaparral 2, also with an automatic, but brake overheating put them out. Two weeks later at Mosport, Hall had a spectacular accident in the standard-shift Chaparral, breaking his arm and putting the car out for the season. For the last two American pro races, Penske took Hall's place and finished second at River-side and first at Laguna Seca. Penske and Sharp also drove the cars at Nassau,

and although Roger won the Governor's Trophy, his suspension broke in the Nassau Trophy race and he took over Sharp's car to share the other win.

At the end of the 1964 racing season, Penske's own personal career analysis was resolved. His driving career had been running in parallel with another successful profession as a sales engineer, and neither allowed time for the sort of growth that Roger was capable of. As he told an interviewer two years previously, "I'm trying to maintain an image as a businessman, a responsible person. Racing, in this sense, is hurting me. I could just say I'll go on racing, but you become a has-been, you turn into a jerk. But racing has enabled me to meet people you've got to know—to have contacts."

One of those contacts, George McKean, the owner of a local Chevrolet dealership, became a close personal friend. When McKean started thinking about retirement, his first choice to succeed him was Roger. In this case, his accomplishments as a driver were irrelevant—he had to stand solely on his ability as a businessman. Although he knew many General Motors people from an engineering standpoint, they had no influence in this area, and could merely nod their heads in approval. Actually, when Penske made the decision to take over the dealership, it was his insurance company and the banks that were financing him who gave him the "either-or" ultimatum. By their standards, Roger was too valuable to risk in a racing car. It had to be the optimum timing for a

Penske had already been driving for Chaparral when Hall broke his arm at Mosport, so he teamed up with Sharp to finish out the 1964 season. Here he drives the automatic to a win at Laguna Seca. He also took second at Riverside.

retirement, however. As one of the very best drivers in America, his next step would have had to be Formula One—and no matter how good a driver he was, he couldn't have started at the top there.

But because of his knowledge and experience, Roger was still in demand as a race team manager. For the 1965 Sebring race, Hall managed to get him to run the operation while Hall/Sharp and Bruce Jennings/Ron Hissom were racing the two Chaparrals. This was not only a new field for Roger, it was a totally new experience for the Chaparral crew. It wasn't exactly the sort of absolute control they were used to—such things as practicing tire and brake changes at 1:00 in the morning before the race. But it paid off. This was the first time that a Chaparral had run an endurance race, and in spite of repeated ignition failures and the transmission locking in first gear, Hall and Sharp won. Actually, they could have finished in a rowboat, as that was the year of the "Great Deluge," and they were so far ahead of the Ford GT's that they spent ten casual minutes in the pits at the height of the storm.

It took less than a year for Penske to get a handle on his new dealership, and then he began considering the promotional value of racing again. Perhaps the interrelation between marketing cars and racing them was not uppermost in his mind when he started in the dealership, but there were other benefits to racing. The Zerex operation had been profitable to both Penske and duPont

Daytona 1966: Roger Penske's first race entry as a car owner and team manager. Dick Guldstrand and George Wintersteen were doing the driving, and in spite of losing the headlights and the radiator, they took a first in class.

in terms of advertising, and now Sun Oil Company was interested in a similar arrangement.

Penske got in touch with Duntov, who recommended a hot young Corvette pilot on the West Coast named Dick Guldstrand. With winter coming on, Guldstrand was installed in a garage in Philadelphia with George Wintersteen's mechanic, Bill Mayberry, and a new 396 Stingray, and he was told to have it ready for Daytona. The car was ready on time, but Philadelphia wasn't, and Guldstrand had to literally shovel the tow truck and trailer through the snow out of Pennsylvania. At Daytona, Penske had his second experience as a team manager, and he managed to generate more excitement than if he had been driving. When the headlights got torn off the car in the middle of the night, and a mechanic poked a screwdriver into the radiator trying to fix them, Roger showed his colors. He taped flashlights to the fenders and ordered the car back out on the track while he searched the parking lot for another production Stingray. By pinning the owner down and forcing money on him, he got the radiator, and installed it in his race car on the next pitstop. Finally, Guldstrand, Wintersteen, and Penske won their class.

Sun Oil was well pleased, so Roger sent the car back to the shops where it was made new again, and it was painted the familiar Sunoco Blue. Sebring was

The Grand Sport Corvette as a roadster. Two coupes had their tops removed before being sold to Penske and Wintersteen. Note the differences from the original coupes—wheels, tires, flares, and extra vents. Chevrolet wasn't at all shy about showing off the cars at an auto show earlier that year.

The GS Corvette roadster looking less like a show car after an off-road excursion. The quick-fill fluid couplings can be seen in the right fender. Dams under the nose seemed to have little effect on front-end lift at speed.

next on the calendar, and first in class wasn't good enough—there had to be a Corvette that could win first overall.

Back in Detroit, the last two of five Duntov/Grand Sport Corvettes were merely taking up space in the Chevrolet warehouse. Both had been converted into roadsters, and one had even been publicly seen at a Notre Dame car show (courtesy of a GM V.P.'s son). But it had been over three years since they were built, and they were rapidly becoming obsolete—destined for scrap. After Daytona, Penske got in touch with the right people at Chevrolet, and he was allowed to buy one of the roadsters. It no longer had the exotic aluminum smallblock engine, but that wasn't important because Roger wanted to install another bigblock like the one that had won Daytona. It was a monumental shoehorn job, as the GS-I was built around the 327 engine, but they had it ready for Sebring. From his previous experience there, Roger knew that the race could be won in the pits, so he also had the roadster equipped for faster action. It had knockoff hubs, naturally, but it also had pneumatic jacks and quick-release couplings in the fender vents where oil and water could be rapidly pressure-injected without raising the hood.

It was a less than spectacular first showing, however. In a straight line, it was without a doubt the fastest car on the track, but the handling had not been adequately sorted and the aerodynamics were still as poor as the coupes had

Sebring 1966: The two Penske-built, Sunoco-sponsored Corvettes getting away as though Roger waved the flag. The GT coupe outran everything else in its class, but the roadster wasn't well enough developed to be competitive.

been. In the early hours it ran in the top ten, until Dick Thompson took it off the course. The exhaust headers were knocked loose, which broke an oil line fitting, and before he got back to the pits the engine was history. But Sun Oil Company was still satisfied with the coupe taking first in class again, and Roger was able to work out a contract with them to run a Lola-Chevy in the upcoming U.S. Road Racing Championship and the new Can-Am series. He traded in his slightly-used Grand Sport Corvette roadster to John Mecom for a new Lola T70. Meanwhile, the only other GS roadster in existence had been bought from Chevrolet by George Wintersteen, to run relatively unsuccessfully in that year's Can-Am series.

Then Mark Donohue sort of ambled in. Donohue and Penske had met in their college days, and they occasionally ran against each other in amateur races when both were driving Formula Juniors. However, Mark had made no great impact in professional racing until Walt Hansgen took him on as a protege. While Walt was the team manager for Mecom he brought Donohue in to co-drive his Ferrari in endurance races, and when Ford hired him in 1966, he insisted that Donohue come along also. It was a profitable arrangement for everyone, as the pair took third at Daytona and second at Sebring in a parade of 427-inch Ford Mark II's. But then, at the LeMans practice session, Hansgen was killed when his car went out of control in the rain. It wasn't the end of Donohue's career, because he had proven his driving skill and engineering knowledge already, and Ford needed all the top American drivers it could get at that time. However, at Hansgen's funeral, Roger started talking to Mark, and he invited him down to a test session. They were running the new Lola, with Dick Thompson doing the development driving, and he wanted Mark to give it a try. It was obviously a very loose association at first, but it didn't take Roger long to see that Mark had the basic abilities he was looking for—and perhaps an even greater motivation to win at any personal sacrifice.

On top of that, Penske was going to try the ultimate weapon in his Lola. He was going to run the bigblock Chevrolet engine that had done so well in his Corvettes at Daytona and Sebring. At that time, the strongest engine you could get in a sports-racer was a bored-out small block Chevrolet, and only Hall had access to the aluminum versions. No one really believed that you could put the monster 427 in a Lola and keep either it or the car together, but Roger had some unofficial assistance from Detroit. When he had first decided to run the 396 Corvette, Gib Hufstader, an amateur race driver in the Corvette Production group, sort of attached himself to the project. Gib was—and still *is*—the sort of enthusiast that Chevrolet couldn't pay to stay away from race tracks, and he was just the sort of experienced engineer that Penske needed around (he was free).

The biggest problem with the bigblock, even in the Corvettes, was not its bulk or weight, but the fact that it wouldn't maintain oil pressure like the small engine. At Daytona and Sebring it was marginal—it had to be driven by the oil pressure gauge instead of the tachometer—but in the Lola it was a

Mark Donohue in his first ride with Roger Penske—the first Lola T70 before it crashed and burned at Watkins Glen. Though they started out with a 427, they had to go back to the more reliable 327 to win any races with it in 1966.

disaster. In the first place, the problems of shoehorning that monster engine into such a tiny car took so much time that they had little left over for testing. They got the car to its first race in such a panic that it didn't even have a tachometer. Mark had never even raced that kind of car before, and he was simply shifting by the seat of his pants. "I'd just run it up until the torque seemed to flatten out, and then shift. We later found out it was running about 7500 rpm— that's quite a lot for the old 427." Pretty soon Mark decided that if he wanted last-minute details like a tach, he was going to have to do them himself—at any hour of the morning. The great problem at the first two races, however, was oil starvation in the corners, causing two blown engines. Hufstader pulled the pan over thirty times, welding in new pickups, new baffles, and larger sumps. But even if they had had a dry sump system in those days they couldn't have whipped it, because it was over a year before R&D discovered that the problem was actually oil *storage—up* in the rocker covers.

Roger, and Sun Oil, couldn't tolerate any more expensive experimentation, so they went back to the basics, and installed the standard 333-inch Traco-Chevrolet to run out the series. And then the roof really fell in. At the next race, the Watkins Glen USRRC, Donohue made his best showing yet. He qualified third, and led the race until he had to pit on the ninth lap to close his gas cap. On the next lap, two cars collided, with one stopping on the track just beyond the crest of a blind curve. The next car over the hill was Donohue, and he clipped the stalled car and spun down the track. As he came to rest sideways on the track, the Lola burst into flames, and Donohue leaped from the car to extinguish his burning driver's suit by rolling in the grass. The Lola was totally destroyed.

Sun Oil was not too happy about the incident, about the gasoline fire and all, but a Sunoco representative visited Donohue in the hospital and speeded his recovery by saying, "We never let anybody down when they're down on their luck. We'll advance the money on future races to rebuild the car." To say that decision paid off for Sunoco is a mild understatement. Broadley immediately shipped them a new chassis, and they were running again for the next race at Kent. Donohue started fourth behind Jerry Grant, Charlie Hayes, and Lothar Motschenbacher, and he won by nearly a lap over John Cannon.

Meanwhile, Penske and Jim Hall had been working out a mutual assistance program. The first Can-Am series was about to begin, and both Chaparral and Chevrolet were interested in finding out how good the Lola was. (It was to win the series that year.) On the other hand, Donohue wasn't familiar with the Chevrolet/Chaparral vehicle development system, and Roger hoped he could learn enough to improve his position. They were going to be competing against each other in the Can-Am, but Hall was preparing the first of the incredible winged Chaparrals, and with the aluminum engines and automatic transmission, he wasn't particularly worried. After Kent, Donohue and the Lola went directly to Midland.

The remains of Donohue's first Sunoco Lola at the Watkins Glen USRRC in 1966. He grazed a spinning car just past a blind crest, and the Lola caught fire while skidding down the track. In spite of painful burns, Mark won another race within a month.

Mark still wasn't a "big name," and he was still driving GT Fords in endurance races, so he wasn't shown around the Chaparral shops too much. Both he and Hall drove the Lola around the test track while Paul Lamar, the resident engineer, instrumented it for aerodynamic lift and a continuous speed recording. Lamar mounted nose and tail spoilers, and the instrumentation recordings showed just where and how it was better. Then they ran it around the skidpad while the mechanics changed tire pressures and anti-roll bars, and it got faster and faster. This was Donohue's first exposure to an organized setup system, and he just stood back and watched. And yet, in all the time he was there, he never drove, nor even saw, the winged Chaparrals. So it's debatable whether Chaparral or Penske benefited more from the session, but the ensuing Can-Am battle indicated that perhaps Chaparral shouldn't have worked so hard on Donohue's car. Mark finished the series second to John Surtees, while Chaparral suffered continual problems with its wings and new engine.

The test trip to Midland was the last outside help Penske was to receive in his USRRC—Can-Am efforts. Chevrolet R&D had all they could handle in the Chaparral project, either in experimental knowledge tradeoff or in the development of new hardware. And anyhow, Penske wasn't particularly interested in running the unproven components that so often caused trouble in the Chaparrals. Not that Donohue needed much help. He practically swept the USRRC in its remaining two seasons, winning every race he finished, and he was usually the strongest challenge to McLaren's domination in the Can-Am series. In addition, he and Penske had the added satisfaction of doing it on their own, except for Sunoco's assistance. Of course, when it became apparent that they couldn't even *buy* the machinery needed to win in the Can-Am, they gave that up to threaten the USAC and NASCAR establishments—but that's a story for another book.

At the end of Donohue's mediocre first season with Penske, things slowed down in the home shops. It was a long time until the Lola could be raced again, and the team wasn't comfortable with the slowed pace. In one of their bull sessions, Mark and Roger started thinking about trying one of Chevrolet's new Camaros against the Mustangs in the year-old Trans-Am series. Roger's primary interest was promotion for his dealership, but Mark had a deeper motivation. In 1965 he had begun racing a Mustang on a very frayed shoestring. He borrowed the chassis, one friend loaned a trailer, another loaned a tow vehicle, and he found a friendly Ford dealer to get the racing parts he needed from Shelby. He spent all of 1965 scrounging up points to go to the National runoffs, and then he got a flat tire while leading Jerry Titus in the Shelby team car. Through 1966, he tried the same thing again, even though he was also driving a Ford GT for Holman-Moody and the Lola for Penske, and again he had a DNF at the runoffs. Shelby wouldn't even give him encouragement, much less team assistance. Now Mark had an opportunity to put together a Camaro, a first-class Penske effort, and he was going to do the job with a vengeance.

For those who may have wondered, four-wheel disc brakes were available on the Camaro. An adapter is necessary for the caliper bracket, and the Corvette emergency brake must be used, but it makes a clean and valuable installation.

This particular Camaro couldn't be any more conspicuous without the tape on its sides, but apparently someone at Chevrolet thought that at least no one could prove it was a race car being tested at the GM Proving Grounds.

There was one small hitch, however. The Camaro 327 engine was over the five-liter limit for the necessary FIA homologation. It wasn't difficult to assemble a five-liter engine, because the installation of a shorter-stroke 283 crankshaft reduced the displacement to 302 cubic inches, but a production run of 1000 cars was needed to qualify. A few people at Chevrolet had already been considering the situation, and with Penske's goading, they went into action. In October 1966, a special production of 1000 Regular Production Option Z/28 Camaros was run off the assembly line. Not only did they have a high-performance 302 engine, but there were optional front disc brakes and steel tube headers. Whether Chevrolet could *sell* them all was another question (although they could be converted back to "production" if necessary), but they had been manufactured and approved for competition, as of January 1967.

Down in R&D, the first I had heard of this mysterious Z/28 car was in November, when I was asked to test the body and to develop a set of aerodynamic "fixes" if necessary. There isn't a car on the road that couldn't use more aerodynamic downforce, and the work I had done on a Chevelle for Smokey Yunick indicated what was necessary—and what Styling wouldn't accept. So I ran the tests, measuring lift and drag on dozens of different combinations of "plows" and "tails," and presented my recommendations. It turned out to be a very rare occasion. In the three and one-half years I worked in R&D, it was the only component I ever worked on that went directly into production—as the optional "Spoiler-Rear Deck Mounted" and "Front Valence," on the Z/28 Camaro. They weren't *exactly* the dimensions I would have liked, but it was better than stock. At the same time, other significant options were listed, such as a larger radiator, a larger fuel tank, bucket seats, and magnesium wheels.

Penske's first Camaro was built the hard way. George Wintersteen went to the factory and drove back an assembly-line stock Z/28, which they proceeded to strip and beef up for Daytona. But before the car was even finished, the Ford team heard about it, and the manager of the GT team gave Donohue an ultimatum: Because the Trans-Ams were to be run the day before the endurance races at both Daytona and Sebring, they couldn't take the chance of Donohue being hurt in the Camaro. (To say nothing of the possible publicity if Donohue *won* in the Camaro.) Donohue couldn't give up the Ford driving, because they were paying him a tremendous figure, not only for racing, but on a daily testing basis, so he told Penske the situation. Roger was annoyed, but he sent Mark back with the word that he would pay Mark the same amount to drive the Camaro, if necessary, and the hell with the Ford GT's. Ford was hurting for top road-racing drivers, especially ones with the vehicle development talents Mark had accumulated, and so they relented. Penske was relieved ... to the tune of several thousand dollars. Not that it came to make much difference, as neither of Donohue's cars finished at Daytona. The Ford GT went out with the plague of transmission output-shaft failures they had that year, and although the Camaro

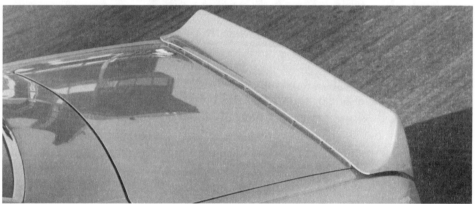

The Z/28 Camaro "Spoiler-Rear Deck" and "Front Valence" were more than mere styling gimmicks. They actually made a measurable contribution to cornering and stability at highway speeds, and were indispensable on a race track.

was able to lead Parnelli Jones' and Dan Gurney's Cougars briefly, it suffered terminal ignition problems after fourteen laps. Then, at Sebring, only two factory Ford GT's were entered, which left Donohue free, and he finished the Camaro second to Titus's Mustang. A few weeks later, Donohue was fourth behind Dan Gurney, Parnelli Jones, and Dick Thompson at Green Valley, Texas, and he began to realize that this Trans-Am was serious business.

The engine was as good as anyone's, but for some reason there were serious brake problems and handling problems. Gib Hufstader had lost interest when they gave up on the 427 engine in the Lola, but because he was quite familiar with the Corvette four-wheel disc brakes, he offered a hand again with the Camaro. Originally the Camaro had rear drums, but Gib produced the necessary adapters and paperwork to fit Corvette discs as an option on the rear. However, the Camaro was somewhat heavier than a Corvette, and they were

The pre-production 1968 Camaro at the GM Proving Grounds with all the Z/28 option pieces. Only 1000 of the 1967 Z/28's were built to satisfy the FIA, but demand became so great that the model supported itself in the market after that.

still running out of brakes. Chevrolet couldn't offer any constructive suggestions without adequate engineering information, so an engineer met Donohue at Bridgehampton on the weekend before the fourth race. Dick Rider was a production brake engineer with little experience in race cars, but he took thermocouple and pressure readings from bow to stern, under the upper limits of braking requirements. This didn't do much good for Donohue, but it gave the Chevrolet test lab something to simulate on their brake dynamometers. At Lime Rock, Donohue stalled on the starting grid and came from the back to finish second to Revson in a Mustang. For the next race, George Follmer drove the Camaro to third place at Mid-Ohio while Mark was driving his last race for Ford— fourth at LeMans, in spite of co-driver McLaren losing half the bodywork.

Meanwhile, politics and personalities were clashing behind the scenes at Chevrolet. Management was upset about the Camaro/Mustang showing in the Trans-Am, and the engineers were explaining that they couldn't solve the problems by telepathy. All their sophisticated tools and instrumentation would be too obvious at any race track and no one wanted to be responsible for allowing Penske's car on the Proving Grounds. Chaparral's cars had seldom been allowed on GM facilities, and even the two times they were taken into the locked shops of R&D, they created a melee of spectators as they entered and left. "Hey *look!* There's the *Chaparral!* Right here at Chevrolet!" But as the urgency of Chevrolet's sinking image won out, the Camaro's race markings were covered with wrapping paper and masking tape, and it was allotted a corner of a small isolated garage at the Proving Grounds.

Rider was again the liaison engineer, and as Donohue explained the problem to him, the car was "... *leaping* and *bounding* out of control, in every corner it went from *understeer* to *oversteer*, and when the brakes were applied the rear axle *banged* into the chassis." Donohue was fresh from the Ford GT program, so he knew what it *ought* to feel like, but he had no idea why it didn't. They spent days working on the car—and nights. By day they would run on whatever straightaway or skidpad wasn't being used, and Donohue and his mechanic, Roy Gane, were continually wrenching until 2:00 in the morning. The answer wasn't simple, by any means, but one of the biggest mistakes had been the anti-windup bar on the rear axle. It turned out to be conflicting with the springs in geometry, binding them up until they had, in effect, an infinite spring rate. And they discovered that the entire chassis was then springing on its own. (This was before the use of structurally supporting roll cages.) But at the same time, as long as they had access to the instrumentation, they took camber-change curves, measured air drag and lift with combinations of spoilers and window openings, and ran extensive brake tests. When the allowed test period was used up, they had reams of data, but the car was still only marginally better. Donohue went to Bryar, and broke an axle shaft in practice. Then he broke another axle shaft in the race.

The axle problem wasn't hard to correct. The factory merely increased a fillet radius, and they magnafluxed them more often from then on. But the chassis was still a major challenge. Because of the rear spring binding, Donohue had balanced the car with incredibly stiff springs in front, and now it all had to be rebalanced. First, however, he had to stiffen the chassis for the stresses of road racing. This meant welding diagonals and braces into the roll cage, making it a rigid structure connecting the suspension points. This doesn't mean he had it done—because neither the racing budget nor time would allow that—it means that Donohue and a welder cut and installed it themselves.

Of course, there were other ways that the Chevrolet engineers could help out without actually working on the car. Mark had been building his own springs, cutting and torching them where necessary, but that was a slow way to sort the handling. The computer simulation of vehicle dynamics was becoming operational in R&D, but no one had, as yet, gathered the necessary input data on a Camaro *race* car for an accurate simulation. So the weekend before the next race at Marlboro, Jim Musser and a technician gathered up dozens of springs of every imaginable rate, loaded them into the R&D tool truck, and set out for the track. (This was no ordinary tool truck. It was a one-ton chassis with a closed bed, and it was equipped with *everything!* Air compressor, arc welder, gas welder, 110-volt generator, engine hoist, floor jacks, dozens of electric and pneumatic hand tools, drawers of parts, and individual tool chests. And yet, with all the panels closed up, it looked like an old vegetable truck.) They met Mark and Roy Gane and the Camaro at Marlboro, and then the fun began. From the skidpad work, Mark knew they needed softer front springs, and Musser was convinced he needed a rear anti-roll bar, so they juggled parts back and forth and back again. Actually, Mark and Roy were doing all the mechanical work— for political reasons, Musser and the technician were relegated to thinking and

Those who envy Mark Donohue might not be willing to sacrifice the fifteen years—and the fortune—he spent buying and building his own race cars. Even today he is still as much a mechanic as he is a driver or engineer.

going out for lunches. But eventually the car began to feel right. Finally they were rid of the *"leaping* and *bounding,"* and Mark declared the car fit for racing. Before they left, Musser asked to drive the car so he could see what it was Mark was trying to achieve. They had been exceedingly cautious about concealing any Chevrolet connection—even going so far as to slip Pennsylvania plates on the tool truck at the track—so it looked all right. But a track guard had been watching all day, and when Musser pulled out, he walked up to Donohue and said, "Say, that engineer from Sun Oil, he's pretty sharp, isn't he."

The race was a week away, and Mark was elated. *Now* the car was *competitive.* They took it back to the shop and rebuilt it completely—engine, transmission, differential, brakes and paint. Still it was just Donohue and Roy Gane doing all the work, and by Saturday morning, after the last two sleepless nights, they left again for Marlboro. They finally staggered in after the last practice session was over, but there was still time to qualify ... and then the factory assistance arrived! Gib Hufstader and Paul Pryor had worked out a new carburetor throttle linkage, and they drove down from Detroit to let Mark try it out. They put the carb on for Mark's qualifying, and he was even faster than before. Mark sat on the pole by almost a second over the fastest Mustang. He stayed awake long enough to call an incredulous Penske, who drove down the next day to watch his Camaro win its first Trans-Am race.

The 1967 season was lost by then, convincingly so after the next race, where they failed a transmission, a fuel tank, a tire, and the steering wheel. But Penske had been asking around, and he finally found out why the Mustangs were hundreds of pounds lighter than his Camaro at pre-race inspection. He started building a new car, only this time he started with an unpainted shell which he first sent to the same weight-reducing shop that Shelby was using. The new chassis was to be ready for the West Coast races, so Penske made arrangements for Bob Johnson and Craig Fisher to campaign the original Camaro somewhat on their own, and they set out for California with the car. They got as far as Reno, Nevada, where the whole rig went over a forty-foot cliff and destroyed everything—the car, trailer, and tow truck. On top of that, the light Camaro wasn't finished yet, and it was getting later every day. Finally they *had* to send it as it was, and there was only time to airfreight it to California. When it arrived on Friday it hadn't even been started, and most of the body was still unpainted. Everyone was up all night, painting and trying to get the wiring sorted out, and when they got it to the track at Crow's Landing (Modesto) the next day, they discovered that the only differential they had was far too low. The only other gear set they could find within 200 miles was too high, but they opted for that, and spent Saturday night installing it. They didn't stand a chance, with only 6000 rpm in the straights, but they made a good showing by conserving tires and pitstops until the Ford team caught on.

Once Penske and Donohue caught on to the West Coast tricks in sedan racing, weights and chassis became equal, and the race was then between drivers and engines. At that point, Donohue and Chevrolet became the team to beat.

The next day, Donohue went to look at the other Camaro. He measured the chassis from corner to corner, and decided it could be rebuilt, with all-new sheet metal. The team was violently opposed to the idea, but Mark insisted it was the *principle* of the thing—all those hours in that chassis—and he backed it up by shipping them an entire body, piece by piece. They were beaten in the series, but they kept on fighting, and although Mark missed the Riverside race because of the Bridgehampton Can-Am, he walked away with the last two Trans-Ams at Las Vegas and Kent.

It was a busy year for Donohue/Penske, as they had been running in the USRRC series at the same time, using it partly as a proving ground for the upcoming Can-Am. That was no challenge, however, as Donohue won six out of the seven races he entered (a pit stop brought a third at Laguna), including the last one at Mid-Ohio, which finally proved that the 427 Chevy engine would work in a Lola after all. But then everything went backwards in the Can-Am. This was the year that team McLaren first came prepared and swept the show, while Mark finished fourth (behind Surtees again), in spite of three DNF's. George Follmer drove the other smallblock Penske Lola steadily to take seventh.

It was obviously an independent Penske/Donohue racing effort in 1967. But there *were* a few curious activities going on at Chevrolet Engineering Center that year. As more and more information about Donohue's Camaro filtered back, a similar test car was set up. It was far from being a race car, but its suspension was much stiffer than production, and at various times it ran with dozens of different combinations of springs, shocks, anti-roll bars, optional geometry, and competition tires. Then, an offspring of that car was the all-independent-suspension Camaro.

Everyone knows that a live rear axle is not as good as independent rear suspension, and the Corvette IRS components were lying around just waiting to be installed in a Camaro. It was easy to justify such a program for possible production because of the anticipated ride improvement, and if it could be included in the optional Z/28 package, so much the better. Al Rasegan got the assignment to produce and test a prototype. The installation was almost a "bolt-in," with a Corvette cross-member and a pinion bracket welded in, to which the differential was mounted, and the Corvette trailing arms pivoting off the old leaf-spring perches. It was amazingly simple … but it didn't *do* anything of any consequence. On diagonal bumps it reduced vehicle "shake" (a torsional vibration), and it eliminated brake hop and power hop at the rear axle, but a judicious installation of shock absorbers could do the same thing. In a straight line, the ride was indistinguishable from the production live axle. But what was worse, the cornering power hadn't improved any. In back-to-back runs with a baseline Camaro, the IRS was occasionally even slower. It might have been improved by experimenting with spring rates and anti-roll bars, but so might the baseline car. And the option price, considering the structure changes necessary on the chassis, would have been difficult to justify. A few years later, Penske tried bending the live axle housing in the middle to get a useful wheel camber at the rear, but even then, the infinitesimal improvement in cornering wasn't worth the over-stressed axles and bearings.

The 1967 Trans-Am series ended on such a strong note that Penske figured Donohue ought to run away from the Mustangs and Cougars in the long-distance races—as long as they played it cool and didn't break. At Sebring, Donohue/Johnson qualified first in class, ahead of Titus/Bucknum in a Mustang. For the first few hours they put on a good show, pushing each other as hard as they thought they could. But the Camaro didn't hold up. Apparently they had ground too much metal from critical areas in the heads, and they both cracked open. At least they learned a lesson, though, and for Daytona they were a little more conservative. Smokey Yunick showed up there also, for the first race with a 1967 Camaro that he had built. He brought in Lloyd Ruby and Al Unser from USAC to run it, and early in practice it was obvious that his engine was assembled for sheer power … and not necessarily durability. However, he was present when the Penske Camaro was weighed in, and he was astounded to learn that it was almost two hundred pounds lighter than his own meticulously prepared car.

Donohue again outqualified all the Sedans, with Smokey's car right beside him on the grid, and Titus's Mustang and the second Penske car were right behind. It was a tremendous battle at first, but soon Smokey's car went down with a bang and the third and fourth running Mustang and Camaro began

Sebring 1968: Fran Hernandez, a key man in Ford's racing activities, intently studying Penske's brake changes, while Roger and Mark converse on the other side. Who would have guessed that the driver was assisting in the job?

fighting it out in the pits. All that pushing kept Donohue and co-driver Fisher on their toes, though, and they ended up taking third overall behind two Porsche sports-racers. The crowd went berserk at the feat, and Penske went home with a large amount of money. Third *overall* at Sebring, in an American sedan. In addition, Penske's second car was fourth overall, with Johnson and Welch driving in just ahead of the Mustang.

Actually the Mustang was somewhat faster, and the success was definitely due to pit work ... or more specifically, a pit *gimmick* dreamed up by Chevrolet engineer Bill Howell. The major pit stop problem for sedans in an endurance race is changing brake pads, or alternatively, conserving the brakes. To speed up the change, Howell devised a vacuum brake-pad retractor that could be controlled by the driver, which speeded up the process by minutes. Every time Titus would catch up, Penske's Camaros would pull away on the pit stops. Fran Hernandez, director of the Mustang effort, just couldn't believe it was possible to change brakes so fast. He ambled over to Penske's pit and watched very closely ... but he still had to admit he was beaten, and he didn't know how. It gave Penske/Donohue good feelings with which to start off the 1968 Trans-Am series.

It's worth mentioning here, that in spite of the amazing performance of Penske's team and pit crews, not all of their great ideas were home-grown. Engineers from Piggins's group watched enough practice and racing, and were detached enough, that they could come up with other productive suggestions besides the brake-change trick. As with Chaparral, sometimes the true parentage of a scheme was indistinct, but there are a few that are generally credited to Bill Howell, Paul Pryor, Herb Fishel, or Jim Kuhn. Though the super-cooled fueling tower was Penske's, the punch-open, cavernous filler neck in the car was built elsewhere. Likewise for the methods of retaining lug nuts on the wheel during a tire change ... and other ideas that may still be confidential.

When Donohue brought his Camaro back to Detroit in the summer of 1968, the climate was a little different. He had already won seven out of the first eight Trans-Am races. The previous year's running had worked out the major problems and the car was both fast and reliable. This time Chevrolet was anxious to see, touch, smell, and measure the car as part of a vehicle dynamics analysis, and to help in the writing of a Camaro Chassis Preparation booklet for general distribution. Because of the quantity of information desired by Chevrolet, an extensive test program was set up and rigidly scheduled. However, there was negligible cost or setup time involved if the timing worked out correctly, because the very same track and instrumentation was to be used for a press preview of the new '69 Chevrolets the same week,

Because "high-performance" Camaros were outside R&D's jurisdiction, Rasegan, now in the Suspension and Steering group, was responsible for the planning of both shows—the press drive, and Donohue's private drive. In both cases, the instrumentation consisted of R&D's telemetry van, which continuously

Jubilant Mark Donohue and Roger Penske in the Winner's Circle at Sebring 1968. Mark Donohue and Craig Fisher placed the Chevrolet Camaro third overall and first in class—an outstanding performance for an American sedan to place this high in an international endurance race.

recorded speed, acceleration and deceleration, lateral acceleration, steering angle, throttle position, and brake points. The course consisted of a foolproof series of high- and low-speed turns, which Rasegan computer-designed to avoid the likelihood of overrevving in second or third gear. For Donohue, there was also a pair of skidpad circles, one 240 feet in diameter and the other 800 feet in diameter, to measure low- and high-speed maximum cornering capability.

A few days after the press had seen the new cars and left, Donohue arrived, fresh and confident after his most recent victory at Mt. Tremblant. Jim Musser and Rasegan were there to run the tests, while Don Gates and I were doing the instrumentation recording. Donohue later recalled his uncharacteristically assured attitude at the time:

"The car was as fast as we could make it. We still had some brake durability problems, but for qualifying there wasn't anything to beat it. I was going to set these blokes on their ear. I went out and ran a bunch of baseline laps as hard as I could and then came in. Musser walked up, and without cracking a smile, he says, 'Well, Mark, I think we can help you out.' I couldn't believe it! But in the next two days we knocked *two seconds off* my lap time!"

This was our first experience with such a complete recording of what a race driver was doing in a race car, and it really told a lot. On the recording, it appeared that there was too much understeer in one direction on the skidpad. By changing the front camber and anti-roll bar, the car became better balanced, and faster. Then the toe-in setting and Panhard rod were changed around, and the car got faster. Then a new type of differential was installed, and the car was faster yet. It was not merely chance, either, as the instrumentation showed exactly where and why the car was faster, and assured us that it was, in fact, the car and not an improvement in the driver. To be honest, a number of changes that were expected to improve handling had a distinct negative effect, but even then, the instruments showed why, and we learned from them.

One of the best lessons was not to put all your faith in maximum cornering on a steady-state skidpad circle, no matter what the speed. To better simulate race-course conditions, a "square course" was marked off, which had four identical corners and four short straights, and allowed a speed range that eliminated shifting. This avoids practically all driver variables, and allows a better observation of exactly what is happening in a repeated transient maneuver.

What was most educational to those of us who studied the recordings, however, was what Donohue himself was doing. He was systematically improving his performance on a very few laps, and then maintaining that near-ultimate level for as long as he cared to run. The recordings were practically identical from corner to corner and run to run—steering, throttle, brake, and acceleration. It was even possible to read out variations in the pavement that were repeatedly run over, such as a minor loss in traction over a bump or painted

Two of the more obvious technical gimmicks that helped keep Donohue in front. The gigantic fuel filler neck not only held a few extra gallons of gas, but it had a latch that was knocked open by the filler spout. The lug holder was a device that allowed all five wheel nuts to be started at once.

line. Since then, I have personally stop-watched many of America's best road-racing drivers through sections of corners and have found no one who can exceed Donohue's level—and maintain it with such precision. At the worst, his elapsed time through any section will not vary more than one-half of one per cent, and in a ten-second-long corner, he repeats within a few *hundredths* of a second—greater accuracy than can be measured with an eye, thumb, and stopwatch. With a test driver such as that, there was no doubt that any changes noted had to be due to the car.

But at the time, what was far more important to all of us, especially Mark, was learning just exactly what the right things were to do, and when to do them, to get a car around a track the fastest. When Mark came to Detroit, he was one of the best drivers in America. But after scientifically learning what the ultimate driving technique is, and then honing that technique to perfection, he became even better. Although I have never analyzed any other driver's abilities to such a degree, scientifically speaking I cannot understand how any driver could be quicker. It is quite possible that right now Mark Donohue may be the best driver in the world. We may soon find out.

Although most engineers at Chevrolet prefer to do their own test driving, only two of us in R&D, Don Cox and I, had any recent racing experience. Even though we were fairly skillful and perceptive, it was still necessary to have drivers such as Hall and Donohue, who not only had far more experience, but who could talk to us in an engineering language. They learned how to drive faster, and we learned how they did it. Not only did those sessions have a profound effect on my own personal racing ability, they provided me with enough insight to create the first comprehensive computer simulation of a racing driver. I still regret leaving the company before having the opportunity to compare the ultimate computer-driven lap to that of Hall or Donohue.

There were other interesting studies performed during Donohue's '68 Camaro test session. The aerodynamic drag and downforce was measured and improved, and the effect was measured on the various test circuits. A little time was even spent establishing a valid brake durability test. When it was possible to fade the current setup, that became the baseline, and various other components were tried. Finally a new pad material was used—and it was an immediate success. Not only was it fade-free, but the wear properties were better. At first, it even seemed to *gain* in thickness. It had one drawback, however. After sitting for a few minutes at the conclusion of the session, four puddles of brake fluid appeared beneath the car. The heat absorption was so great that it literally melted the seals and dust boots right out of the calipers. End of test session 1968.

The pamphlet that resulted from that examination and analysis was quite a success, if it can be judged by the number of independent non-factory-prepared Camaros that were built. It probably revealed more about the preparation of a competition chassis than anyone had ever made public before. There were

Riverside 1968: Penske/Donohue/Team convincingly wrapped up the '68 Trans-Am Series, but not by a runaway at any race. It was always good spectator appeal to make it look hard by letting the Mustangs and Cougars run close behind.

pages on "Spring and Sway Bar Rates," "Shock Absorbers and Bump Stops," "Front-End Geometry and Chassis Balance," and "Subframe Preparation." There were recommendations for front-end alignment, spring rates, wheel offset, and all the "right" part numbers. What's more, it was available to anyone. All you had to do was write a reasonably convincing letter to Chevrolet Engineering, and if your letter reached the right person you got an anonymous copy in a plain brown envelope. Even if you drove a Mustang.

The Penske/Donohue Camaro won ten out of thirteen races in the '68 Trans-Am, and the Penske/Donohue McLaren-Chevrolet also did fairly well in sports-car racing that year. Mark won five out of nine races to take the last U.S. Road Racing Championship. Then, in the six-race Can-Am series, Donohue put down Chaparral with his totally non-Chevrolet-influenced car, finishing just behind the factory McLarens and just ahead of Hall.

For the 1969 season, Penske Racing took a new approach. Because McLaren only sold "last-year's" cars, Penske dealt with Lola for all his activities, including a T70 Coupe for Daytona and Sebring, a Can-Am car, and an Indy car—the last of which was to be powered by an Offy. As it turned out, that was a little more than even Penske/Donohue could handle. The coupe won Daytona and failed at Sebring, while the rest of the team was trying to get two new '69 Camaros ready for the Trans-Am and the Lola ready for Indianapolis.

When the Trans-Am started, everyone was ready, but perhaps a little tired and absent-minded. The first race was lost on rain tires and a pit stop. For the second race, Mark and second driver Bucknum were at Indianapolis. At the third, Bucknum won, but Donohue lost a wheel bearing. At the fourth it was one broken engine and one broken rocker arm. Then at the fifth race another engine blew. People at Chevrolet began to wonder what was going on. There had hardly been a failure in the previous year, and now everything was going wrong. Penske's people had obviously made some of the mistakes, and Traco was still building the engines, but it was claimed that they were getting some misleading information out of Chevrolet—like about the wrong connecting rods and rocker arms. Penske and Vince Piggins, his liaison at Chevrolet, were hardly speaking, and Penske wanted to deal directly with R&D. The issue soon became rather academic, as DeLorean came to Chevrolet and put Musser in charge of all performance work including Piggins's group *and* R&D, so that both became one.

Musser immediately called a meeting with all the interested parties. He wasn't too happy about Penske going to Indy while the Camaros were losing, but he was optimistic. "They've beat us four out of five, but we're using the right approach. We *are* making progress and we will have to start winning."

Part of the right approach he was speaking of had already been involved in Bucknum's single win at Mid-Ohio. Because the track is only a few hours drive from Detroit, Don Gates had driven the instrumentation van down for a special test session preceding the race. Donohue, Bucknum, and Gates had the track to themselves, trying to make both cars as equal as possible. While one car was being worked on, the telemetry gear was installed in the other, and full lap recordings were made of speed, lateral acceleration, steering, throttle, and brake points. Two competitive drivers such as Donohue and Bucknum are naturally curious as to where their differences lie, and so they began driving the same car and comparing the details of their techniques. Although he was consistently faster overall, there were a few places where Donohue was not as quick as Bucknum. Therefore, by working back and forth, each was able to lower the other's laptime. For the race, Mark was able to qualify ahead of Parnelli Jones, and for rare moments at that stage in the series, both Camaros were able to lead the race—Bucknum doing it for the finish, after Donohue burned a wheel bearing.

If there had been enough time, the van might have been loaned out for other races, but there were other nagging vehicle problems that required investigation at the Tech Center. When Musser consolidated all the "outside" activities, Camaro performance could be researched in R&D. Don Cox had just finished up the basic design of the "sucker-car" chassis, and so he was assigned to liaison with Donohue. Because Donohue's racing Camaros were always either in Philadelphia or at the races, Cox had a "simulation car" put

Ontario Motor Speedway 1971: Where Donohue and the Chevrolet V-8 came up against Formula One cars and drivers, and the battle wasn't too lopsided until the Chevy was hit with fuel starvation. On the right is engineer Don Cox.

together. Cox's Camaro was sort of an oddity, with competition suspension, brakes, and tires; production body, chassis, engine, and driveline; and no roll cage, fuel cell, or upholstery. It was necessary to get a test car going as soon as possible, and for rattling around the Tech Center, durability or comfort were of minor importance. Besides, if racing tires are conspicuous, a roll cage is a dead giveaway.

Right away, Cox knew he had a good simulation. In the first brake test session the rear axle hopped violently, and then finally the brakes overheated until the pedal went to the floor. That was a familiar problem to most sedan racers in any make, and it was usually compensated for by pumping up the brakes with the left foot while still accelerating with the right foot. It was hardly confidence-inspiring, however, and so Cox launched into a serious research program. By building a complete brake system on a bedplate, he was able to measure just exactly where all the fluid was going, and by using the brake dynamometer, he found why it was going there. Slowly, small "fixes" improved reliability. Finally, Cox realized that the two pistons in the dual master cylinder had different capacities, and the smaller was plumbed to the front brakes—where the requirements were greatest. Donohue was a little skeptical when Cox called and said, "I've got the final answer to all your brake problems. Switch the hydraulic lines at the master cylinder." But at the end of the season, when Roy Woods and Milt Minter were test-driving Penske's Camaros prior to purchase, they were both incredulous. "That's fantastic, Mark. The brakes work *every time.*"

Concurrently, Cox and Donohue were improving other areas. Alternate front-suspension attachment points were resolved for better cornering geometry, although there was no time to incorporate them that season. The rear-axle hop was cured by the right type and arrangement of hydraulic dampers. Experimentation with shock absorbers also gave them enough knowledge of the requirements, and what was available, to be able to replace the ubiquitous Konis with their own "Penske" shocks.

Going into Bryar, the sixth race, the situation looked bleak for Camaro. The two Mustang teams of Shelby and Bud Moore had been practicing all week, while Donohue was incorporating changes and working out at his skidpad. Then the game changed. Within ten laps, Mark was faster than anybody. In the race, he fought it out with Parnelli until the Mustang brakes gave up, and, with Ed Leslie's help, Camaro finished one-two. Two weeks later at St. Jovite, while Mark was leading, Follmer's second-place Mustang blew, and the resulting oil slick wiped out four of the two Ford teams' cars. From that point on, Mustang was never quite able to recover, and Donohue or Bucknum won each of the remaining races. Penske/Donohue Camaro won the Trans-Am again.

However, whether that was due to any individual, or teamwork, or a better car, or superior engineering—or a single broken Mustang engine—is a moot question. On the other hand, the initial frustration and near failure had opened

Due to running in two other series, Penske's chances looked dark in the 1969 Trans-Am until four of the Ford factory cars were wiped out in one accident and the odds were evened out. Mark motored home in all the remaining races.

A typical Penske pit stop. Earl MacMullin pumps 22 gallons of gas in the car and five gallons on the car, faster than Woody Woodard can wipe the windshield. Total time from wheel-stop to wheel-start is less than six seconds.

fundamental disagreements between Penske and Chevrolet management ... and the seeds of change had been planted.

It cost a minimum of $300,000 to run a competitive two-car Trans-Am team when the factories were directly involved, and no amount of Penske/ Donohue engineering services or consultation could cover that sort of a budget at Chevrolet. The actual dollar distribution is proprietary information, but Chevrolet's contribution to Penske's racing activities was never much compared to that of Sun Oil Company, Sears, Goodyear, Champion ... and the SCCA race purses. Roger Penske flatly states that without Sunoco, he never could have run the Camaros in the 1968–69 Trans-Am Series, much less won them. Ford's budget for the Mustangs—at times there were five factory-sponsored cars—ran into the millions of dollars, while the most useful assistance to come from Chevrolet was engineering research and the right production parts when necessary. Penske's Chevrolet dealerships helped in that respect, because the right pieces could come through authorized channels, even though it was Roger's personal contacts which caused them to flow in the first place. And yet, it was only near the end that Penske was able to break into the great storehouse of tricks— Chevrolet R&D. The rest of the time he had to go through the Product Performance liaison group, which had no direct facilities with which to build or test high-performance components. People like Piggins, Howell, Pryor, Hufstader, and Kuhn, did everything they could, but they had no "hands" with which to produce hardware, and even advice had to be dealt out with great discretion.

With those obstacles, it's surprising that Penske would run a race team at all, especially considering the additional aggravations and opportunity for disaster. But Penske is, above all, a businessman, and what racing successes do for his reputation, his reputation does for his professional activities. In the seven years since he retired from driving, his empire has grown to three Chevrolet dealerships and a dozen other operations from a Hertz agency to the board of directors at Ontario Motor Speedway. When Penske decided to race American Motors' Javelins instead of Camaros, the situation was certainly well-understood at GM. There were no conflicts in the corporate operations. Roger Penske races for its promotional value, and the fact that he can win with any vehicle, only says that much more for his automotive endeavors—and for the Chevrolet product that he prefers to market. To Roger, racing is a tool, but for it to be an effective tool, he *has* to *win*.

At this point it's interesting to compare the Chaparral and Penske operations with respect to Chevrolet. Basically, Chaparral was an outlet through which Chevrolet R&D could experiment with high-performance, advanced concepts, while Penske, through promoting his own operations, promoted the Chevrolet product. It is unlikely that the two could have been combined, and it is inconceivable that they could have been transposed. Hall was always anxious to try any new, faster device, at frequent high cost in reliability, while

CAMAROS CAPTURE SCCA AWARD --- Chevrolet Motor Division has be honored by the Sports Car Club of America (SCCA) as the manufacturer of t most successful cars in the over-2 liter class of the club's 1968 Trans-America Championship competition series. Chevrolet General Manager John Z. DeLorean (right) accepted the manufacturer's trophy from Jim Kaser, SCCA director of professional racing. Camaros won 10 class victories in the 13-event series.

Chevrolet Motor Division   General Motors Building   Detroit, Michigan 48202

Penske was usually very cautious with any new development. It's almost as if they had two totally different philosophies of racing.

To Hall, if nothing broke they weren't learning anything, and with Penske, if anything broke, they weren't working hard enough. Hall was always trying something. Penske is always proving something. Hall had an obsession to innovate. Penske has an obsession to win.

But is it possible to call either one … a Chevrolet factory racing team?

Two of the best showmen in the old NASCAR tradition. Curtis Turner was more a "reputation" or a legend than a race driver in later years, and Smokey still manages to get more exposure than the first place finishers in racing.

6

Smokey Yunick
Comes and Goes

Smokey Yunick really gets around. As owner of "The Best Damn Garage in Town" at Daytona, he is right in the heart of NASCAR racing, and for the past twenty years he has made it a point to run the fastest make at all times ... the hell with corporate allegiances. When Hudsons dominated in the early 50's Smokey was right there. When Chevrolet came out with a V-8 he saw the light and ran with them. In 1957, it looked like Ford had a better idea, and Smokey ran two of their cars until they were both totaled at Darlington the same year. Then Bunkie Knudsen decided to change Pontiac's image, and Smokey helped him out in NASCAR from 1957 until 1962. About then Knudsen was promoted to Chevrolet, and shortly after that Smokey was loaned some of the rare new "porcupine" Chevrolet engines around which to build cars. That began a long association between Smokey and Chevrolet, but when Knudsen went to Ford, he asked Smokey to help over there—for as long as that lasted. And now, finally, Smokey is building Chevrolet engines again, although not nearly as closely with the factory as in the mid-1960's.

After returning the special 427 engines he ran with at Daytona in 1963, Smokey decided to stick with Chevrolet products for a while. The new medium-size Chevelle was about to appear, and he probably had good inside information on the return date for the "porcupine" in production numbers. In addition, he had friends at Chevrolet who knew his capabilities as an engine developer and could contract for them in one way or another. In 1965 the SS 396 Chevelle was storming the country, and Smokey began modifying one for high-performance testing. Actually, he had gotten the car in pure-stock form even before it had been officially announced, so he had a running start at the latest version of the bigblock engine. The working arrangement with Chevrolet was necessarily loose and/or quiet in this period, but engines did pass back and forth between them. It was always possible to identify a Yunick engine at Chevrolet Engineering because of the characteristic holes in the headers. About two inches from the flange on each tube, there was a 3/16" hole ... which was supposedly a top-secret tuning

Daytona 500, 1966: Mario Andretti tried a NASCAR race in the legitimate Smokey Yunick-built Chevelle. He wasn't doing too well with the 405 cubic inch engine, however, when he was hit and had to retire early.

trick. If anyone adopted Smokey's "trick," however, they probably could not detect any difference. Not unless they stuck thermocouples through the holes into the exhaust gases and recorded individual cylinder combustion temperatures during testing.

Not even Smokey's dynamometer could determine *everything* of interest, though, so the Chevelle was prepared for NASCAR competition. For months the car was seen around the circuit, running engine tests, tire tests, and driver tests, but few races. Paul Goldsmith, Smokey's best Pontiac driver, was usually the test driver, although a number of others were rumored to have tried it out. Even Mario Andretti drove it for a short time in the 1966 Daytona 500, but they were never competitive, and dropped out after a collision on lap 31.

At one point, they needed some really high-speed private running room and some specialized instrumentation to go with it. Smokey had been to Firestone's Texas proving grounds, and that seemed about right, so they set out for Texas. Before they could get on the track, though, some sort of schedule conflict came up and they were shut down. Firestone's facilities are not far from Midland, Texas, and Chevrolet had some test gear there at the Chaparral track. But the track was owned by Hall, and there was no great friendship between Hall and Smokey. Finally Winchell, Musser, Hall, and Smokey made suitable arrangements, and the Chevelle was dropped off in Midland.

The Chevelle was not a road-racing car, and it did not take well to Rattle-snake Raceway. Even worse was the reaction of the track to a two-ton race car, because the asphalt had been designed for the tiny racers of the early '60's, and the big stocker was tearing it apart. They did the skidpad work first, and that was not too harmful. It was a big enough chunk of asphalt that the car couldn't move it around very far. The next test was to measure high-speed aerodynamics, and they discovered that the straightaway was not long enough to get the Chevelle up to speed, nor straight enough to keep it on the road.

So Smokey gets the idea to use Texas's long, straight, deserted back roads for race-car development. This is not a souped-up SS 396 ... this is an all-out NASCAR stocker, and Smokey is driving flat-out on two-lane roads. An engineer is buried in the roll cage, reading gauges, and Smokey yells above the screaming exhaust, "Hey, watch this guy." Before the passenger can look up, they rocket past a slow-moving farmer, doing well over 160 mph, and disappear over the next hill.

Hall was concerned that the sheriff would soon be in the neighborhood, but they never heard of the incident again. After all, put yourself in that farmer's position—being passed by a NASCAR sedan out in the middle of nowhere. Would *you* have believed it?

Smokey was an "insider" at Chevrolet, but he was not in as far as Research and Development. Still, he knew enough people to know fairly closely what was going on in there, with respect to Chaparral. This was late 1965, when Chaparral was wrapping up its most successful year ever, and Smokey was interested in picking up a little of that technology for his own NASCAR efforts. It made sense on the surface—that the same knowledge could (and should) be applied to stock-car sedan racing—and a few people began thinking that R&D's engineering development ought to produce a stocker that handled better than anything ever seen before. Winchell and Musser might have had some reservations, but it was an intriguing challenge that offered a broader education in vehicle dynamics, and they adopted it—with a little outside influence.

Jim Musser was given the responsibility for engineering and design, with George Caramanna, an old stock-car driver himself, in charge of construction. But this was in the middle of Musser's ascent, and before long he was put in charge of the entire department. Vic Hickey, of off-road-racing fame, was working in R&D then, and he got the project next. But Hickey was more urgently needed on some production problems that cropped up, and finally Musser got Frank Boehm to see it through. The whole project was handed around too fast for anyone to even get acquainted with it. To further complicate the situation, it was being handled with even more secrecy than the Chaparral project. Because of the visibility of such a large and obvious vehicle, it was given a separate assembly room off the regular locked R&D shops, with even greater inaccessibility. For months, there were not more than a dozen people in all of Chevrolet who knew exactly what was being built. And, correspondingly, none of the other specialists was able to contribute any constructive criticism in the early stages.

There weren't many people who could have offered too much, anyhow, as this was a totally foreign project, even to the road-racing research engineers. It was to be twice as heavy, use the bigblock engine, turn left only (hopefully), and carry a production 1966 Chevelle body. But it promised to produce a lot of new knowledge.

It started, as they say, with a clean sheet of paper. Between Smokey and the engineers, the NASCAR rules were interpreted in light of reports regarding accepted "rule-bending" practices. Because the frame could be modified and strengthened, it was decided that it might be quicker to start from scratch. The shape was the same—roughly—because it had to fit most of the standard components such as engine and suspension mounts. But because low-carbon steel channel rails are not the strongest design possible, chrome-moly steel was Heliarced into complete box section rails throughout. It was not obvious, but since it seemed like a logical interpretation of the rules, no special effort was made to conceal the fact. Roll cages had long been mandatory in NASCAR, and because one had to be there, it might as well be put to good structural use. There were frequent heated discussions over exactly which tubes went where, but the final result looked suspiciously like a tube space frame (birdcage) with square tube rails at the bottom. There was not an ounce of fat in it, either, as Boehm had used his considerable experience in engineering the early Chaparral suspension components to produce the maximum strength and rigidity for a minimum of weight. There was a minimum weight specified in the rules, but it is always better to put any ballast, if necessary, where you *want* it to be.

The computer suspension-analysis system was barely operational at the time, and no track recordings were available from NASCAR circuits, anyhow, so the suspension was designed somewhat intuitively. Up front, the geometry was only slightly changed. The camber-change curve was modified, anti-dive was increased, and, of course, the springs and shocks were beefed considerably. Naturally, all the components were hand-built from chrome-moly plate and tubing for maximum strength. At the rear axle, they were temporarily stumped, since it did not seem like adoption of the popular inboard transaxle and independent suspension would pass unnoticed. However, the live axle was coil sprung, and the rules were liberal enough to allow practically any sort of locating linkage. The greatest problems with a live axle seemed to be that torque reaction loads the left rear tire more heavily, and the axle tends to hop under hard acceleration or braking. Under the latest theories, these effects could be negated by using axle wind-up torque reaction through the proper arms mounted to the frame, and that was what was built (the first time)—a four-trailing-link rear suspension.

When all that was finished, they had to make the thing look like a Chevelle. The roll cage/space frame was laid out to clear the internal dimensions of a Chevelle body, but getting it on was something else. Acid-dipping of body panels had not been adopted yet, so they merely took an assembly-line body shell, stripped it of whatever interior panels were not absolutely necessary (or required by the rules), cut out the entire bottom, and dropped it over the naked chassis. When it was sitting in about the right place, a new firewall and floor pan were made up to match and welded to the frame.

Smokey was busy developing the engine down in Florida. It was the first year of the 427 cubic inch version of the new "public" porcupine bigblock, and that was one of the reasons that Chevrolet, Smokey, and NASCAR were anxious to see Chevrolets back on the track in force. Smokey and his competitors could still recall the effect that a similar engine had at Daytona three years previously, and this year the plan was to do it with a single car.

Time was running out, however. The goal was to have it built and developed by the July 4th Daytona Firecracker 400, a very prestigious event. But the car simply could not be built any faster in Detroit, what with secrecy, overtime policy, limited manpower and all that. Finally, the decision was made for Smokey to finish the car at his own place. He was going to have to do all the detail work, anyhow, since Chevrolet really had no experience in final assembly and rigging of a real NASCAR race car. And, incidentally, up to that point they were still "clean." To a racing enthusiast, what they had was obviously a competition chassis, but to anyone else, it could have been any sort of prototype heavy-duty chassis. What left Detroit was hardly recognizable, anyhow, as everything left in baskets and crates. The chassis and body were still separate, Smokey had the engine and transmission, and all the suspension components were not even welded up yet, many of them being shipped days later. Caramanna went with the "kit," to make sure it was assembled approximately the way it was designed, but down in Florida the atmosphere was a little different. The only people there who objected to two shifts working 24 hours a day were the mechanics.

At the same time as the car was being built, I had a production 1966 Chevelle to use for aerodynamic development. Because lift and drag are of primary importance in superspeedway stock-car competition, and because we were currently gaining considerable experience with sports cars, it looked like a valuable area of investigation. There was already an extensive wind-tunnel report on the aerodynamics of the Chevelle, as almost all serious prototype bodies are now tested by GM Styling before they reach production, but Winchell had developed some doubt as to the accuracy of their figures. Besides, they had not covered some of the areas that we were interested in. Nothing but actual, on-the-road data was good enough for extrapolation to 180 mph.

Instrumentation for lift was simple and well-proven from all the Chaparral testing, but the measurement of air drag was a little more complex. Don

Gates and I had been trying to develop an accurate system for some time experimenting with electronic coast-down speed traps, strain-gauged axle shafts, and taking the slope of a coasting speed curve. The GM Proving Grounds was trying strain-gauged rear wheels, and Styling had tried mounting the body on force transducers. Finally, Gates came up with an extremely precise electronic system that automatically differentiated the coasting speed, and recorded it as negative acceleration, or g's, which could be converted into drag in pounds. It was accurate and precise, and it had good repeatability … as long as all other variables could be controlled: temperature, pressure, gradient, wind, tire growth, chassis friction, lubricant temperature, etc. What's more, the entire lift- and drag-recording system could be rapidly set up, calibrated, and operated by one man.

The hard part was finding minor changes in the body that produced major positive benefits in lift and drag. If it wasn't for racing rules and production limitations, the approach would have been obvious, but NASCAR could get sticky about unusual body configurations. The baseline production Chevelle aerodynamics were about average for the class, although there was lots of room for improvement. Therefore, the first step was to get it into the common racing configuration—lowered and raked forward—and it was immediately better. From there it was mostly a case of testing "tack-on" devices such as plows and spoilers and trying to balance front lift, rear lift, and drag for the optimum net gain. Of course, some of the trials went to ridiculous extremes, such as a plow that scraped on the ground and a tail that obliterated rear vision, but they did contribute to the basic understanding. Other nonacceptable production changes were also tried, such as major vents in the hood, and even no hood at all, and finally, full-length belly pan. It is not inconceivable that a belly pan could be offered as an option—perhaps to someone who felt that fuel economy demanded the reduced air drag. However, it contributed far less than some of the other more subtle devices. Its greatest value was in demonstrating just why the "inverted airfoil" theory had failed on previous high-speed designs. For structural reasons, the underpan was somewhat airfoil shaped, and when it produced questionable results, I took pressure readings across its length and breadth. As it turned out, the presence of wheels and the ground passing by at a high rate made it act very much unlike any airfoil. While the pressure recorder was out, I also took readings all over the hood and grill and cowl plenum to determine the best carburetor air inlet, but that had already been established on the first 1963 porcupines that ran at Daytona.

So what happened? Not much from that. The production group apparently decided that one Smokey Yunick Chevelle was not worth tooling up and producing any large quantity of aerodynamic gimmicks. Not that they were standing in Smokey's way, anyhow. Rule-bending eventually reached such proportions that he finally achieved almost as much by minor body tweaking here and there. What is the difference between a bumper and a plow? Only the height at which it is bolted on the front end.

Eventually they got the car running down in Florida, and it was time for the research engineers to get back in the game. One problem in the development of a superspeedway car is that you need a superspeedway to test on, and the few that exist are not very private. It's bad enough that vehicle secrecy is impossible, but in this case they also had to conceal the identity of the engineers. Someone might get the idea that Chevrolet was going to field a team of race cars, when in fact they were only investigating vehicle dynamics. For the first test, Daytona was rented and Frank Boehm went down to observe while Don Gates handled the instrumentation. It was a totally new field to everyone in R&D, so they concentrated on getting as much information as possible: speed recordings, suspension travel, lift and drag, steering angle, and throttle and brake application. This was before the telemetry truck was built, but the size of the car meant it was possible to use onboard instrumentation without serious weight effects. The primary tool was a continuous ten-channel oscillograph (an extremely precise and responsive strip-chart recorder) backed up with every sort of transducer imaginable. Because it was a brand-new car designed by inexperienced people, the first test really did not resolve much, but they did get the car halfway balanced, and they got a lot of data to analyze back up in Detroit.

This brought about a number of changes before the next test trip at Charlotte. While Smokey was rebuilding the engines, Boehm studied new approaches in weight jacking and oversteer/understeer, and Gates was building a new tire-temperature recorder. Tires are every bit as critical as engines and aerodynamics on the superspeedways, and yet what little the tire companies knew was based mostly on trial and error. Chevrolet R&D knew from road-racing experience what could be done in this area, but there was no data on these tires under these circumstances, and it is pretty hard to get data on a tire at 180–200 mph. The most valuable indicator of tire performance is temperature of the rubber—but at the *instant* it is working, not later in the pits. So Gates assembled a row of infrared sensors aimed at the spinning tire, to measure the temperature continuously … without even touching the tire. After a little debugging, they took the gear and the car to Charlotte for tire tests.

Most of the sessions were supposed to be tire tests, but Smokey was interested in making the car as fast as possible by any means, and all the chassis changes tended to eat up time. However, Gates's new device permitted an immediate evaluation of a set of tires, as one good, hard, high-speed corner would suffice—instead of taking the average of a large number of lap times, which were strongly influenced by driver repeatability. A great deal of very educational data came out of that session, enough to generate many new ideas in both tire design and suspension geometry. But the session had to be cut short. Smokey had a new test driver named Earl Balmer, who had just won a preliminary race at the Daytona 500, and he ran into a little difficulty with the Chevelle and the wall. A tape recording of the incident got wide circulation at Chevrolet.

Daytona Firecracker, 1966: Curtis Turner in the nearly sponsorless Smokey Yunick Chevelle. If it seems to be the same Chevelle that Mario drove, compare the roll cages and the clearance between the front tires and the bumper.

Smokey: "Looks like we better call him in on the next lap." rrrrrrrrRRRRRRRRRRRR BAM! ... Silence ... "Well, that was just one lap too many." The body damage was not too serious, and the car was soon running again, although the next time out it had legendary old Curtis Turner at the wheel.

Smokey was getting ready to make his entrance at Daytona, and not only was Turner one of the best and most experienced drivers available, he was also one of the most colorful. If the car only lasted five laps it would still get as much "ink" as the winner, because it was a Chevrolet and because Turner was driving it. The instrumentation was used one more time while he was getting familiar with the car in Daytona practice. By that time they had enough experience that the gear was telling as much about the driver as it was about the chassis, and yet the engineers had to be subtle about it, since *they* were not the ones out on the track. After the first runs someone casually asked Turner why he had to back off in the middle of the turns, to which he indignantly replied that he *wasn't*. Yet the recordings definitely showed a dip in the throttle application. So Turner went back out and turned even faster laps ... and still there was the dip in the curves. Eventually they decided that the lateral "g" forces were causing the tension cable between the throttle and the instrumentation to sag, giving an erroneous readout, but Turner got some extra speed from *somewhere*. His best practice speed turned out to be 179.3 mph, over four mph faster than the track record, and it brought out all the spies and tipsters. Everyone was quite willing to assume that all the unidentified people who were working the instrumentation (Gates, Boehm, and Musser) were actually Chevrolet engineers.

After all the sightings and rumors, the Chevelle finally appeared in public at the July 4th Daytona 400, and the audience was well-primed. If it wasn't for

Turner on the banks at Daytona ahead of a fastback Charger. In four races, this was the only finish for the Chevelle—in fourth place, in spite of making a number of extra tire changes for safety's sake.

the spectator demand for a GM product to challenge the Chrysler factory cars (especially because Ford had gotten mad and gone home), there might have been more difficulty in getting the Chevelle through technical inspection, due to a number of innovations. However, the same was true for most of the other entries, since NASCAR inspection seemed to have been more concerned with equality of competition than strict rule interpretation. In practice, Turner was down a fraction from his test sessions, and Lee Roy Yarbrough and Richard Petty qualified ahead of him, although it was still sensational to see a Chevrolet in the top three places again.

For the race ... the debut of the Chevrolet R&D-designed Chevelle ... there was not a Chevrolet engineer around, not even in the grandstands. They had done their jobs and they had gathered all the information they needed. Now Smokey could do what he wanted with the chassis. It was not a bad first showing. Turner was in contention for most of the race, and even led for a moment, but with "insurance" tire changes on every fuel stop, the best he could finish was fourth. The race was won by Sam McQuagg, driving the new fastback Dodge Charger—in the first appearance of a lip spoiler on the back, which was acceptable because Chrysler was offering it as a production option.

The next major Grand National race was the Dixie 400 at Atlanta a month later, and by then Yunick and Turner had their sights adjusted. However, they were about to be caught up in someone else's battle. NASCAR had announced rules for 1967 that were more acceptable to Ford, and Ford responded by returning to the 1966 series. But the car that was brought for Fred Lorenzen to drive had the most flagrantly modified body ever seen in "production" racing. The nose was tilted down, the rear end was bent up to act as a spoiler, and the top had been chopped by inches. Because NASCAR had asked for them to return, there was little they could do but accept it, but they handed out warning lists for *everyone* to get straight before the next race. Smokey ended up with about twenty points that had to be changed, including the location of the wheels with respect to the door jamb. That was small consolation to their competitors, however, as Turner easily put his Chevelle on the pole, setting a new track record, and Lorenzen for all their trouble) managed to qualify third. From the start of the race, Turner ran away from everyone, and there might have been a real post-race confrontation if Turner and Lorenzen hadn't both expired at about the halfway point.

Smokey was adamant. If it was legal the first time and acceptable the second time, and the rules did not change, why should he? He skipped the next major NASCAR race at Darlington to go to a USAC race. Because he could not get a driver to jump fences, the car was not raced, but it did pass technical inspection in spite of the fact that both sanctioning bodies had the same rules. As the USAC inspectors said, it was obvious that the frame had been altered, but "... it is permissible to reinforce the frame." Then the whole group got a little quieter as NASCAR, Yunick, USAC, Chevrolet, Ford, and Chrysler perhaps decided that it was wisest to hang together and follow some sort of agreement, instead of publicly berating everyone else. The final coordinating body, the Automobile Competition Commission of the U.S. (ACCUS), established more explicit rules concerning induction, frames, and bodies for the next season.

There were two more big races left in 1966, however, and while Turner went over to drive a Ford for Junior Johnson, Smokey and the Chevrolet engineers decided to have another look at the engine and suspension. Again, the racing engine was Smokey's responsibility, but the car was shipped to Detroit where it could be more closely and quietly examined. In spite of ... or perhaps *because of* ... its speed, Turner was occasionally commenting that it felt "twitchy." Turner was not a development driver who knew all the terminology necessary to communicate with engineers. He might comment, but he never made excuses for his performance or blamed the car (maybe all that "Detroit brainpower" was too intimidating to refute). But because he was such a good "compensator," it was quite possible that there was something seriously wrong with the Chevelle and he was just learning to adapt to it. Also, on one of their test trips, Boehm and Gates began to suspect that the rear roll center was too high, which could cause a transient instability at the limit.

When the Chevelle got to Detroit, a number of engineers drove it, and the learned consensus was that it felt ... "twitchy." In a series of high-speed laps on a banked track at the Proving Grounds, Vic Hickey lost it slightly and clipped a guard rail with the right rear fender. He accepted responsibility for the accident, but it was time for some changes, anyhow. Boehm finally concluded that the exotic four-link rear suspension was geometrically fighting itself, and they gave it up to a more easily analyzed design. The new geometry had two trailing links to take thrust, a single upper link to absorb axle housing torque, and a Watt linkage for lateral forces and location of the roll center. The front suspension seemed to be working correctly, but while there was time, it was redesigned to be more easily adjusted during track tests. After all that work, it was taken to the skidpad to be set up with the same basic stability it had before. Then, when that was taken care of with new spring rates and anti-roll bars, it was taken back to the high-speed tracks, and it was like a new car. It no longer felt like it could spin on a whim. It promised a breakthrough in driver confidence.

But it didn't work out quite right. Possibly Turner had gotten so accustomed to the car as it was, that he couldn't believe it could go faster and yet feel more stable. Without the continual warning, he might have expected it to sneak up on him and pull a surprise. Smokey took the car to Charlotte and Rockingham in October, and they only qualified third and tenth. On top of that, Smokey started having problems at his end of the deal. In both races, the 427 engine lasted less than two hundred miles before coming unglued. The Chevrolet/ Yunick/Turner Chevelle wrapped up the year by finishing only one of four races—the fourth place at Daytona.

Meanwhile ... back in the pack ... while all eyes were on Smokey's Chevelle, a couple of very independents were coming up from nowhere. J.T. Putney kept hammering away at his 1966 Chevelle, finishing in the top ten nine times, placing himself eighth in the final points standings. Also, in midseason, Bobby Allison switched from Ford to Chevelle and *won* three of the shorter races with a 327 engine in a lighter chassis. While Chevrolet was learning about its new engine, the old one was doing all right on its own.

The problem with the new 427 was not a lack of power. Smokey and Turner could outrun anyone with it whenever they chose ... for a few laps. Instead, it was a question of where to balance power versus reliability. The first DNF at Atlanta was merely a random ignition failure, but in testing, and at Charlotte and Rockingham, the 427 showed a definite tendency to come apart at the connecting rod. If not constrained by the rules, Smokey still had a professional obligation to stick with the production rods until he could make them live. After the ordinary techniques of magnafluxing, polishing, and shot-peening, all he could do was experimentally determine how many rpm they would take and still last 400–600 miles. He usually worked around in the 6800–7200 rpm range, but there were a lot of broken engines before one could stay together at 7200. For one race, Smokey actually destroked the engine by about twenty cubic inches for reduced rod stress. It looked like it was going to run the distance, too, but Turner got excited and pushed it, and it also went up. In addition, they were having some problems with valve float at those speeds, although later accomplishments with the engine make one wonder just how accurate their tachometers were. Finally, between Smokey's engines and the new aluminum 427 engines being built for Chaparral, they got most of the bugs worked out, but it was just about too late for the Chevelle.

Over the winter, ACCUS, NASCAR, and USAC had carefully defined exactly what the rules were going to be in 1967, and no deviations would be permitted by anyone. They allowed a 1-1/2 inch spoiler on the back of all cars—production option or not—in the "interests of safety and handling." Absolutely no external body modifications were allowed, and there would be templates to check the shape on every car. However, because it was sometimes difficult to correct bent bodies in a hurry, a car could run on one warning as long as it carried a "penalty spoiler." This was a 2-inch by 50-inch vertical flange attached to the nose, which supposedly cost 5 to 7 miles per hour top speed.

Smokey sat out the Riverside opener so as to have everything in order for the Daytona 500. There was an additional $5,000 award for the fastest qualifier, and he knew the money was his already. A lot of work had been put into the car, not only in speed development, but in satisfying the regulations to the letter and the spirit. However, when he got to the track, the *gosh-darn* body template did not fit his Chevelle, and he had to wear the penalty spoiler. No one from Chevrolet was around, naturally, so Smokey called Detroit and a

Daytona 500, 1967: NASCAR inspection, in which templates are used to identify illegal body modifications. Smokey's Chevelle didn't seem to fit too well. Barely visible behind the template in the bottom picture is Fran Hernandez, and perhaps even John Holman, watching intently.

In 1967 the Chevelle looked a little better-sponsored and a bit more stock. Still, at Daytona Turner was by far the fastest on the track in qualifying and he led at different times until the engine blew near the end of the race.

bunch of us got on the phone for a "brainstorming session." We went over every nickel-and-dime aerodynamic gain we had come up with over the last two years, and tried to think of ways to incorporate them. As it turned out, there *were* things that helped which were legal, but which could not be used for the duration of a race. Anyhow, to make a long story short, the car was "adjusted," and Turner went out and picked up the $5,000. He set a new track record; it was the first time a stocker had broken 180 mph, and they sat on the pole for one of the most hard-fought Daytona races ever. In the race, Turner led the first laps, but he was soon passed by A.J. Foyt, who was then passed by Lee Roy Yarbrough, who was passed by Buddy Baker, who was passed by Mario Andretti. Then it was Turner in the lead again until he was passed by Paul Goldsmith. David Pearson, Cale Yarborough, and Fred Lorenzen also led a few laps each. In all, the nine drivers swapped the lead almost forty times in the 200 laps. Unfortunately, the Chevelle broke a connecting rod on lap 143, and Andretti was leading at the finish.

The worst was yet to come. It was five weeks until the next 500 miler at Atlanta, and Smokey spent the time trying to get just a few more miles out of the engine, and trying to figure out where the body was wrong. When they showed up at Atlanta and the template still didn't fit, they tried it on a production Chevelle and it didn't fit that one, either. So Turner ran without the spoiler, and it looked like he was going to run off with the game. Turner and the Chevelle had the old track record at 148.3 mph, but while everyone else was practicing at 149, Turner was up to 151 mph. He never even got to qualify, however, because of a little trouble on the track.

Cale Yarborough was following Turner through the last turn, when suddenly the Chevelle went out of control. It skidded up the banking and rammed the wall, and then literally took off into the air. As Yarborough watched, the Chevelle was catapulted off the wall, and it disappeared over his head. As he said later, he expected it to come down right on top of him, but it cleared by at least a foot. The Chevelle came down on its nose the first time, but it was still traveling well over a hundred miles per hour, and it pounded end over end down the straightaway. On one of the eight or ten flips, it cleared the pit lane guardrail, and finally stopped not far from a horrified Smokey Yunick. No one expected Turner to come out of it alive ... much less help himself out, and walk to the first-aid station to find out if anything was wrong.

There wasn't enough left on the car to ever tell exactly what happened. To the best of Turner's memory at the instant, he thought something had broken on the suspension. On the other hand, Smokey was watching and he thought Turner simply lost it. At the very least, the incident certainly proved the strength of that very special hand-made frame and roll cage. Drivers have been killed in lesser accidents, when the roll cage was designed and built with just a little less care. Smokey himself was so shaken by the violent, spectacular scene, that he vowed

on the spot to dissolve the team. Turner wasn't troubled, though. He kept driving for other teams until he finally used up his luck in a light plane crash in 1970.

A lot of people in Detroit were struck by the Atlanta report, and then relieved that it was over and that it hadn't been any worse. At last they were free of any implied responsibility. Chevrolet engineers had done all the research they were interested in on superspeedways, and the Chevelle had served its original purpose. Frank Boehm had suggested earlier that as a final test, they ought to point it toward the Atlantic and turn it on to see how far it could get before it sank. There was some question as to what to do with the remains, as there wasn't much purpose in shipping it back to Chevrolet, but Smokey took care of that in short time. He made a door stop out of it. What was left of the engine and transmission was removed, and he had a local salvage yard compress the Chevelle into a one-ton block of steel, which was deposited just outside his shop doors.

Bobby Allison went on to win three more Grand National races in his Chevrolet that year, and with other wins in a Dodge and a Ford, he finished fourth in the final championship points. But Chevrolet had totally lost interest in speedway racing. They hadn't gone in to show off, or for product promotion. They went to learn. As the bigblock engine and the Camaro showed in later years, they learned a lot, but there was not enough to the game to justify continued research. There are no major handling challenges, the cars seldom utilize brakes or transmissions, and the suspension counts little. The only significant vehicle parameters are aerodynamics and engines, and road racing puts greater demands on even those. It is no wonder that NASCAR concentrates on a *driver* championship—they don't even *want* to have any technological advantage from one make to another. Except for spectator product-identification, they might as well have every car be exactly equal. They certainly put on a good show, though.

Smokey couldn't really quit racing. After the Chevelle got rolled up, he started looking at a pre-production 1967 Camaro that he had gotten to evaluate. The Trans-Am had just started to grow, and there were also the Sebring and Daytona Manufacturer's races right close by. Slowly, the Camaro began looking more and more like a Trans-Am car. Near the end of the 1967 season, the Camaro showed up at the Riverside race, and everyone was unpleasantly surprised. SCCA was not used to the NASCAR way of rule-bending, and they flatly declared the car unconstitutional. As long as Smokey was out West, however, he decided not to waste the trip, and he stopped off at Bonneville to wipe out some old Ford and Pontiac speed records … under USAC jurisdiction.

For his next act, Smokey chose to run the 1968 FIA races at Daytona and Sebring. Hulme and McLaren were supposed to drive the Camaro, but there was a disagreement over appearance money and it came down to McLaren and Hall instead. It didn't make much difference, as the car did not pass tech inspection. At Sebring it finally got in the race, and with Al Unser and Lloyd Ruby driving, it qualified right behind Donohue/Fisher in Penske's Camaro. It was a

This is the path Turner's Chevelle took coming out of the fourth turn at Atlanta. The broken guardrail shows how it became a takeoff ramp.

A photograph taken from the final resting point indicates just how far the car traveled while performing non-standard maneuvers.

The only thing left standing on the Chevelle was the roll cage inside the passenger compartment. Nothing else was worth salvaging.

fairly even contest for a while. Smokey's car was lightning on the straights and Penske's would eat it up in the corners. However, after two or three hours of that, Yunick's Camaro engine went up in a big way and Donohue cruised on to win the class with a spectacular third overall.

For the next few seasons, Smokey stuck to NASCAR's pony-car series, the Grand-American. He would carry the Camaro around to the bigger tracks and qualify for the small-car race on Saturday. Then he would try to deal the track promoter into letting him run against the big cars in the Grand National race on Sunday. Anyway ... even first place or nothing in the purse. Eventually, NASCAR tried it a few times, but Smokey had gone elsewhere by then.

In one of the biggest corporate tradeoffs of the year, Bunkie Knudsen left General Motors to become President of Ford Motor Company. No matter how skillful or experienced a man is, he is sure to have personnel problems when he enters a company at that level, and so he tended to draw certain talented individuals from former associates at General Motors. Larry Shinoda was one of the earliest and then, after about a year, Smokey Yunick was brought in to run a Ford competition program. All too soon Knudsen was laid off (in the *second* biggest automotive story of the year) and Smokey was free again. But not for long. A man with that much experience is valuable no matter what his politics are, and if he was able to help Ford with what he had learned at Chevrolet,

Smokey Yunick's Chevrolet Camaro, driven by Lloyd Ruby and Al Unser, retired after 43 laps in the 1968 Sebring race, with a case of engine failure.

perhaps he had also gained useful knowledge there that Chevrolet could use. If Smokey Yunick is racing Chevrolet products today, it isn't because he wins a lot of races, but because he and Chevrolet can learn a lot from each other.

7

Other Racers

Racers tend to be a loyal breed. Whether drivers, builders, or team owners ... they show extreme loyalty to the highest offer, for as long as it lasts. That is not necessarily negative criticism, because professional racing is like any other business in which the first goal is to survive. Therefore, during the quiet years at Chevrolet, the decision as to who were "insiders" and "outsiders" was based largely on estimated loyalty factors. It was bad enough that Chevrolet in general was involved in activities about which they had reason to keep out of the public's attention. But in Research and Development, the problem was particularly sticky, because most of the projects there (high-performance and otherwise) were not even known to the rest of the engineering staff. This meant that there always had to be various levels of "insiders."

At the top, R&D always needed to be 100% certain that any outside contacts would give absolute fidelity. They simply could not afford to work with anyone who might take their fresh, valuable information and run. [No technology I'm revealing in this book is either fresh or valuable to anyone.] Jim Hall was an obvious candidate, because he didn't need any of the outside financial assistance that someone else might offer. He *had* that—what he wanted was the knowledge, which only Chevrolet could offer him. In addition, he owned a Chevrolet dealership, which indicated the strength of his financial involvement with the company. Toward the end of the game, Roger Penske disproved that theory, but that was under slightly different circumstances, and Roger never had quite the access to the facilities and information that Hall did. Smokey Yunick was also an exception to policy because of his Pontiac and Ford ties, and he ended up knowing a little too much when he went back to Ford. But Knudsen brought him in, and the general manager carries quite a bit of influence at Chevrolet.

At a slightly lesser level was the Product Performance group, under Vince Piggins, which screened all incoming requests and offers, and all outgoing information. Because of the transitory nature of Chevrolet's *de facto* policy, all

Jim Travers, left, and Frank Coon make up world-famous Traco Engineering, a small machine shop in Culver City, California. Although they are not engine designers, they are the best racing engine rebuilders in the business.

inflow and outflow had to be evaluated with respect to possible future reversals. Personal selectivity was based on the assumption that in racing there are *no* patriotic allegiances. From the time when the group was first established, many came … but precious few were chosen. Chevrolet was simply not in a position to dole out sponsorships to everyone who had a good idea for a competition activity. Any parts or money that might have changed hands was determined strictly on the basis of what *real* benefits were to be gained—engineering or technological studies or rare, exclusive consultation services. And those were usually *initiated* at Chevrolet.

What few dollars left the building in this way were nothing compared to other outside services and parts that were purchased, such as production proto-type accessories, tooling dies, fiberglass mockup pieces, cutaway and promotional cars, show vehicles, and university professor or research firm advisors. The Product Performance finances came out of the Engineering budget—not the advertising budget—and if it looked as though there was little to be learned in a particular area, the money might as well be spent on internal engineering projects. The specific programs might have been of meager cost compared to Chevrolet's total operations—although major to a racing team owner—but they always got their money's worth in engineering feedback … or the flow *stopped*.

A Penske Camaro engine being set up on the Traco dynamometer by the more visible partner, "Crabby" Travers. For all the engines they turn out in a year they have an extraordinary record of successes—and few failures.

The relationship with Traco Engineering is a good example. Traco is one of racing's oldest teams, and is made up of Jim "Crabby" Travers and Frank Coon, working out of a modest little shop in Culver City, California. For over twenty years, these two have established an unquestionable reputation for building the strongest and most reliable racing engines of all makes and sizes. In the beginning, they assembled Ford flatheads for the more serious pre-war hotrodders, and from that, they grew through midgets up to race-winning Indianapolis cars. Ford hired them to build a desmodromic-valve engine shortly before the AMA ban, and they then used that experience to build a Formula I version for Reventlow. After Reventlow folded, Traco began modifying Chevrolet engines for other customers, such as Jim Hall and Roger Penske. Through them, they came into contact with Chevrolet engineers, notably Frank Winchell, Jim Musser, and Vince Piggins.

Neither Travers nor Coon have much to say about any of their customers. They build engines for many different people, and they maintain their market by respecting confidences between all of them. It is a small secret, however, that Chevrolet Engineering is one of those customers. Exactly what dollars and components are exchanged is proprietary information, but it's an obvious fact that Chevrolet doesn't know *everything* about their own engines. When they discovered that Traco not only knew how to significantly increase the durability of a Chevrolet V-8, but could make it produce more power, they started working together a little more closely.

As it turned out, it is a mutually beneficial arrangement. Chevrolet is not in competition with Traco, and Traco must count on Chevrolet to produce the most workable—or the most easily modified—components. But it's not collusion or even a violation of the spirit of the AMA resolution. It is simply a profitable business arrangement. Chevrolet buys Traco's engines to see how they work, and perhaps buys some consultation, but they are just like any other customer. Chevrolet doesn't tell Traco how to get more power, and they neither race the purchased engines, nor give them to other potential Traco customers to race with. If a modification seems worthwhile, and it can be economically incorporated, it may become "production," and all engine modifiers (including Travers and Coon) are that much further ahead. But Chevrolet remains a very small portion of Traco's income, and everyone prefers it that way. The adoption by Ford and the subsequent rapid abandonment was enough of a financial shock to their tiny operation that they would rather stand alone. They currently build, or rebuild, hundreds of engines a year for many scattered buyers, and the loss of any one of them would be tolerable. The worst loss, of course, would be Roger Penske, as he has been a dedicated customer for almost ten years, and the association alone is worth a lot to their current status. Conversely, the association has also done a lot for Penske's current position.

But Traco will build any engine for any person—as long as they respect the buyer's ability to treat a racing engine as it demands. They get enough work from the "big-buck" professional racers, that they can turn away the "flakes," or bargain-hunters who don't want to pay for what they are getting. Traco builds Ferraris, Porsches, Offys, American Motors, Volkswagens, and even Fords, but their unsolicited testimonial is in favor of Chevrolet. As Travers says: "Just about any engine is good enough for a production car. But when you modify them for power and strength, the smallblock Chevy is the best there is. Don't ask me why, because I don't even think the engineers back there know." You can't buy a seal of approval like that.

One of the very best illustrations of recent Chevrolet high-performance policy—the history, progression, and decline of—is the very public example of Jerry Thompson's racing activities. Shortly after Thompson joined Chevrolet as a development engineer, he began racing Corvairs and Corvettes in the SCCA. By 1965, he was a Division Champion in his own Corvair sedan, and people within Chevrolet Engineering were starting to notice. Coincidentally, he was also a dyno engineer on the Chaparral engine project, but that was totally unrelated to any of his outside operations. What *was* related, was history. Thompson and Don Stoeckel had been development engineers on the Corvair Monza SS (XP-777) project of a few years previous, and they were using the experience to "prodify" the Corvair sedan to the absolute peak of performance. Not only were they cleaning up with it in American SCCA racing, but across the border in Canada the sedan rules were a little more open, and they were terrorizing the competition. The inconspicuous Corvair was a sensation with a Rochester fuel injection setup as designed for the XP-777 by Dick Rutherford. Naturally, everyone thought that it was at least partially factory subsidized, but the only thing the team could take out of the plant was their memories.

In the fall of 1965, Don Yenko, a Chevrolet dealer near Pittsburgh, conceived an even faster production Corvair called the Stinger. It was based on the Corvair Corsa, but it was extensively modified before delivery from his dealership. To be classified as a "Production Car" under the current SCCA rules for competition, a minimum of 100 cars had to be built. The SCCA had been deceived under this rule before, however, and they were reluctant either to approve or classify the car. It wasn't until a passable number of identical Corvairs was sitting in Yenko's lot, that they recognized his sincerity. At that, they felt the car had enough potential to run in D-Production, although Yenko had requested F-Production. Classification of a new car is based on estimated performance, and the Stinger seemed to be a limited-production *race* car.

The Stinger was available in Stages I through V, depending on the level of performance desired, and the dollars available. All of them looked the same, with identical paint jobs and body modifications. To make them "sports cars" instead of sedans, the rear seat was removed and replaced with a package shelf, and the rear pillar was widened with a fiberglass panel. For aerodynamics and cooling, the rear deck was replaced with a lighter fiberglass lid which incorporated a spoiler and air ducts. But the most distinctive feature was the standard white paint with a blue hood and racing stripe.

Beneath that, each one was practically custom-built. They all had heavier springs and shocks and anti-roll bars and a quicker steering ratio, and were available with heavy-duty brakes, wider wheels, and a limited-slip differential. The "Stages" referred primarily to engine equipment. Stage I was for street use, with the basic engine built for turbo-charging, and running four carburetors, exhaust headers, and a larger oil pan. Everything else was built on this, and the racing version, Stage III, finally had an all-out competition engine. It was magnafluxed, zygloed, shot-peened, lightened, and balanced. It was ported, the carburetors were modified, a cam kit installed, and the compression raised to 10.5 to 1. With all those engine and body modifications, including bucket seats in Stage III, it weighed 300 pounds less than a stock Corvair, and it was a *lot* faster. Stages IV and V were beyond SCCA racing, with a bigger bore and fuel injection.

The Yenko Stinger made its first racing appearance at Marlboro in January 1966, with Yenko driving, and it came within a second of the current pacesetter, Bob Tullius's TR4. Yenko had neither the time nor experience to campaign the car, however, so he asked around at Chevrolet. Thompson's championship made him the obvious choice, and so he, Stoeckel, and Rutherford formed RST Engineering to make their racing a little less unprofitable. Not only was the Stinger competitive in DP under RST, it was almost fast enough for C-Production. In the first few races the Stinger was so far ahead that Yenko got on the phone and dropped his pride to insist that RST shouldn't try so *hard. Just win.* And so they did just that—Thompson drove the car to an easy Divisional Championship in 1966. They only managed a fifth in the National runoffs, however, and so they ran through the whole thing again the next year to get another chance at it. In 1967, Thompson's Stinger was declared National Champion at the Daytona ARRC over the best import efforts by Tullius, Kastner, and the Huffaker Healey.

That was all that was necessary. Yenko had sold all his cars and made a profit at it, which was his primary intent—not winning races. The production Corvair image hadn't been hurt a bit, and Chevrolet was absolutely "clean." And Thompson had firmly established his reputation as a top driver/engineer. RST Engineering shut down at the end of the season, returned the Stinger, and divided up the remains. Since then, Yenko has gone on to repeat the system with other Chevrolet products such as a Chevy II (Yenko Deuce) and the Vega (Yenko Turbo Stinger), but he hasn't seen fit to promote them with an extensive road-racing program.

Thompson had sold his own Corvair, but 1967 had been such an easy year that he began picking up other rides. He drove a Camaro in a few Trans-Ams, and he began co-driving with Tony DeLorenzo in a 427 Stingray. Thompson and DeLorenzo first met when they were both driving Corvairs in 1965, and it seemed like an ideal relationship, with Thompson an "inside engineer," and DeLorenzo's father a vice president of General Motors. But Tony's master's degree in public

Daytona ARRC, 1967: Jerry Thompson wraps up the Championship for Yenko's Stinger, with the help of RST Engineering and Chevrolet wisdom. It looked a little strange next to all the European sports cars, but it worked.

One of the more successful amateur production Stingrays, driven by Tony DeLorenzo, son of an embarrassed GM VP. Still, every part on the car was bought through normal channels, and it was built in a private garage.

A common sight in 1969 Midwest and Eastern SCCA events—the two O-C Fiberglas 427 Corvettes driven by Tony DeLorenzo and Jerry Thompson leading the field; finishing first in a long succession of races, and taking the National title that year.

L to r: Jerry Thompson (Chevrolet engineer)-Tony DeLorenzo (General Motors VP's son) and Dick Lang-Gib Hufstader (Chevrolet engineer) placed second and third in GT at Sebring, providing great exposure for their sponsor O-C Fiberglas.

relations turned out to be of far greater value than his name. Tony *bought* his 1967 L-88 Corvette from Hanley Dawson Chevrolet, and the only "favor" that might be attributed to his father, was getting the Engineering Center to evaluate the car after it had been set up for racing. At that, all it consisted of, according to Tony, was "… running it up and down the straightaway to see if it would blow up." The car had come through normal channels, and Tony listened to rumors that there were inherent problems in the aluminum-head engine. But, as it turned out, so few of the "heavy-duty" Corvettes were built that the factory and the assemblers took great care in setting them up correctly. It didn't matter *who* you were (or weren't). Hanley-Dawson paid the way that first year, while DeLorenzo took second place in the National Championship, and he teamed with Thompson at Elkhart Lake, Daytona, and Sebring.

Thompson was using his engineering to keep the car running, and DeLorenzo was using his salesmanship to keep the sponsorship flowing. For 1968, they brought in Z. Frank Chevrolet of Chicago, which allowed them to run two cars: the '67 with a small engine, and a new '69 with the large engine. That season they were both second at the Nationals, Thompson in B-Production and Tony in A-Production. But that season they were also able to sell Owens-Corning on the idea of using a Corvette racing team to promote Fiberglas. With this, they were able to run two late-model 427 Corvettes throughout 1969. Tony gave up his full-time job to form Troy Promotions, and they really promoted the daylights out of Owens-Corning.

The team looked about ten times as strong as it actually was. They bought a semi-trailer for $100 to haul the cars, and painted it and the cars in O-C-F colors. There was a crew of up to a dozen (depending on how close to home the race was) talented people to support the operation, although they were largely unpaid volunteers. And Thompson/DeLorenzo were the ubiquitous showmen, selling Owens-Corning at business meetings, shows, and even in the pits.

Even if they had earned their successes the long and hard way, even if they weren't ten feet tall, they could have cowed the competition into submission. But when they won eleven National races in a row, and the Championship, and also took second at eight of them, everyone was saying, "Well, no wonder! Look at all the help they're getting from Chevrolet."

It didn't really work quite like that, however. The amount of help they got was roughly equal to the amount of help they *gave*. Chevrolet couldn't have made the Corvettes go any faster within the given rules but they could help keep the cars together. As an engineer, Thompson might not subscribe to such an unqualified statement as "Racing improves the breed," but he does have a history full of examples to support it. One of the first was at Daytona in 1967. Going past the pits at about 175 mph on the banking, Tony hit the brakes and the front wheels went into full toe-out, sending him spinning off into the infield. The steering relay rod had buckled in compression. So they straightened and reinforced it, and reported it to Duntov, who rapidly had heavier ones made. They were proven in the next race, and were soon in production.

A similar incident was responsible for heavier front-wheel bearings. One was lost under stress on the banking and it practically melted a corner off the car. The same was true for the driveshaft, and then the rear spindles, and, of course, the disc brakes. The team would uncover weak links, carry them back to Chevrolet, and get stronger ones to replace them. It was a conscientious exchange—a proper two-way relationship. Chevrolet was getting low-cost development through known engineers and technicians, and the team was getting first crack at the stronger components. But they had no speed equipment or knowledge that wasn't available to everyone else. When it came to building the cars, neither Thompson nor DeLorenzo was in a very good position to expedite parts. They frequently found salvage yards to be the quickest, most economical route.

Then the shock came, late in 1970, and the true picture became apparent. The team had no competition in amateur racing, so they were anxious to take on the pros. Trans-Am seemed like the most familiar game, and it paid well for a good finish. But the decision was made too late, and the two Camaros were never really completed, even at the end of the season. Owens-Corning went along with the gag for a while—promoting Fiberglas with the Corvettes *and* with a pair of steel Camaros—but both teams were weakened and they had a disastrous season. There simply wasn't enough time or dollars for both efforts. After Daytona '71, Owens-Corning decided that they had gotten enough out of it, and they got out. There was very little time left before the start of the '71 Trans-Am season.

So DeLorenzo bought a pair of Bud Moore Mustangs, which certainly proved a point, if nothing else. Just how much Chevrolet racing support can there be when two such "insiders" buy Fords to race? And it wasn't that Mustangs were basically any faster, because Parnelli Jones and Mark Donohue had already resolved that. It was a case of trying to sell sponsorship on race cars that were bastard children of an uninvolved manufacturer. Everyone knew that Chevrolet wasn't going to help any. Of course, the Ford engineers weren't going to get too close, either, but they weren't that involved, anyhow. Bud Moore built the cars, and Kar Kraft had most of the racing talent, and between them they managed to help out considerably. DeLorenzo's father must have had some difficult times at General Motors executive meetings, but he finally admitted that it probably was a good move, because no one could then question his own involvement. He never wanted Tony to race *anything* in the first place. Thompson had the worst time of it at work in Chevrolet Engineering. His superiors were so out of racing that they couldn't have cared less, but to the friends who accused him of desertion he simply said, "It was either stick with Tony and drive Mustangs—or go off on my own and drive nails." Everyone knew about the incredible amount of help he *wasn't* getting from Chevrolet by then, anyhow. Thompson and DeLorenzo did somewhat better with the

Mustangs, but it's impossible to conclude anything from that, as most of their factory-supported competition had left the Trans-Am series.

In the field of drag racing, Chevrolet has been even less concerned with any specific individual or team activities. In the first place, there has never been any need to. Chevrolet products continually win championships in all the "stock" classes they can compete in, solely on their inherent strength and the skill of the independent professionals who campaign them. Of course, the fact that Chevrolet products usually outnumber their opposition by the same ratio as new car sales doesn't hurt a bit, either. But as long as stock-car drag racing is primarily dependent on engines, weight, and tires, Chevrolet will continue to dominate. Tires are equal for just about everyone, weight-reduction tricks are obviously common to everyone, and the Chevrolet engine has established itself as the baseline for power per pound and reliability—in class racing, that is. In unlimited drag racing, there is nothing to beat the Chrysler hemi, but when you get in the 1500-horsepower-for-six-seconds area, that's not too closely related to automotive use ... it's more like a semi-controlled explosion in a barely reusable container. Because of all the Chevrolet successes, everyone naturally assumes that they are pulling the strings, which means the company can sit back and take credit for what all the independents are doing.

However, the biggest reason Chevrolet doesn't get involved is that there is little to be learned from it. For their highly specialized purpose, the drag-engine builders have developed an art of producing "flash" horsepower that is far more advanced than the science of engine engineering. After all, they have numbers on their side. There are hundreds of engine builders trying all kinds of random tricky experiments, and the results are quickly and easily evaluated. Some manufacturers have attempted to break into all the free publicity generated by drag racing, but they haven't stood a chance against the old-line intuitive builders. Ford made the mistake of announcing the "world's fastest" dragster before they built it, and then had to quietly lose it and all its better ideas. There were too many ideas and too little development to beat the amateurs, and there was not enough "spin-off" into production engineering.

What is there to be gained by an automotive manufacturer getting into drag racing? What kind of engineering exchange could there be? Aside from engines and tires, not much. Vehicle dynamics studies are rather pointless, because the ideal condition is a perfectly straight path for less than a mile. Transmissions are highly specialized, to the extreme case where direct-drive is used with a calibrated "slipper" clutch. In aerodynamics, the drag racers are only beginning to catch up to road racing's current state of technology. The drag chute is more efficient and more stable than any mechanical brake system, but hardly applicable to production. Even where there might be some valuable knowledge—engine durability or tire traction—road racing is far more representative of the most extreme public demands.

On the other hand, Chevrolet wouldn't know there was nothing to be gained if they didn't keep their eyes on the game. There have been some covert exploratory incidents. In the fall of 1966, an attempt was made to completely instrument and analyze a typical drag run. A computer program which simulated a vehicle accelerating at full throttle had recently been completed, and it was necessary to verify it with actual tests. It had already been checked out with production Chevrolet vehicles, but for credible advanced work with the program, it had to be proved at higher limits.

It wasn't hard to find and rent one of the quickest Camaro drag cars, and it wasn't hard to rent some privacy at a nearby drag strip. The instrumentation was quite straightforward, with a continual speed recording, continual accelerometer readout, shift points, and elapsed time. A considerable amount of data was also taken on what the chassis was doing: aero lift, wheel hop, and weight transfer. Then, to be able to simulate the car on a computer, information was needed on the engine torque curve, tire traction coefficient and radius, and chassis dimensions such as center of gravity height, wheelbase, etc. It was a load of knowledge, and, in itself, told a lot about current drag science.

The hard part was getting the computer to agree. It took many changes and reruns to correlate the output with the actual test data, particularly with respect to starting-line techniques, but each change told more about what was going on. Once the computer program was checked out, however, the matter rested. The information was only of academic interest to Chevrolet R&D, and the drag-car builders saw no useful results. The program could have been used to evaluate future vehicle configurations, but actual back-to-back comparison runs were almost as easy. No one was pounding on Chevrolet's doors for engineering help … they all wanted financial help.

A few years later, "Grumpy" Jenkins heard about the R&D instrumentation van, and asked for help with his Chevy drag cars. There weren't any specific areas that anyone wanted to investigate, however, and so the test program was rather flexible. This time, the instrumentation had been advanced to where far more data could be taken on each run. In addition to all the previous readout, a typical recording might include engine speed, speed of both rear wheels, engine torque, and axle torque. Still, little was learned. It was discovered that there was an unexpected amount of horsepower being lost between the engine and the axles, and that led to more investigations into gear-train efficiency. It was also interesting to note that the engine overruns quite a bit more than expected in wide-open-throttle speed shifting. Regardless of the quickness of the driver, declutching at a 7200 rpm shift point will allow the engine to "spike" up to almost 9000 rpm.

But simple drag racing never meant much to Chevrolet engineers. It is a difficult task to win repeatedly, but it is not a *complex* task. There is little use for advanced technology and even less demand. If the racers think Chevrolet is actively or intentionally developing a winning product, it is because they grossly underestimate their own abilities.

The situation has always been somewhat similar with regard to USAC Championship or Indianapolis racing. It is highly competitive racing, and a challenge to build a winning car, but it is too far removed from production to justify any serious involvement. There was one false start toward an open-wheel version of the aluminum monocoque Chaparral, which *might* have been raced at Indianapolis, but there was not sound enough research justification to keep the project alive. The closest that Chevrolet ever got, perhaps, was in the Corvette SS aluminum blocks that were shipped to Mickey Thompson, and even that was an extremely casual affair.

Thompson had done surprisingly well at Indianapolis in 1962. Dan Gurney had qualified his unconventional new rear-engine Buick V-8 car eighth, and it held its own fairly well against the Meyer-Drakes until the transmission failed. Naturally, there were spectators there from Chevrolet and Ford, and they all went home with engineering figures dancing in their heads. Shortly after that, the new Stingray was announced and Duntov arranged for Thompson to run one against the Cobras. Therefore, when rumors began to pass back and forth between Chevrolet and Ford concerning engine development for next year's Indy, Thompson was the most obvious candidate to try out a Chevy engine there. The engine make was probably of minor concern to him, because over the winter he was coming up with an even more radical vehicle, which theoretically could win with *any* engine. That was the year Thompson showed up with a car built around Firestone's controversial new 12-inch tires (22 to 24-inch rolling diameter, on a 12-inch diameter wheel). But the engine he ran with could have had an effect on his parts business, because he specialized in speed equipment for American V-8's—not Meyer-Drakes. Ford was busy preparing an aluminum block engine for Colin Chapman to run, but they hardly had time to build enough for him, whereas Thompson knew that Chevrolet had a number of well-proven aluminum smallblocks on hand.

Practically all he got from Chevrolet was machined blocks and heads. There were no specifications, instructions, or recommendations as to assembly or operation limitations. If Chevrolet knew, they were not about to officially endorse whatever Thompson was going to do with the engines. Not that he needed much help in that direction, anyhow. He already had a complete development shop with all the dyno and machining equipment he needed to produce the special components he was marketing. Because he used all his own pistons, rods, and crankshaft, it was easy to sleeve and destroke the 283 engine down to the 255-cubic-inch limit. Of course, Thompson also had to do extensive power development on the new engine, during which more than one of the rare light-weight blocks was ripped open by sustained high rpm on the dyno.

When everyone got to Indy with the new cars, there was more noise in the pits than on the track. The establishment could not take both Thompson/Firestone/ Chevrolet's new ideas and Chapman/Ford's new ideas all at once—especially

Mickey Thompson's version of the Chevy aluminum smallblock 283 engine, with his own pistons, rods, and crankshaft, sleeved and destroked to 255 cubic inches to meet Indianapolis "stockblock" limits.

The Chevy 255 engine fitted to Thompson's Indy car for the 1962 race. Plagued with failure, Duane Carter got the car qualified only to lose the engine during the race. Mickey's other car finished ninth overall—the only time a Chevrolet engine finished.

when they ran so *fast.* Jim Clark and Dan Gurney in the Fords were the most worrisome, because Thompson was having considerable problems with his three new and two year-old cars. For various reasons such as chassis breakage, engine breakage, and lack of familiarization, Masten Gregory, Graham Hill, and Billy Krause were never able to qualify three of the Chevy-powered cars, while Clark and Gurney sat fifth and twelfth on the grid. Fifty-year-old Duane Carter finally got one of the Thompson cars in the fifteenth spot, and then, on the last day, rookie Al Miller made the grid with Gurney's 1962 car (on 15-inch wheels). Miller's time was only 1 mph slower than Clark's, for ninth fastest overall, and so surprising, that the Chevy engine was protested, torn down, and found legal.

The race was almost anticlimactic for Thompson. Carter lost his brakes and spun, breaking a hub carrier against the wall. It was replaced in an hour, and he went back out again dead last, only to lose the engine a few laps later. Miller, starting thirty-first, due to USAC's odd qualifying arrangement, ran a cool, steady race to finish ninth as other cars fell down around him. That was all overshadowed by the battle for first place, as that was the year of the great "Parnelli Jones-oil leak-Jim Clark" flap in which Clark's Lotus-Ford had to settle for second. So Jones's Meyer-Drake was first, Clark's Ford second, Gurney's Ford seventh, and Miller's Chevy ninth.

A comparison of years at Indy. In the foreground is Thompson's 1962 car, updated with a Chevy engine, and behind is his 1963 racer with the low-profile body which was built to accommodate the tires he developed with Firestone.

Indianapolis 1963: Duane Carter in the new Thompson-Chevy qualified fifteenth, but broke in the race. His teammate, Al Miller, was faster in the older car, and came in ninth—the only finish to date for a Chevrolet engine at Indy.

It was not exactly an equitable comparison between Chevrolet and Ford, however, with Thompson, Miller, and Carter on one side and Chapman, Clark, and Gurney on the other ... and dubious contributions from either manufacturer. Still, that has been the best showing ever for a Chevrolet V-8 at Indianapolis—the only time one has ever qualified for the race, much less finished in the top ten. Ford went on to bigger and better things, such as the very non-"stockblock" 4-cam engine that eventually won the race for them, and Chevrolet was escalated out of even the most minor interest. The next year, Thompson made a logical switch to factory assistance with the Ford engine. But 1964 was the race in which one of his cars was involved in the first lap melee, and everyone at Chevrolet certainly had lots of intense personal feelings about participation after that.

Over the years, many other USAC racers have vainly tried to make the cast iron Chevrolet block competitive at Indy, as the displacement limit on "stock-blocks" rose. The most persistent has probably been Jerry Eisert. When the first 6-cylinder Corvettes came out, Jerry began racing them in drags and at Bonneville, and when the V-8 became available Chevrolet went to Eisert with a specific assignment. He was to run the new Corvette against a Mercedes 300 SL at Bonneville and produce an honest independent evaluation. It wasn't even a contest, as everyone was soon to learn from open road-racing competition. A

Indianapolis, 1965: The familiar Harrison Special Chevy trying to make the grid. For years the cars just never quite made it—even when they switched to an overhead-cam Ford. Builder Jerry Eisert is at the left rear.

few years later, Eisert became more familiar with Chevrolet as he worked with Jim Rathmann on the NASCAR circuit.

By 1965, Eisert had been through road racing and had settled in USAC. That was when he began building his own complete cars, and the first one was Chevrolet-powered, naturally. For the championship circuit, 305-inch engines were allowed, and relative newcomer Al Unser had a mediocre year in the car. The best they could do against the Meyer-Drakes and 4-cam Fords was a seventh place at Milwaukee. At Indianapolis, only 255 inches were allowed and the car didn't even make the grid. For 1966, a "stockblock" limit of 305 inches was permitted at Indianapolis, also, and Eisert tried again. Still the engine was not competitive, and Eisert switched to the 4-cam Ford—which didn't make the grid, either, as it turned out.

For the next couple of years, Eisert stuck to the Championship trail with his familiar Harrison Special, although none of a number of top drivers could get any Chevys into the first five spots. Then USAC upped the displacement limit again, to 320 inches in 1969, and 203 inches for a supercharged stockblock. Eisert took turbo-Chevys to Indy in 1969 and 1970, and *still* could not qualify. But Roger Penske was getting interested in USAC money by then, and he and Donohue were Chevrolet-powered by tradition. In 1968 they squeezed in a couple of USAC road races with a Chevy-Eagle, and Mark picked up a sixth at Mosport and broke at Riverside, while getting to know the cars and drivers.

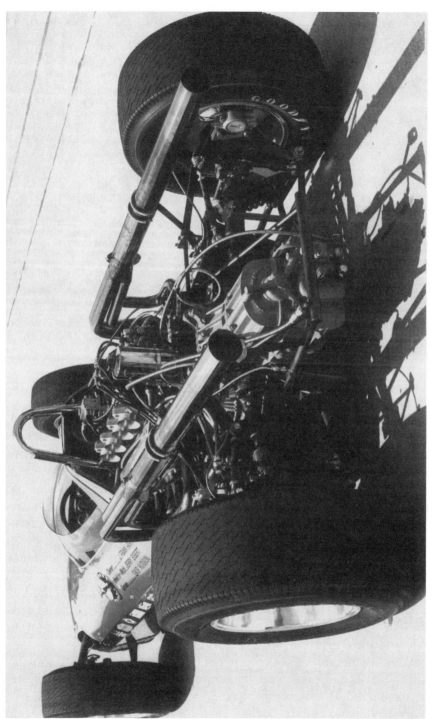

The Harrison/Eisert car was able to run a 305 Chevy on the Championship Circuit, where it was more competitive, with Al Unser driving. When the limit was upped to 320 inches, Follmer finally won with a Chevy at Phoenix in 1969.

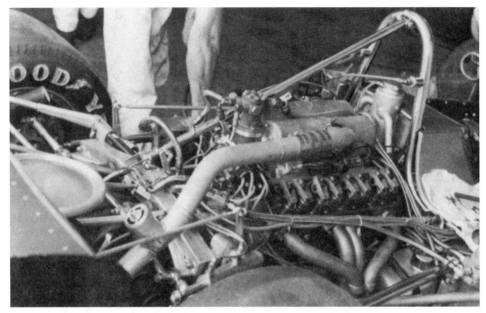

A Smokey Yunick-prepared turbocharged Chevy USAC car at the Ontario 500. The obvious pressure duct comes from a turbocharger at the end of the right tailpipe, and incorporates a "blow-off" valve.

In the first USAC race with the 320-inch stockblock limit, George Follmer astounded everyone by winning with a Chevrolet at Phoenix, as Foyt, Andretti, and Al Unser dropped out. But the Meyer-Drakes and Fords still had the advantage, road course or oval, short track or long. At Indianapolis, Donohue tried his best with the Chevy, using it to pass his driver's test. However, to be competitive in the race, he had to switch to the turbocharged Meyer-Drake with which he qualified seventh. For the remaining USAC road races that Donohue ran that year, Penske opted for the 320 Chevy, although probably for the economic logic rather than the likelihood of winning with it.

Chevrolet need not be embarrassed about the performance of the smallblock engine in USAC. The Meyer-Drake and 4-cam Ford are *racing* engines, built specifically for that purpose, while the Chevrolet is by far the strongest production engine challenging them. When USAC comes up with an equitable relative displacement for overhead cams versus overhead valves, the game will not only be a lot more competitive, but a lot more inexpensive.

Chevrolet Engineering is not ignorant of the situation, either. It shouldn't be any surprise that they have experimented with practically every configuration of engine, including the smallblock in 255, 305, 320, and 350 cubic inch versions, on alcohol and with turbochargers. It makes sense ... why not learn what the engine does under such impossible stresses, as it is subjected to at Indianapolis? But all that has ever passed out of the building is perhaps a little information on what was done and how it was done, and the performance results. Possibly that inside information is what keeps the independents' faith up against the USAC odds.

Surprisingly enough, there is not much to say about Team McLaren in the story of Chevrolet racing research. For one reason or another, the two companies have not found it profitable—from an engineering standpoint—to get together very closely. Bruce first became familiar with American V-8's when he bought Penske's aluminum Zerex Cooper-Oldsmobile, but it was not until 1966 that he found it necessary to switch to the larger cast iron Chevrolet smallblock for the Can-Am series. It didn't do much for him at first, as John Surtees won that first year with a Lola-Chevrolet, but Bruce was merely getting his ducks in a row for a major assault in 1967. When they came back with the new M6A and Denny Hulme as a team driver, out of six races they won six fastest laps, five races, and the championship. Suddenly, they were a major power in American racing.

McLaren was quite aware of the Chaparral aluminum engines he was competing against during the 1967 season, and although he didn't have much difficulty beating them, he still felt that the McLaren's successes had earned similar cooperation from Chevrolet. However, because of his lack of knowledge of just exactly who the responsible people were, his first contacts at Chevrolet were through Vince Piggins. McLaren was a very big name then, and he was doing a lot for the Chevrolet image, but however much Piggins might have wanted to help, he didn't have access to Research and Development's experimental pieces. Meetings were arranged with R&D, although everyone was playing his cards pretty close. McLaren had won the series, true, but what could he offer Chevrolet R&D in the way of engineering knowledge? In addition, he was a little too flexible in his dealings with other companies, such as Ford Motor Company and their 4-cam Indy V-8, which he was using in Formula One. R&D was getting all it needed from the Chaparral operation, and they were loaning it all they could spare at the moment. R&D could not take a chance in expanding the program, especially for someone who had other ties. Besides, if there were any leftovers, Penske was probably next in line.

That did not keep Piggins from cooperating as much as his budget and facilities would allow, though, and for the next few years there was sort of an odd, undefined competition between the two departments. McLaren and Penske were racing standard, conventional chassis and aerodynamics, using familiar suspensions and the ubiquitous Hewland transaxle. They both did a lot of detail development, but no major innovations, and they consistently finished ahead of Chaparral in Can-Am racing. Depending on the criteria for interpreting "success," it would look as if Piggins's group, and/or racing team contacts, were

In 1968, the aluminum 427 was made available to McLaren and Penske, and McLaren began building their M8A around it, using the engine as the rear chassis. The only reinforcement was the tubes seen passing through the headers.

The McLaren/Chevy engine was a great success from 1968 on—after Chaparral had suffered the majority of "teething" troubles throughout 1967. Of course, engine builders like Bolthoff, Knutsen, and Traco had a lot to do with it's wins.

producing more. That is a *statistical* analysis, however, and it disregards the true inside operation. In fact, much of what Piggins passed on in information or parts, was that which had previously been designed, engineered, and painfully developed through Chaparral.

The bigblock engine development is a good example, as explained in the next chapter. After Chaparral spent a year breaking practically everything on it that could be broken, McLaren and Penske inherited the proven product. Not that it was easy to break the engine loose from R&D. It was forces outside their control that finally made the aluminum 427 available to other teams, and eventually anyone with sufficient money. But, as in the smallblock development success story, the major contribution finally reversed itself with the bigblock, also. While Chevrolet engineering was cautiously experimenting with the first 454-inch blocks, McLaren's remarkable Gary Knutsen and George Bolthoff (both formerly at Chaparral or Traco) were running 465-inch versions on their own.

Because of the working arrangement between Piggins and McLaren, then, it was agreed to let Chevrolet put one of McLaren's engines on its dynamometers for a power check. When the engineers saw the engine, they were a little concerned with external appearances: "The flywheel and vibration damper are too tiny. They're going to blow up and scatter the engine." But Bruce was there with his baby, and he assured them it would do what he said. After they

Edmonton 1968: 4, 5, 6, 66. Any race-watcher in 1968 could have told what the numbers stood for, and they were frequently in that order. However, Chevrolet preferred to have Penske concentrate on the Trans-Am in following years.

installed it on the dyno and made a few warm-up runs, they ran a quick power test ... and the engineers were incredulous. They thought about it for a minute, and then someone said, "I thought I heard a funny rattling noise. Maybe we had better look inside to see what the problem is." But Bruce said no thanks, and he allowed them fifteen minutes to get it crated and back out to the shipping dock.

That isn't to say that there was not a lot of exchange of information and parts between Chevrolet and McLaren. A large percentage of their Can-Am engines were Chevrolet limited production, and, as with Traco, many of their modifications and suggestions were incorporated into production components. However, when it came right down to the track, McLaren, Penske, and Chaparral were in direct competition for very large dollars, and they were not about to relay any minor engine assembly secrets through Chevrolet Engineering.

When Jim Musser was given charge of all Chevrolet high-performance activities, the question of degree of cooperation arose again. McLaren still had an inflated idea of what he could use out of R&D, and Musser had a natural professional curiosity about the details of McLaren's success. But no one quite trusted anyone else enough to believe that any information would only travel so far, not only in engines, but in chassis development, also. It was apparent to Chevrolet that McLaren knew all the basics in chassis—whether from extensive experience or perhaps from observing what seemed to work at times on the

Chaparral. Aerodynamics was obviously the key, and McLaren was not at all shy about adopting the suspension-mounted wing after Chaparral's had broken in every conceivable fashion. They showed no great innovations in suspensions, either, where it is mostly a matter of knowing what is wrong ... and not doing that. And McLaren had adequate facilities of its own with which to experiment and refine the basics. They did not ask for much help, they did not seem to need any, and therefore Chevrolet did not offer much.

There was one near exception, however. Team McLaren had heard of the legendary instrumentation van, with its ten channels of telemetered information, and there was something they wanted to know about their M8B that their own equipment could not handle. So they were able to make arrangements for Don Gates to help them instrument the car and run it at Michigan International Speedway ... keeping the results confidential. But before the act could be consummated, Gates had to confess that he was about to leave Chevrolet to work for Chaparral, and that sort of cooled the deal.

Musser's juggling act between Chaparral, McLaren, and Penske, and Can-Am versus Trans-Am, was eased somewhat with Penske's unintentional departure. Then, when Musser left and Piggins was alone with the problem, it got easier yet when Hall retired. It is unfortunate that all that talent could not have worked harmoniously, but everyone saw things they wanted in other organizations ... only not badly enough to give up some of their own stuff in exchange. The fact that everyone was using basically the same engine from the same source was not common enough grounds for a group marriage. At least it created some occasionally stiff competition while it lasted.

Of course, that is not all of Chevrolet's covert outside assistance. To cover all areas of Chevrolet's involvement means that the amateurs have to be considered, also. According to the AMA resolution, no one was to "... encourage or furnish engineering ... assistance ...," and by common agreement that meant that all technical inquiries of a racing nature would be turned away. However, when Ford pointedly and publicly broke its end of the agreement, people at Chevrolet decided that the least they could do was reply courteously to customer problems. By all rights, any engineer could discuss racing theory with any outsider, so why not have an organized amateur information system?

The result was sort of a technical racing-knowledge clearinghouse. In addition to all the engineering research (intentional and otherwise) that produces race-car advances, Chevrolet people keep an eye on what the professionals are doing in all forms of racing. Can-Am, Trans-Am, NASCAR, USAC, Formula One, Bonneville, Drags, etc., can all contribute something useful to the loyal Chevrolet performance enthusiast's activities. There are certain people within the company who therefore consider it part of their profession to keep up with the state of the art by *going* to the tracks and *looking* at the most current racing machinery. The pros tell Chevrolet a lot, and Chevrolet passes it all on to the amateur who asks. Sometimes it requires working with the pros, instrumenting their cars or doing computer analysis, and sometimes it includes homework research.

The best example of this was a test engineer at the Proving Grounds named Bob Clift, who was also an experienced amateur road racer. Because he was addicted to racing, and since he did test work on Corvettes under Duntov, he usually knew most of the answers to practical questions involving the setup of competition Corvettes. Independents who have road raced Corvettes from Waterford to LeMans owe a lot to the pages of competition specifications and preparation checklists that Clift produced as a byproduct of his own investigations.

- 15/16″ front anti-roll bar in bronze bushings.
- 3/4″ rear anti-roll bar in rubber bushings.
- Grind off welds where tires may contact.
- Break in spare differentials.
- Remove all rotor rivets for quick rotor change.
- Safety wire the block drain cocks.

… and on and on. Hundreds of points, tips, and specifications that the amateur Corvette racer would take years to discover by trial-and-error. It was sort of a "hobby" version of the Camaro preparation pamphlet that was produced from the testing and measurement of Donohue's successful 1968 Trans-Am Camaro. Maybe these papers are still available, and then again, because of the death of racing interest at Chevrolet, maybe they aren't. But the fact remains that among the millions of Chevrolet owners, there are enough who are performance-minded to keep the small group of "Product Information" engineers constantly busy. When the phone stops ringing, there are enthusiasts waiting in the lobby to explain their dreams or problems. It is one hellava job to be the guy who has to keep saying—as politely and apologetically as possible—"I'll see what I can do, *but* …"

For those who are so brash as to insist that they be *sold* certain parts that they *need*, whether Chevrolet makes them or not—well, why shouldn't Chevrolet profit from a demand if there is a legal and socially acceptable outlet for the hardware? Certainly they sell heavy-duty components that will make a car more durable under the roughest treatment. But where necessary, they include a warning that such components or some modifications may not be legal under some state vehicle codes, for ecological or bureaucratic reasons. And, like it or not, some customers are going to use Chevrolet components in competition, for which Chevrolet feels compelled to make sure they have the strongest equipment possible. When a Chevrolet fails, it usually is not the owner who gets the bad image. Likewise, it is sound practice to keep an eye on the speed equipment industry, and on what they are selling to be bolted on or in the production vehicle. Chevrolet cannot market anything that is strictly *race* oriented. There is nothing in the parts warehouse that is not "streetable." However, there are mutual benefits of cooperation between Chevrolet and the speed equipment manufacturers. Chevrolet can sell raw connecting rod forgings or unmachined crankshaft billets to other manufacturers and make a profit. What *they* do with the raw materials is none of Chevrolet's business ... directly. If they finally appear as lightened rods or stroker cranks at a reasonable price—who loses?

If there is ever any reason to have a public or court hearing concerning any of Chevrolet's competition interests, I could personally testify as to the seriousness of their purpose. While I worked for Chevrolet, I built up an old Stingray for amateur racing, and the list of what I got is rather short. Occasionally, I was allowed to borrow a company trailer to tow it with. And that's all! It wasn't possible to get leftovers of any kind ... not so much as a used head gasket. Years ago, employees had been allowed to take home anything that was destined for scrap, but when perfectly good parts began leaving that way, Chevrolet clamped down. Now all scrap parts are positively destroyed. At one time I even tried a written request to evaluate the old racing tires lying around the shop, before they were scrapped, but that offer didn't even warrant a formal reply. And I was an engineer in Research and Development, the source of most competition parts and knowledge.

Neither my amateur status nor company position had anything to do with it, either. Later, when I was driving a Camaro in professional racing, there came a time when I needed some scarce brake parts in a hurry. I knew *all* the contacts personally—I had worked with them—and the best they could do was to get a Chevrolet dealer to open up on Sunday and take my check. And yet there couldn't be any bitterness there because no one else in my position was getting anything I wasn't. There was lots of advice ... good, sound, valuable advice ... but that's *all* there was.

8

A Tale of Two Engines

The smallblock Chevrolet V-8 must be one of the greatest production engines ever built. Not only from the standpoint of production economy—its original major purpose—but it has probably won more races than any other engine of any kind. It was certainly never intended for competition, as the Chevrolet of those years was a staid economy car. But it accidentally filled a certain need among the automotive enthusiasts. The familiar flathead Ford V-8 had been first in the hotrodder's heart since 1932, and then the overhead-valve (ohv) Oldsmobile engine began taking over in 1949. The new ohv engines were just too heavy and too expensive to become very popular, however, until Chevrolet announced its lightweight block late in 1954. So, the immediate response from all the racers was not simply a Chevrolet-owner backlash against the flathead Ford. The engine obviously showed tremendous potential from the very beginning. It was small and light, it ran to high rpm, it was strong, and most of all, it was cheap.

That wasn't good enough for Ed Cole, though. He suspected that an all-aluminum engine of the same design might not only be lighter, but cheaper yet. This was about the time of Duntov's Sebring Corvette SS, and so he used that as partial justification and initiative to build the engine. The idea was to make it *all* aluminum to hold down costs. This meant no valve seat inserts, no pressed-in valve guides, and no iron cylinder liners. Because aluminum has very poor wear properties, GM Research had come up with the idea of using a high-silicon alloy, which would form a hard bore surface, and eliminate the need for liners. But they ran into problems immediately. The engine was to be cast in the same configuration as the stock 283 cast iron engine. Its complexity, however, demanded the use of sand cores, and the sand-casting process demands extensive final machining. But sand-cast aluminum is low in density—or high in porosity—and the machining opened up even more cavities. It was a vicious circle, and there was no answer other than accepting a high rejection rate, which was far too expensive. Then, too, there is nothing harder to lubricate than aluminum on aluminum, and in cold-starting, the pis-

The first appearance of the aluminum-block Chevy V-8 in Duntov's CERV-I, as a linerless 283. It was also a test-bed for revisions on the Corvette fuel-injection, which was concealed (at the time) by the headrest fairing.

tons would scuff the bores in spite of the silicon. It took over ten years for GM to develop dense die-casting, a suitable alloy, bore etching (to "eat" the aluminum away from the standing silicon particles), and iron-plated pistons, to make the linerless engine a reality.

When they gave up on the linerless V-8, there were still a few 283 blocks left that had survived testing, and Duntov installed one in his CERV-I in 1959. The same year, they began making the aluminum cylinder heads available on Corvettes because the wear problem was not as critical there. But even in that case Chevrolet couldn't make them standard equipment, and finally had to stop selling them because in cold weather the valves would hang open. The valve stems would literally freeze in their guides.

The Indianapolis displacement limit for stockblock engines at the time was 255 cubic inches, which was pretty close to what they had. So a couple of the 283 engines were saved from scrap and shipped to Mickey Thompson, who was building his new "roller-skates" for Indy. If the block survived machining, it was suitable for racing, because there the lubrication and temperature could be carefully controlled. But Thompson needed less displacement, so he bored them and installed sleeves to reduce the bore.

Roger Penske also managed to get one of the aluminum 283 blocks, and he shipped it to Traco. In his case, he figured he only needed to get 300 horsepower out of it to make his Cooper Monaco unbeatable, so they built it rather conservatively. That amount of power may seem ridiculously low for a 283 engine today, but that original all-alloy engine had only weighed 350 pounds—the lightest V-8 engine Chevrolet has ever built.

At various times, many people received credit for building the aluminum-block Chevrolet V-8's: Jim Hall, Roger Penske, Mickey Thompson, Harvey Aluminum, Alcoa, and Reynolds. But the idea that anyone could produce a Chevrolet cylinder block without Chevrolet's help is ridiculous. It takes extensive drawings just to produce the patterns for the molds and water-jacket cores. And that is nothing compared to the task of machining the rough casting without the factory tooling. In the first place, you have to know where to start, so that the accumulated machining operations will all have enough material everywhere. You cannot afford to get halfway through and discover that the head-bolt holes are tapping through into the water jackets. Yet it is no great effort for Chevrolet to loan molds and cores to an aluminum foundry and then slip the rough castings into the production line during a normal maintenance shutdown. The factory numerical-control machines can probably automatically finish a cylinder block in a few hours. To anyone starting from scratch, the cost of building such an engine would be far more than any possible worth.

That only pertains to the original linerless 283 blocks, which were exact copies of the production engine, and therefore inherently weak. To produce anything better would have been even more difficult. Those first engines (for as long as they ran) pointed out a number of weaknesses in design which were

The machined aluminum smallblock Chevy with cast-iron cylinder liners as it was raced by Mickey Thompson and Chaparral. The extra bosses on the bellhousing indicate that this block was not used with an ordinary transmission.

A raw aluminum smallblock casting. The latest version, with full bearing webs, reinforced sidewalls, dry sump oil passages, and no fuel pump bosses. It is also available now in Reynolds' linerless 390 alloy.

not apparent in cast iron. When Duntov began to build the one hundred Grand Sport Corvettes, then, he decided that it wouldn't take much work to produce their engines in aluminum. By that time, the basic block had been expanded to 327 cubic inches, and so that was to be the size in aluminum, also, which would allow the use of production pistons, rods, and crank. Duntov had left R&D for the production Corvette group, but he had taken all his engine designers with him. Fred Frenke was given the task of beefing up the new block.

Because of inherent porosity in the sand castings they had to use, the cylinders were to be cast oversize, and "dry" steel liners pressed in. Any other porosity problems were found by carefully pressure-testing the water jackets, oil galleries, and crankcase, and if they could not be fixed by welding, the block was simply scrapped. Also, the main bearing webs needed to be thicker, partly because they were aluminum, and partly because of all the increased power they expected. In addition, for the first time, the main bearing caps were held down with four bolts each. New cylinder heads were designed and cast, utilizing the stagger-valve or "porcupine" layout of the recently developed bigblock design, but they never flowed air as well as the production design in aluminum. Eventually, they settled on a relatively stock design, except for fully machined combustion chambers and revised oil drainback passages.

The interim Chevrolet 409 "truck engine" that served in passenger cars from 1958 to 1964 while the new 427 engine was being developed. This engine didn't perform too badly, but it didn't have enough potential for the future.

A total of twelve blocks designated "A" through "L" were successfully cast and machined in the second, four-bolt main bearing 327 design. There might have been more, but that was the point at which the Grand Sport program was cancelled. A few were temporarily installed in the Corvettes, but they were never raced, and the rest were stored.

At the same time, they also cancelled a program that didn't exist—the 427 Mark II engine. Back then, Chevrolet's heavy-duty engine was based on a heavy, oddly designed 348-cubic-inch block that came from the truck division in 1958. After five years of development, it had grown to 427 cubic inches, but it was still by no means a high-performance engine, and it was nearing the end of its expansion potential. An engineer named Dick Keineth and a General Motors Institute co-op student named Mike Pocobello had been quietly working on an all-new design, however, which was more strongly related to the

A "porcupine" about to be installed in Rex White's stocker at Daytona. Note the four-tube cast-iron exhaust headers with a GM part number. As might have been expected, none of the all-new engines went 500 miles.

great smallblock. It had the same crankshaft and bore of the truck engine, but the block was lighter and the heads were more adaptable to high airflow at high rpm.

During the fall of 1962, one of them was assembled, and after extensive dynamometer testing it was installed in a very special heavy-duty sedan chassis and road tested at excessive speed at the Proving Grounds. On the dyno, it was quite a sensation, as it was the first Chevrolet engine to exceed 500 horsepower. But it still had not proven itself in extensive durability runs, as the smallblock had before its introduction. Meanwhile, the 1963 Daytona 500 was approaching. Whether the purpose was to get a lot of free durability testing, or for comparison with the competition, or simply to show off, is disputable, but someone decided to try the Mark II in competition. Shortly before the race, a few were shipped to selected car builders in the South. If anyone thought that they could be passed off as production 427 engines ("All that's changed is the block, and heads, and intake manifold."), the idea was soon dispelled by the sensation that was created. The cars running them were so incredibly fast, that the only thing that avoided a complete entrant revolt was their breakage in the race. But after that week, they all disappeared, never to be seen again. A couple of years later, a very similar engine was made available to the public as a 396-cubic-inch "Mark IV," but it was a new block, with a larger bore spacing to allow greater

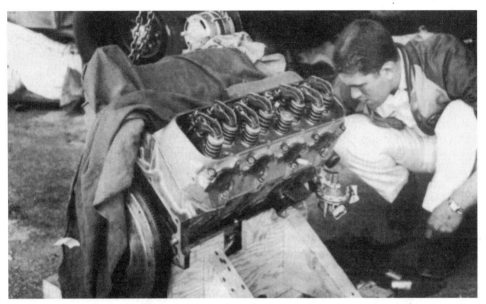

Chevy's new mystery engine at Daytona in 1963. The "porcupine" derivation is obvious from pushrods, valves, and rocker arms that stick up in all directions. Minor casting differences from the later engine are apparent.

expansion. And expand it did, eventually reaching 510 cubic inches in the final aluminum alloy version for Can-Am racing.

Almost a year after the cancellation, Frank Winchell began working on his mid-engine sports-car design, and the aluminum 327 engines were resurrected for this project. Taking advantage of the security of R&D, and disregarding the possibility of publicity for Chevrolet, Winchell began loaning them out to Chaparral for some free durability testing. In its first racing season, 1964, five engines of that design were loaned to Chaparral, and they ran a total of 6000 practice and racing miles with no failures other than a cracked head. Early the next year, however, cracks began appearing in the internal crankcase bulkheads, so a slightly thicker casting was drawn up by R&D, and four new engines were built. Before they could be shipped, the first total failure occurred in engine "H." While leading the race at Mt. Tremblant, Sharp's engine developed what was frequently referred to as a "terminal oil leak," whereby a broken rod pokes a hole in the pan. Since it had been showing low oil pressure, the cause was not certain, but development began on new connecting rods and rod bolts anyhow. The new rods were an experiment in the use of vacuum-induction-melt (VIM) steel, to insure that there could be absolutely no impurities in the raw forging, and the bolt size was increased to 11/32-inch diameter. But before the year was out, Ronnie Hissom had another engine blow on him in practice at Elkhart Lake. This time, the bolt failure was obvious. Eventually, after months of experimentation with different bolt designs and materials, running in the millions of stress cycles on a test fixture, the real problem was stumbled upon. By accident, a pair of bolts was re-magnafluxed just before installation in an engine—and it was discovered that cracks had appeared while the bolts rested on the *shelf.* What was happening was that the bolts were stored while still torqued down in their connecting rod, and the most minor corrosion was starting stress cracks. Meanwhile, Hall lost the third engine for the same reason in practice at Mosport. From that time on, the connecting rods and bolts were so well-understood and overdesigned, that their durability was never in question.

At the same time, however, other aggravating problems were cropping up. A rocker arm galled and tried to saw its way off the stud, so a crash program was needed to find a better lubricating method. That was no sooner solved than a valve spring broke, and the VIM steel was used again in custom-wound and polished springs. Then there were a couple of electrical failures in the early transistorized regulators and ignition amplifiers. The exhaust headers were cracking at the ports, and that turned out to be a metallurgical problem, which was cured by a different welding technique.

The most persistent problem, surprisingly, was in the camshaft gears. When the first dry sump oiling systems were installed, engines started losing power throughout a race. Before long, it was discovered that because an extra set of pump gears was necessary to pump the oil out of the engine, the load on the oil pump was causing excessive wear on the drive gear at the camshaft. Because the distributor was driven off the same gear, the ignition timing became progressively more retarded. John Nolte had designed the camshaft, so he was given the problem, and after destroying the gears on over a dozen camshafts, he finally whipped it by pressing on gears made of a more compatible steel, instead of machining the gears on the shaft.

The third year of the aluminum smallblock was a charm, relatively speaking, for the engine. Most of the possible problems had been worked out, and all that happened was an alternator failure at LeMans, a blown head gasket at Mosport, and a cracked cylinder head at Laguna Seca—which was still good enough for Hall to finish second behind Phil Hill in the other car. Of course, all the engines run in 1966 were of the third block design, since most of the original castings had cracked. In all, there were twenty-two 327 aluminum blocks cast, of which perhaps ten exist today, stored and forgotten somewhere in the vast warehouses of Chevrolet Engineering.

As coveted as the aluminum 327's were, few people ever knew that they never would put out as much power as an equivalent cast iron engine. The problem never was adequately resolved, but there was no end to good excuses. The most common explanation was that valve lash was upset by dynamic heat expansion of the block and heads. That theory was popular because it was very difficult to prove—or disprove—on a hot, running engine. Another obvious factor was in the heads. Because they were aluminum, and had a tendency to crack, more material was needed around the bolt holes and combustion chambers. This meant that less material could be cut away for the ports, and in spite of the very best design, they simply would not flow quite as well as a cleanly ported cast iron head. My own layman's theory was that the better thermal conductivity of aluminum was allowing more of the power to pass into the cooling water and out the radiator. This was never checked, either, and the fact was allowed to rest—aluminum blocks cost ten to twenty horsepower.

If the sole advantage was lighter weight, it was a big advantage—at first. The 327 aluminum racing engine weighed under 400 pounds ready to run, complete to the flywheel. This was almost 150 pounds less than the identical engine in cast iron. There was another drawback to aluminum, however, and that was in displacement. Because of cracking problems in the pressed-in dry steel sleeves, the block could never be safely enlarged to anything greater than 327 cubic inches. When other road racers started opening up their iron blocks, the overall advantage began to shrink. When McLaren was running a 360-inch engine, he had almost 50 horsepower over Chaparral's lighter 327.

A complication in producing the aluminum 327 for competition use was the sad fact that for many years, Research and Development never had a dynamometer cell of its own. Although there was a row of two dozen dynamometers right next door, they were under the Engineering Laboratory jurisdiction, and R&D did not even have its own dyno engineer or operator, but had to use the ones supplied by the lab. Most often, however, they were given Jerry Thompson and Tom Collins. The project was so theoretically secretive, though, that the R&D project engineer, Leonard Kutkus, would not even admit to Thompson what these Weber-carbureted aluminum engines were being built for. This made it somewhat difficult to exchange meaningful information, even though Thompson, as a racer himself, knew exactly what was going on. Because he is an entertainer of some established wit, he took great delight in putting Kutkus on the spot, with something like … "Look Len, this doesn't make sense at all. This engine is going to stall at every traffic light. It won't take much work to get it to run smooth at low rpm. Let me talk to Winchell about it." Whereupon Kutkus would blanch, and insist that he just accept it as it was.

For the first couple of years, the aluminum 327 engines were never developed for power. It was largely a durability program, and so they were simply assembled, broken in, and shipped out. All that was done in the dyno cell was a ten-hour run-in schedule, adjustment of carburetors and timing, a power check, and a leak check. Occasionally, something was changed, and Kutkus would get a report on the power increase (or decrease) before the engine left, but what was important was how the engine returned a few months later. And considering

A two-carb Trans-Am Chevrolet engine on the dynamometer at Chevrolet Engineering. The cylinder at upper center is a pneumatic throttle actuator which controls engine speed during pre-programmed high-speed durability runs.

the conditions under which they ran, they did very well. The Chaparral mechanics would simply plug them into the car and turn them on, not even so much as changing spark plugs unless something sounded wrong.

Naturally there was other high-performance work going on at Chevrolet on the smallblock engine, but it was all based on the cast iron version. It was not until engine M-4 (the fourth rebuild of block number 13) that there was time or money, or a dyno, or interest, in power-developing the aluminum engine. That one finally produced a peak of just under 500 horsepower at 7200 rpm.

But by then, the search for power was so important that Chevrolet had become somewhat questionably cunning. In the last year of 327 development, one of Penske's 327 Traco engines was intercepted, and it showed up in the R&D dyno room. In a back-to-back test with a supposedly identical R&D engine, the Penske/Traco version had more power. Then, in an attempt to learn *why,* it was torn down to the last gasket, measured, and reassembled. When Traco discovered what had happened, its irritation was mollified slightly by the report that Chevrolet found *nothing.* However, the investigation led to further studies of the shape of torque curves, as opposed to just looking at the peaks. Computer runs were made on the effect of all possible combinations of curves in an accelerating vehicle.

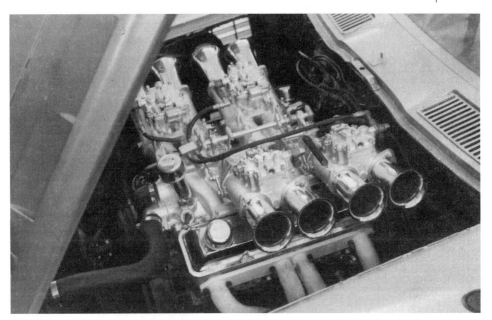

The smallblock Chevy with 58-mm sidedraft Webers in the GS Corvettes as they were run at Nassau in 1963. Unfortunately, the 58's weren't suitable for the smaller-displacement aluminum engines with automatic transmissions.

One of the greatest influences on the torque curve is the configuration of the induction system. Early in the game, 48-mm downdraft Weber carburetors were felt adequate—partly because Weber did not make a larger downdraft. There was a 58-mm sidedraft available, but in adapting it to a V-8 manifold, the runners became too long for proper tuning. Therefore, when the rpm were raised to the point where it was felt that the carbs were choking, R&D cobbled. By casting and machining a few new pieces, it was possible to adapt 58-mm bores to the 48-mm vertical float bowls. This did raise the horsepower peak, but it also lost torque at lower rpm. Because of the few transmission ratios and the torque converter, it was eventually necessary to return to the broader-torque 48-mm Webers.

To anyone who has ever worked or lived within a mile of the Chevrolet Engineering Center in Warren, Michigan, it is no surprise to learn that Chevrolet has built engines that were used in racing. What other explanation would there be for bypassing the normal dynamometer exhaust collectors, removing the dyno room windows, and running huge, straight exhaust collectors out the opening. The burbling and popping usually started about 4:00 in the afternoon, and after a short warmup, windows would begin to shake with the roar. On a cool night, you could recognize the sound for miles—the sound of a large 8-cylinder engine, running at very high rpm, for a very long time … like the length of a long

A cast iron test engine set up with 48-mm downdraft Webers and a dry sump oiling system. The headers were usually installed backward for dynamometer use. The particular setup was being tested at Bartz's engine shop.

straightaway at LeMans. Sometimes the sound would continue for a full 24 hours. The first time it did not. But there was always a houseful of bets on how long it would run, and the second time out it made it.

The schedule was controlled by a computer tape which followed an actual lap-speed recording from the particular track. Various cams and levers operated the throttle, brakes, and speed for as long as the engine might last. Some of the schedules were not recognizable, but all were obviously of an engine running through an automatic transmission. The noise outside was bad enough, but standing next to one of those engines running at over 7000 rpm in a closed room would be enough to induce internal damage. It is hard to imagine that thing inches from a driver's head at 200 mph.

Eventually the aluminum 327 reached a point where it was hard to find new areas in which to increase its performance. The basic heads and block were nearing optimum development. The phrase "optimum development" is a little too casual to really describe the program, however. Any new vehicle, any new engine, any new device, is automatically an incredible collection of development problems to be solved. In high-performance, the greatest problem is in achieving the most power or the least weight for a given durability. But when you get down to the fine edge, no engineering or mathematics is accurate enough to reliably define the limits. The only way to find the optimum is by continual, repeated tests to destruction, until *every* component is the lightest and strongest possible. And yet many components in a race car, such as a connecting rod or suspension arm, cannot be made fail-safe because if it is too heavy you lose— if it is too light it is a tragedy. Ideally, it is like the proverbial "one-hoss shay." Everything works perfectly until it has completed the last trip, then the horse dies and everything else collapses from fatigue at the same time.

To try to make an engine perform like that was a very expensive education. It was a good education for those involved, but it pointedly demonstrated the consideration of cost as a function of performance. For example, there was the engine weight-reduction program, which researched materials and designs that would have cost perhaps a thousand dollars per pound of weight removed. One aluminum block was completely machined—externally—to remove every bit of superfluous, unstressed material. Also, at one time, heavy metals such as depleted uranium were even considered for crankshaft counterbalancing, because a greater density at a longer throw would allow less total weight. It may sound ridiculous, but until someone goes through the mathematics, you cannot be positive it won't work.

In spite of the educational value, the lightweight smallblock finally priced itself out of racing. To be sure, everyone made damn sure that the same failure never occurred twice, but the total end result was a terminal case of overengineering. When it was finally phased out, there were practically no production pieces in the entire engine. The only known components that were absolutely stock, were the head bolts (although they were magnafluxed), and a few seals.

In the last year of concentrated development on the aluminum 327 engine, other interesting new approaches were taken. A low center of gravity (c.g.) was very important to the competition cars, and a flat, opposed engine such as the Corvair was ideal in such an application. The engine men looked at the Corvair six and the aluminum V-8, put the two together in their minds, and cast up a flat-opposed-8, aluminum 327 Chevy. Practically all that was needed was a new cylinder case and a crankshaft, and new intake manifolds were fabricated for the Webers. It got through a break-in schedule before it was noted that somehow it had gained almost 100 pounds over the equivalent V-8. At that, even if it could be developed down to the same weight, calculations showed that it would only lower the vehicle c.g. by 0.4 inch. Parallel mockup of the proposed chassis for it was also showing problems in clearance for tires and exhaust headers now that the heads were so broad. The tradeoffs simply were not healthy enough. It was sent to storage without even a power check.

Another engine turned out even worse, but it eventually advanced an engine that went into production five years later. A *die-cast* aluminum 327 V-8 was known as "the chewing-gum engine." To avoid the necessity of sand cores for water jackets, the block was cast with an open deck, or in other words, the cylinder liners were free-standing. To get water jackets in the die-cast heads, they were cast in two pieces, and held together with the standard

The mysterious porcupine engine first returned with 396 cubic inches, and it was a racing sensation in the Chevelle, Corvette, and then, Camaro, as it grew to a 427.

head bolts. Of course, all the ports had to be straight so that the mold could be removed. The reason it was known as "the chewing-gum engine," however, was that it was difficult to avoid casting porosity, and it leaked *everywhere*— patches and sealant notwithstanding. On its first run-in, both the radiator and crankcase were soon filled with the same murky white mix of oil and water. Only the fact that it had the standard iron cylinder liners kept it from pumping the mixture out the exhaust pipes. It, at least, was eventually dynoed and installed in a chassis for test, but never raced. The same basic idea is being used today in the aluminum Vega engine, but in that case, General Motors' new Accurad casting process assures dense, leakproof blocks.

At the close of every racing season, everyone at R&D would suddenly conclude that Chevrolet had shifted too close to being a "parts supplier" for racing teams and had neglected the advanced thinking. Fall 1966 was no exception. The Can-Am had not gone too well at Chaparral, and everyone decided that something even more exotic and educational than the wing was needed. More horsepower was always demanded, but development on the aluminum 327 was nearing the limit, since that basic block would not take a displacement increase. The 427 engine had seen a lot of racing development in the Chevelle for Smokey Yunick's NASCAR racing, and it assured an easy 100 horsepower gain. On the other hand, it weighed a few hundred pounds more in cast iron, and necessary chassis strengthening would rapidly add more weight. Then, someone facetiously suggested that if one 327 was not enough, two of them ought to be plenty. As ridiculous as that sounded—two 327 Chevys in a Can-Am car—no one was quite sure why it wouldn't work. One of them could be hung out the rear, driving through the same transmission, and it would not require more than a few hundred pounds worth of added structure. Imagine—*twice* the power with only a 600-pound weight gain, and no increase in air drag.

There was the option of producing the 427 in aluminum, at little more than a sixty-pound weight gain over the 327. But Frank Winchell had made his feelings well known about that. "Putting a 427 cubic engine in these little cars is *immoral!*" So the matter was resolved purely objectively. The two proposed cars were designed mathematically. That is, the attainable specifications were drawn up, and both were run around a typical race course by computer simulation. The twin 327 had fantastic acceleration—where not limited by wheelspin— and an unheard-of top speed, but the single 427 car was not all that bad, with better braking and faster cornering due to less load on the tires. To no one's surprise, the 327s won, but not by very much. In fact, they were faster by such a small margin, that no one wanted to take a chance on all the possible vehicle-dynamics unknowns, recalling poor experiences with previous radical prototypes. Besides, the engine group was a powerful lobby, and they were anxious to dig into a new powerplant. The aluminum 427 won for losing.

The production cast iron 427 had certainly shown its potential in NASCAR racing already. But that engine was nothing like what was allowed under Can-Am rules. Can-Am had no regulations covering production derivation or quantities, nor induction system or other internal modifications, so it was wide open for all the imagination and experimentation Chevrolet cared to attempt. Pocobello, an engine specialist, had just taken charge of the program, and Kutkus was busy keeping the aluminum 327s together to finish the season—and as backup in case the 427 did not make it. Fred Porter, however, had spent some time engineering weight out of the small engine, and so he was given the task of converting the 427 into a lightweight.

The 327 Chaparral engine may not have contributed many components to production, but it certainly aided in the initial construction of the 427. All the cracked blocks and heads, the rod and crank and bolt failures, the false approaches to power, the superlight materials attempts—they all saved man-years of development the second time around. For as much as they appear to be the same, the aluminum engines required all new patterns for casting both the heads and block. While the new castings were being designed and machined, work progressed on the induction and exhaust systems, using the old cast iron pieces. Carbs were tried at first, but because of the vast volume of air required, anything that had adequate flow suffered in response. Besides, if the Can-Am allowed fuel injection—why not experiment with that.

The aluminum 427 Chevrolet block, with four-bolt mains, and oil galleries for a dry sump system. The lessons learned from smallblock racing engines guaranteed this version to be a success—once the minor bugs were whipped.

Daytona Continental, 1967: The first appearance of the aluminum 427 in the Chaparral 2F, Phil Hill and Mike Spence driving. Hill set the fastest lap and new record at 118.5 mph; the car was retired on the 93rd lap.

By the start of 1967, the first all-aluminum 427 was running on the dyno. There was no joy, however, because its 500 horsepower was no more than the 327 could do. But it was *strong,* and it had 100 extra cubic inches for only a 65-pound gain in weight. Obviously, it was going to take some detail development. Right away, Porter began working on improving the ports and combustion chambers, and although the 427 started the season in the new Chaparral 2F at Daytona in February, it was months before even the iron development engine broke 600 horsepower. At that, as on the small engine, it was proven that identical heads in aluminum lost over 15 horsepower, though they more than made up the difference in weight. Power increases were hampered all along the way by the niggling detail problems that kept cropping up in the field—the ordinary, underrated, "debugging" process.

There were oiling problems, gear failures, a chronic, elusive high-speed miss, cracked camshafts and dampers, cracked pistons, and on. Even with the best pedigree, racing engines do not spring as champions from a designer's pencil. It took the entire year to discover and fix every one of the unanticipated weaknesses. When the oiling deficiency was cured with a larger pump, the distributor drive gears failed under the added load on them. The ignition system also had a tendency to quit completely and then recover for no reason whatsoever. By using a heat lamp on a dyno engine, Gates finally found that heat caused enough expansion in the distributor to short it out, but that wire cost one race. Engines developed a misfire and failed due to pre-ignition in race after race, until the fuel pumps were redesigned and intolerable scatter was worked out of the distributor firing. Then, because the bottom end was so strong, peak rpm were raised from 6600 to 7000, for the extra power there. But then the "accessories" started failing. New vibration frequencies caused the vibration damper to crack, and when it was redesigned, the camshaft snapped.

All those failures in the new engine were bad enough, but what really made the situation embarrassing was the *leaks.* When the car is steaming around the track setting records, and it breaks—well, it was just from trying too hard. But when it goes from race to race with oil not only drenching the engine and smoking on the headers, but streaming out all over the body—that *really* looks sloppy. All sorts of sealants were tried, cast rocker covers were held down on machined surfaces with more bolts, and everyone accused everyone else of poor assembly. It was not until the engine was installed in a "rocker" that the real problem surfaced. Because of his experience with the smallblock, Kutkus had stayed with it and investigated possibilities for Trans-Am and USAC. To work out problems of oiling under high lateral acceleration, he had built a gimbal which could rock a motor-driven engine up to 50 degrees in any direction. This allowed him to install plastic windows and pressure gauges everywhere in the system and observe exactly what was happening under accurately simulated race conditions. What was happening was that under braking and cornering, the rocker covers were holding the oil, and building pressures up to 90 psi in there.

The new aluminum 427 was a "leaker." On the dyno it was spotless, but on the track it spewed oil regardless of care of assembly or type of gaskets. Finally, the answer was discovered on a "rocker," or gimbal mount.

The subsequent relief system not only eliminated oil loss in the 427, it was one of the reasons why the 302 was so successful in the Trans-Am—it was able to corner consistently at high g's without losing all its oil from the pan and burning up.

This is just one of many good illustrations of why Chevrolet engines have proven so popular with racers. Once all the expensive, complicated durability work had been done by the factory, it was relatively easy for independents and speed shops to coax out the necessary power. By concentrating all their high-performance and durability development on only two basic engines over an entire fifteen year span, instead of trying many different sizes and designs, Chevrolet attained an incomparable reputation. Not only do the engines have an amazing power-to-weight ratio, but they are practically bulletproof, the latter assuring the former.

That finished up the 1967 season, with the aluminum 427 showing a poor record, but becoming a highly developed package for the coming year. Chevrolet, with Chaparral help, had done the hard part, getting it to live. Research was continuing on detail improvements in power and durability, but Chevrolet was not interested in marketing the engine because of the high price and limited demand. Hall was offered the exclusive market, if he would purchase the components, assemble them, and manage the whole program. However, he was extremely busy already, trying to finish his 2H, the first all-Chaparral vehicle since he built the original rear-engined car. He might also have been slightly reluctant to sell to his competitors. At that point the potential market for the engine in Corvettes caused Chevrolet to reconsider quantities. Tom Goad returned from personnel management to handle the distribution; casting and assembly was transferred to the production engine group; and it became known as "slightly available" through the proper channels for the proper price. Penske immediately picked up a half-dozen which were shipped to Traco, McLaren bought a bunch, and the 1968 Can-Am season was off to become a relatively competitive series.

After Chevrolet and Chaparral had spent an embarrassing year with the engine, Penske and McLaren then got the credit for the engine being so successful through the 1968 season. R&D and Chaparral attempted to defend their honor by continuing power development, but that was the year in which the 2H was a last minute drop-out, and the year was spent alternately between getting the old 2G up to date, and debugging the 2H. Still, a great number of improvements were made in the engine and passed along to everyone concerned—because it *was* a Chevrolet benefit.

Increased oil pump requirements had put too much strain on the distributor and cam gears, so the engine was converted to an externally driven pump. Pistons had continually cracked around the bosses, although not badly enough to fail, and that was cured. John Nolte, who had designed the cams for the smallblocks, came back to scientifically develop a .600-inch lift camshaft which broadened the torque curve on the 427. The connecting rods and bolts were improved for insurance, and the resulting engine could be reliably run on a 24-hour LeMans schedule, holding 7000 rpm.

Because it had some production possibilities, research continued on the port-type fuel injection, and as part of that effort, many new manifolds were built. One of them was designed specifically for Hall's new low-profile 2H. To allow a very low, smooth rear deck, for better airflow to the rear radiator, a crossover manifold was built with sidedraft stacks. This allowed the rear deck to be only five inches higher than the valve covers. It had reduced area in the stacks where they crossed, and so it never produced the power the vertical stacks were capable of on the dyno, but it was hoped that ram air ducting would make up the difference.

The production aluminum-block 427 Chevrolet engine was finally made available to the general public. Most were sold across the counter at around $2000 for the short block, but some were built in Corvettes and Camaros.

The Chaparral 2H, with its low-profile cross-ram fuel injection stacks. The idea was to reduce frontal area and to avoid obstructing the rear radiator (bottom), but the reduced inlet area cost quite a few horsepower.

In addition to work spent reducing frontal area on the 2H, many man-hours were spent in getting the engine down for a lower center of gravity. With a dry sump, there was no oil pan depth requirement, but it took a lot of engineering and experimentation to create a pan that would pick up all that oil being thrown around inside, without gobbling air and vapor locking the pressure system. For a long time, everyone else had an engine height (or ground clearance) advantage with the small-diameter multiple-disc Borg and Beck clutch as opposed to Chaparral's torque converter. Finally, Kurleto was able to get the converters from 12 inches down to 10 inches in diameter, which was only about an inch greater than the smallest clutch. The reduced starter gear diameter then made it necessary to gear the starter motor down, which was accomplished by adapting the Delco motor to a Chrysler starter gear assembly. It got to the point where the next lower limit was going to be the clearance needed in the pan for the connecting rod bolts at bottom dead center.

In the evolution of the bigblock engine, continual efforts to reduce weight had naturally brought about the use of magnesium alloys. Magnesium was tried, at one time or another, practically anywhere aluminum had been used. It was used to cast oil pumps, water pumps, valve covers, gear covers, and inlet manifolds. In many cases, casting porosity prevented its use, unless considerable time was to be spent pressure checking, patching, and remachining each component. The most interesting experiment with magnesium was in the casting of a pair of cylinder blocks. It might have resulted in a considerably lighter engine, at far greater cost in material and machining—if it had worked. The first running engine not only leaked, it destroyed itself on the break-in dynamometer. Kutkus announced at the post mortem that unexpectedly great bore distortion was the problem, and due to the problems and cost, the second engine was never even assembled.

Obviously, not all of the engine development effort was productive. For one reason and another—usually cost and production applicability—many projects were abandoned with no more benefits than the knowledge of new problem areas. Fred Porter was often an uncomfortably vociferous proponent of the advanced layout engine, and along with Earl Rohrbacher, the department's engine savant, was at least able to begin a number of interesting investigations. The single overhead cam V-8 was designed in both 327 and 427 sizes, but never pursued. Porter campaigned for a year to build three-valve heads for the bigblock, and some were cast and flow tested, but never ran on an engine. Rohrbacher came up with new ideas for rotary valves, and Porter, anticipating the value in racing, got involved. Experiments never got further than a 4-cylinder "half-block" dummy before wear and sealing difficulties overcame them.

In 1969, the emphasis on engine development versus engine assembly began to change. While Hall was recovering from his Las Vegas accident, his brother, Chuck, rehired Gary Knutsen from McLaren. The idea was to try to make Chaparral profitable by building and marketing racing engines to the independents. Chevrolet R&D was no longer interested in the basic aluminum 427 because it was literally unbeatable in its class. It was only competing against itself. Besides that, there were other more exciting areas to explore. Over the next year or so, there was considerable talk about turbocharging the aluminum 427, and about an optional overhead cam kit for the smallblock, and an optional 327-cubic-inch aluminum block for production. There was very little action taken, however.

The primary research done in that period concerned bore/stroke ratios versus maximum rpm and power. The production bigblock was soon to be stroked to 454 cubic inches, and it was unknown whether it would live at the 7200 rpm that Can-Am racers were turning. At the same time, it was also possible to increase the bore from 4.250 to 4.375, and reduce the stroke to maintain about the same displacement. This would seem to be wasted effort, except that it gives the same bore/stroke ratio as the all-conquering 327, and allows the maximum rpm to be raised by 300 for the same piston speed. So three engines were built to compare power and durability for different rpm, with the different ratios:

4.375 bore × 3.470 stroke = 430 cubic inches (7500 rpm)
4.250 bore × 3.760 stroke = 427 cubic inches (7200 rpm)
4.250 bore × 4.000 stroke = 454 cubic inches (7000 rpm)

As is well known, the 430 engine won—for the time being—with an output of 680 horsepower at its 7500 rpm, and that is what was built by McLaren

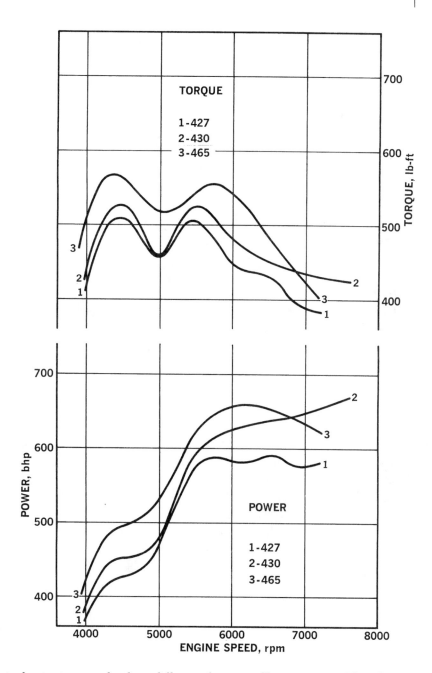

Typical output curves for three different aluminum Chevy engines. The advantage of the 465 is obvious—at a sacrifice in reliability—but note the difference between the 427 and a 430. Eventually, however, they got bigger.

Two McLaren engines showing the ultimate progression of the Chevy 427. At the bottom is a 465-incher with overlapping iron liners. Above is the same block cast in Reynolds 390 alloy to eliminate liners—and gain 45 more inches.

and Hall for a few seasons. Before long, however, the knowledge and parts got around to everyone else, and to keep an unfair advantage, *both* bore and stroke were increased. Everyone also began taking more risks than Chevrolet appreciated, and they ran the biggest engines up to 7500 rpm. And most of them still survived. Considering that the 327 was seldom run over 7200 rpm, it was an amazing accomplishment.

But what little that Chevrolet was contributing to racing was now stopping altogether. Through all the "quiet years," very few engines were actually built specifically for racing. Chevrolet concentrated on making the absolute lightest V-8's available, and making them as strong as technology would allow. Sometimes power was part of the consideration, but strength and lightness were above all. Therefore, not only did race-car builders prefer the Chevrolet product, but it benefited production vehicles as well. Another consideration that was always in the engineers' (and managers') minds was that any benefits from racing wins were not as important as the potential humiliation from a product that continually broke in competition. The independent racers took it from there.

Not that it is a sin or a crime for an automobile manufacturer to be interested in racing—for whatever benefits accrue. Ford, Chrysler, American Motors, and many Europeans have gotten heavily involved and no one has ever persecuted or prosecuted them. The very *worst* that Chevrolet could be accused of would be hypocrisy, and yet even that is explainable by the difficulty in communications—intentional or unintentional—within such a huge organization.

Still, through 1968–1970, the primary interests in engine development began to shift. Slowly, insidiously, more and more engineers, technicians, and dollars were being redirected toward vehicle emissions research. Power development practically came to a stop.

The two-speed version of Chaparral's automatic in the first appearance of the 2C chassis. As more ratios were needed, the rear cover was extended to contain the third and fourth gearsets, and the case was strengthened for larger engines.

9

The Incredible Acquisition

When it comes to the acquisition of engineering knowledge that can be applied to automotive competition, there is probably no other organization in the world to compare with Chevrolet. In their day, Mercedes may have been the intellectual leaders in the field, and today there are a number of astute, experienced race teams and constructors: Lotus, McLaren, Ferrari, Lola, and March; and you can't deny the accomplishments of Ford with its GT Coupes and Indy engine, and those of Chrysler in oval track racing.

There is an important difference, however, which may be confused in the semantics of the word "engineering." When an engineer has accumulated enough experience working around mechanisms or systems in his field that he can design a slightly different device intuitively, he is not "engineering." And when engineers build a dozen different configurations to see which one works the best, that's experimentation, not engineering. Instead, engineering involves research, the formulation of theories, mathematical modeling, design, construction, development, testing of the theory, rejection or advancement of the theory, and most important, the accumulation of valuable quantitative knowledge that can be used in further engineering.

This isn't to imply that all the world's successful race teams don't follow this technique to some degree. It's just that they have not had the facilities nor spent the man-years on it that Chevrolet has in the last two decades. Even before the first Corvette was conceived, the groundwork of research was being laid in the basic understanding of how and why vehicles perform as they do. The former head of Chevrolet Research and Development and former Rolls-Royce engineer, Maurice Olley, spent his career developing some of the first theories of automotive vehicle dynamics. There were others in other companies working in the same area, but when Chevrolet began to convert from racing for advertising and entertainment to studying racing for the advancement of engineering knowledge, they had Olley's papers to start with.

The ordinary, taken-for-granted automobile is an extremely complex device to understand or even to study while in motion. The combination of four fairly independent tires and suspensions, plus aerodynamics, plus road variations, plus the infinite number of control inputs from drivers of varying competency, make it far more indeterminate than trains, ships, or even aircraft. Even to begin to understand it, an engineer needs a few thousand bits of information on the basic subsystems such as: mass distribution, suspension geometries, tire characteristics, compliances, aerodynamic performance, driver limits, road surfaces, ad infinitum. But this is all very difficult information to get, and only an automotive manufacturer would be interested enough ... and it is therefore highly restricted within each company. So it shouldn't be presumptuous to assume that the world's largest corporation has the world's largest source of basic test data on automotive components.

For example, when the first mid-engine test vehicles were being built, it became important to know the handling effects of "polar moment of inertia," or resistance of a vehicle to rotate about its center of gravity. Tucked away in General Motors' Research Library is a technical paper on the influence of increasing polar moment of inertia on a Cadillac ... dated 1934. And there have been many studies since. Without such sources of previous test results, any theories of vehicle performance are based on accumulations of guesswork.

Of course, in a field that demands advances as fast as automotive competition does, each component or subsystem develops at its own rate, also. Recently, because of the tire companies' interest, characteristics of racing tires have improved by two or three steps in one short season. So it is imperative to know exactly what a tire, or body shape, or fuel mixture, or alloy is capable of, *right now.* This is where Chevrolet shone in their brightest hour—the almost unlimited budget to develop the tools, the equipment and facilities with which to attain specific, necessary knowledge. The budgets that other companies spent on racing experiments, or conquest by brute force, were equaled at Chevrolet in the establishment of hardware and theories which are still useful today on production vehicle problems.

One of the first basic areas of investigation was tires. No car company makes tires, or designs tires, or even tries to ask for specific performance characteristics. But it is very important to know which of all the tires available is best in any particular application. In this case, the application was racing. As it turned out, however, tire companies put more dollars into direct competition than Chevrolet did, and so individuals or teams became aligned with the manufacturers for financial, rather than performance, reasons. But at any time, Chevrolet could say, "Brand X has more cornering power on asphalt at 190°F, with an 850-pound load and 1/2° negative camber than tire Y." And the tire companies themselves didn't even know that. The tire companies don't care about the details—all they care about is winning, and if they have to take three different tire designs in four different rubber compounds to a track and experiment—at least there's no question then about which tire is fastest. But Chevrolet had to know *what and why.*

At first it appeared that Goodyear, Firestone, Dunlop, and the others were being coy with the necessary data. But when it became obvious that they didn't *know,* the first racing-tire test machines were built in Chevrolet R&D. General Motors Research has test machines that roll a tire on a six-foot simulated surface, or roll them on a drum, or tow them on a trailer behind a truck, but they weren't equipped to handle the sizes or the forces and characteristics you see on a current racing tire. In the early 1960's, road-racing tires were little more than high-performance street tires, but as they began to grow sideways, they demanded very special test facilities.

The first machine was a trailer, built to accommodate the low-profile Firestone Indy road-racing tire. After it did little more than point out the difficulties of testing, however, it was used simply to roll tires steadily across a glass window. Every tire company has a window surface, but this is used primarily to study production tires, and having our own device gave us the opportunity to draw our own conclusions on all racing tires. And they were very interesting. Since then, however, the interests of public safety researchers have revealed most of the theories, and even disproved some, in fact.

The best instrument was a centrifuge. Previously, the cornering capability of tires had been evaluated on a skidpad, by driving a car around a constant radius at maximum speed. That only gave one figure, however—maximum cornering coefficient in g's. To properly engineer race cars you need to know cornering power versus slip angle, versus camber angle, versus normal load, versus temperature, and versus tire pressure—just to mention a few unknowns in each tire design and compound. So, a self-propelled "trailer" was built which drove a single test tire around a circle at the end of a tethered boom. Controllable variables were load and camber angle, and a curve of cornering force versus slip angle was automatically plotted for each run. To get complete data on all variables for each tire required so many runs, however, that it was one of the worst assignments in the department. Especially if an engineer were susceptible to dizziness, as the operator had a seat on the boom at its pivot point. Eventually, the quantity of information requested, and the impediment of Michigan weather, made it necessary to move the entire rig to the Chaparral skidpad in Midland where the next season's experimental tires could be tested over the winter. Still, the distastefulness and boredom of the work meant that the engineer who needed the data usually was responsible for getting it. Don Cox eventually compiled some of the most productive data and conclusions, and the fact that he subsequently was hired by Penske could have had some small bearing on the eventual success of Goodyear tires in road racing.

Not that one machine told everything about tires. Although a provision for driving and braking the test tire was considered from the beginning, that meant multiplying the test effort by two or three times. Instead, general conclusions were projected from the GM tire test machine, which could spew out thirty pages of three-variable carpet plots on a single tire—all tested automatically and analyzed and plotted by computer.

That wasn't all. When specific bits of information were needed, special test rigs were devised. To obtain the spring rate of a tire for suspension analysis, a tire was deflected while rolling on a steel drum (static spring rate is higher than rolling spring rate). And when longitudinal slip rate versus braking coefficient was needed on race tires—necessary data for developing anti-lock brake systems—an instrumented race car was towed behind a truck while the brakes were slowly applied.

So there were vast quantities of information. Reams of it on just a few tires. Some of it was obsolete before it was printed, as the tires became obsolete. But generally speaking, it gave the engineers a feel for what tires could do and how best to accommodate them in suspension design, and it gave the systems analysts an accurate mathematical model of tires for computer simulation of the entire vehicle.

Aerodynamics was another area where data had to be taken firsthand on a specific design. Not only was preliminary research meager, it was practically impossible to extrapolate it into current design, or even to rely on it in a slightly different variation on the same vehicle. Every aerodynamic device or shape had to be tested as a whole entity on each car. The first rear-engined Chaparral (2A) was a prime example. It had a high nose and the underside of the car was supposed to act like one-half of a venturi, sucking the car down. But it worked just the opposite, and it took a lot of pressure-testing on the road and model work in a wind tunnel to find out exactly why. From that point on, the accumulation of relevant test data kept Chevrolet/Chaparral preeminent in aerodynamics.

From the beginning, wind-tunnel testing was recognized and highly regarded—but only after being verified on the road. The very earliest tests that were related to racing were quarter-scale clay models run in rented aircraft wind tunnels by GM Styling staff. It was merely in the interest of "general research," however, and took a back seat to the mundane "proposed production" sedan tests. It *had* to be secondary, because the rental on aircraft tunnels is astronomical, partly because of the energy required to move all that air, partly because of the overhead in a building the size of a gymnasium, and partly because of the necessary computer analysis of the output. Just the data on one basic vehicle, in 30 configurations, would take a week to run, and fill a 200-page book with graphs, pressure plots, photos, and conclusions. Multiply that times two or three vehicles a year for the past ten years and it amounts to a lot of information—on everything from semi-trailer trucks to (believe me) a streamlined dragster.

When aerodynamic ideas started getting more radical at Chevrolet, however, Winchell decided to try to cut test expense and keep all the data at home. He decided to hire his own aerodynamicist and build his own wind tunnel.

A one-quarter-scale clay model of the preproduction 1967 Camaro in a rented aircraft wind tunnel. Aerodynamic forces are measured (through the pegs hidden by model wheels) by a force balance beneath the floor. Ink drops spread out across the surface, indicating airflow direction.

A one-twenty-fifth scale plastic model Corvette in the Chevrolet wind tunnel. The results are somewhat less accurate than in a larger tunnel, but they are quick and easy to obtain, and they cost practically nothing by comparison.

The ones that were being rented cost a few million dollars to build, but they were large enough to run quarter-scale models. So, Winchell settled on one-twenty-fifth scale at correspondingly less cost. After a year's construction and development, it was operational, and actually ran the first tunnel test of a wing mounted above a race car. However, about that time, Winchell was promoted to head up GM Engineering staff, and he took the tunnel with him, where it too became a corporation facility.

Because of the known significance of aerodynamics, and the unknowns of testing, parallel development was being carried out in full-scale vehicle evaluation. Strain gauges were attached to axle shafts, wing struts, and suspension springs to read out air drag and lift on a number of vehicles, both production and experimental (rear-engine type). Then, as Gates added to the instrumentation capabilities, it became possible to accurately measure drag by "coast-downs" from high speed, and measure lift by suspension deflection.

Likewise, pressures were being read on full-scale race-car bodies. The total air force in any direction is an integration of varying pressures all over a body, but knowing the specific pressure in a specific area, such as behind the fenders, or above the nose, offers solutions to pressing problems. Pressure and flow in ducts was also recorded for the radiator, carb inlet, brake ventilation, and driver cooling, to improve their efficiency.

To any automotive engineer in the world, especially a race-car engineer, this is invaluable data that would take years to collect. In fact, even if he knew where it all was filed, it would take an astute GM insider a year or so merely to assimilate it. Yet all those tools, all that data, were not the creative force behind the aerodynamic advancements such as spoilers, wings, plows, radiator ducts, the "sucker" ... The tools merely made the construction and development faster and surer.

The design of race-car suspension used to be an art. Now that the characteristics of tires can be determined, it has passed beyond a science, to the point where Chevrolet computers can produce any suspension geometry that is mechanically possible. That even includes the consideration of compliance, or the deflection of supposedly rigid components (and flexible insulators), which in some cases is designed into a suspension for vehicle stability. Of course, every suspension system is a gaggle of compromises, with your production vehicle oriented toward economy and comfort. But in race-car design, where there are two criteria, "stay together" and "win," suspensions are purely a function of what the tire needs to maintain the maximum traction for the maximum length of time.

Back in the days when the proper geometry was considered far more important than other design criteria have proven to be, so much time and thought was expended that the subject has lost its glamour. Not that you can throw a suspension together and make it work, but for all the different layouts seen, the fastest thing about any one is probably the driver ... or the aerodynamics ... or the tires ... And the slowest thing about any "different" geometry at this point is probably a lack of common knowledge in development.

Springs, shock absorbers, and anti-roll bars are a little more open, particularly in their relation to aerodynamic downforce. However, if it's important to get the handling "perfect" before the car touches the track, a Chevrolet engineer can just make successive runs with DK-4, the mathematical car and driver in an IBM-360 computer, and modify any component in the vehicle until it works right. One of the drawbacks to using a computer, though, is that you seldom learn "why" it came up with a particular "what." The intermediate steps and sub-conclusions are all buried in millions of digits on a stack of printout sheets two inches thick. For the engineer who has the time and wants to gain an in-depth knowledge of what's going on as, say, the left rear tire hits a bump while accelerating out of a right-hand turn, he has recourse to one of the earlier, more basic programs. Then again, if he wants to *watch* his mathematical model of a suspension operate, before it is even drawn, it can be simulated on an analog computer, which will illustrate the movements on a cathode ray tube, even slowing them down to whatever oscillation rate can be visualized.

Then, when it comes to visualizing the final suspension, comprehending it in three dimensions, and working out the space requirements on an actual chassis, stacks of working drawings can be bypassed through use of the "erector set." Since it takes time for technicians to mock up a proposed suspension, a kit was built with hundreds of fully adjustable links, struts, brackets, knuckles, ball joints, steering arms, axles, hubs, etc., which can be quickly assembled into probably any suspension configuration—independent, swing axle, live axle, deDion, and even some that are nameless.

Once a suspension layout is finalized, it's time to put all the pieces together with a chassis. Perhaps here the technology in Chevrolet R&D was a little lax—computers were never used. Chevrolet does have computer simulations of chassis structures which can be stressed and analyzed, and, actually, the aircraft industry was using the technique years earlier. But in the racing game, where stress inputs are more indeterminate, chassis design was more or less intuitive, based on extensive experience and comprehensive testing of previous designs. To avoid gross errors, there was a check-step along the way— the plastic model. By the proper selection of plastic material and scale thickness, an accurate scale model could be built from the earliest layout drawings. Then, after each model panel was plastic-welded or plastic-riveted together, it could be loaded, twisted, and shaken just like the full-size chassis, and the data scaled up. Deflection at any point could be electronically measured at any vibration frequency and subsequently stiffened before the design reached final assembly. On a competition-type chassis, this was quite straightforward—there were few and simple pieces—but a model of a production sedan had to be seen to be believed. Every last sheet metal panel and spot weld down to the headlight buckets reproduced in translucent plastic to a precise quarter-scale.

A large part of the education in chassis requirements came from previously successful (and unsuccessful) chassis which were borrowed or purchased, and stressed full-scale. There were some very good ones and some very weak ones, but even the worst produced guidelines and pointed out areas to be wary of. The major criteria, of course, is stiffness per pound—first in torsion, then in beaming—and by establishing baselines, it was then possible to balance out the other compromises, such as material cost, ease of construction and maintenance, durability, and space requirements.

Materials selection, whether for body, chassis, driveline, or miscellaneous components such as wings, was always an interesting game. The materials specialist, Joe Kurleto, was a fanatic for advanced types of fiberglass; the technicians preferred familiar sheet aluminum; fiberglass was better for compound aerodynamic curves; aluminum was cheapest; and then there were the expensive alloys of magnesium and titanium which were difficult to fabricate. Toward the end, experimentation and experience boiled it all down to the right material for each particular application. Along the way, however, there were running chassis made of sheet steel, wet lay-up fiberglass, sheet aluminum, steel tube space frame, sheet aluminum with titanium panels, honeycomb panels, and preimpregnated fiberglass cured in ovens. The last technique developed from

Kurleto's continual experiments to reduce wing weight, finally producing a 14-pounder with a foam core and "prepreg" skins. Hall's very own Chaparral 2A was the first wet lay-up plastic chassis, and also one of the very strongest, but prepreg avoided the excess nonstructural resin which was a weight penalty. A considerable amount of time was spent in the development of construction techniques, learning about such surprises as mold warpage in the curing oven, but eventually it produced the technology for Hall's structurally brilliant Chaparral 2H.

When it came to structurally testing a completed vehicle, the stress rigs used may have appeared crude, but they were highly educational. The most sophisticated test setup was conceived by Cox and produced all the loads that a vehicle could be subjected to on a track. Bump loads, cornering forces, braking forces, acceleration forces, and in any combinations, all while the operator sat right there and watched the reactions—if he dared get close. It is amazing to watch what happens to structures and components under the stress of competition, and it's frightful to listen to. Panels buckle, castings flex, ball joints and pivots lock up, control arms twist—all to the tune of a horrible creaking, groaning, popping. It's fortunate for the driver that the engine drowns most of it out.

And then there was the ridiculous "great secret," the automatic transmission. No one could have anticipated the years of absurd speculation regarding its origin and operation, because it was no greater an engineering triumph than any of the other subsystems that made up the whole effort. How did it work? Any good transmission mechanic could tell the basics of its operation, merely by looking at the external case and shift linkage, and by listening to it run. The torque converter was visible through cooling vents in the bellhousing, and anyone could distinctly hear how many *manual* shifts were made. The many writers who explained its "epicyclic gearsets" obviously had never seen either a planetary gearset or the transmission case, because there's no way the former would fit into the latter. There's no secret to its operation—the layout is similar to earlier transaxle layouts used by Hewland, Colotti, Z-F, Halibrand, Sadler, and other constructors. It's just that a torque converter was added. Ford must have thought there was a secret, however. When a Chevrolet R&D employee was terminated after expropriating junked test parts for his own use, Kar Kraft, then building the great LeMans GT Coupes, immediately snapped him up. But it still took them man-years and many prototypes to discover the real secret.

The great Chaparral/Chevrolet/automatic transmission secret is this: a torque converter ahead of a simple manual transmission ... and a masterpiece of engineering development! That's all.

The advantages and disadvantages of an automatic in racing are well known: more torque multiplication, easier driving, no brake balance effects, and later on, freeing the driver's left foot for wing actuation. On the other hand, it didn't save shift time, there was increased rotational inertia, and a lot of horsepower was wasted in heat due to slippage in the converter. In addition, there were familiarization problems when other drivers were needed. Even at the end of the season Phil Hill spent in the Chaparral 2E, he would occasionally jab at the brake pedal on an upshift.

The casual observer's naivete can be understood, however, because of the number of different versions. At the beginning, when tires were the limiting factor in acceleration, and the smallblock engines were being used, a simple single-speed transmission with a wide-range torque converter was adequate. But then tires began developing and traction increased, and before long, a two-speed and then a three-speed were necessary. And then there was a four-speed, along with continual changes in converters. At one time, even a manual clutch was tried, although never in competition. Over a period of years, it seemed as though converter design advanced monthly. They were built with different diameters, with different stall speeds, different torque ratios, and varying efficiency, and each was best suited for a different transmission, or a different track, or engine. Some were adaptations of production converters and some were hand-built, but in spite of the cost and time, lessons were learned and the state of the art improved correspondingly.

The same was true in the manual end of the transmission. There were 14 gearset ratios available in any gear, plus two ratios for the differential, plus variations in tire diameter. Combined with different torque curves available from the engines, the entire driveline could be tailored to any track or conditions. It might seem impossible to fit that many combinations into a meaningful whole, and it might be, if not for the detailed Chaparral records of previous performance; computer plots of all combinations of engine, converter, and gear ratios; and the ability to predict track performance by computer simulation.

But the real reason it all worked right, was the detail execution—the development. First Jerry Mrlik, then Joe Kurleto, masterminded every last seal and bearing to take what the engine could put out, what the driver could dish out, and what the tires could absorb, and no more. In the seven years that the same basic design was used, engine output nearly doubled, and yet Kurleto was able to keep just ahead of disaster by anticipating weaknesses. Better metallurgy, stronger converters, improved lubrication, bigger gears and bearings, made it one of the most dependable components in the car. It also allowed less weight in driveline components, in that the converter absorbed vibration and shock loads from the engine. And yet, if the interest in competition had continued into 1971, the automatic probably would have disappeared.

In the first place, the basic housing couldn't take much more stress from larger engines, nor from suspension loads when it became a structural member. The gear case had been extended twice, to house extra gears, and it had been reinforced to the limit. Gear shafts were as large in diameter as could be allowed by bearing size, and converter diameter was keeping the engine from being lowered in the chassis. It was losing its advantage in performance, too.

Developments in other areas, especially the broadening of engine torque curves, were eliminating the necessity of a converter. And finally, had all else remained equal, the power lost in heating up the converter at supposed "lockup" was becoming intolerable. Even when a converter is running at its most efficient, there are still a few rpm lost in slippage, which means a couple of percent of wasted horsepower. A few percent, even out of 600 plus can be sorely missed. There were solutions in the works, naturally, but the end result probably would not have been worth the necessary development at that stage.

To this point, we have only looked at a few examples of the race car subsystems that the Chevrolet team concentrated on researching and developing. There are many others that deserve mentioning. Brakes were a constant area of investigation, from both a performance and durability standpoint—especially because of the lack of engine braking with an automatic transmission. Different disc materials and pad materials were experimented with, not just by "cut and try," but by programming brake dynamometers, instrumenting the brakes with thermocouples, and recording temperatures and friction coefficients. Theories were established for the energy absorption required at various tracks and the possibilities of energy dissipation. Ducts, fans, and heat sinks were designed accordingly. Those photographs you see of flaming discs on a dynamometer? … they're not passenger car tests—they represent the upper limits of racing usage. Cox and Pocobello had a collection of cracked discs, scorched pads, and melted seals. But that established the ultimate capabilities for future production development.

Variable-rate steering systems, driver packaging and comfort, load-leveling devices, fail-safe wiring systems, windshield cleaning—how do you keep a wiper blade on the glass at high speed in a pouring rain? All these were individual and interesting challenges to be met. Not only that, but they contributed to the great bank of basic knowledge which may or may not eventually be needed in the engineering of your everyday passenger sedan.

However, the greatest challenge—and the greatest opportunity—was always the creation of an entire, all-new vehicle. And there were plenty of them. Considering everything from experimental production prototypes to all-out race-car design, it's safe to say that Chevrolet has built at least one of just about any possible basic vehicle design. With one exception that comes to mind, that is— there never was a rear-engine, front-wheel-drive car. A few were only built on paper to be run and evaluated by computer, such as the race car with two smallblock engines fore and aft of the rear axle, and the smallblock go-kart with a flexible chassis instead of suspension. But there were open-wheelers, three-wheelers, four-wheel drive, front-engine, rear-engine, mid-engine, engine next to the driver, driver ahead of the front axle, driver behind the rear axle,

The Chaparral 2E on a "tilt-table" to measure the center of gravity. By balancing it in different positions, it was possible to measure the height of the center of gravity—a critical dimension in computer analysis.

unsprung engines attached to the axle, engines as structural members, backbone chassis, tube chassis, monocoque, rollover cars, crash cars, vacuum-traction vehicles ... Many were stillborn, some are still in storage, a few are still running, but most were scrapped after giving up all their particular characteristics to engineering analysis.

A few of the most commercially feasible designs became production prototypes, but the most successful performers were returned to be tested and documented to a degree that no other race car in the world has ever been studied. They had to be. Hundreds of accurate bits of information were necessary to build mathematical models of the cars for computer runs.

For example, before one of the later-model Chaparrals was retired, it was subjected to weeks of detail testing. Of course, much of the data on its components was already available, such as complete engine output curves, records of engine assembly, torque converter performance, gear ratios, brake coefficients, weight of each individual component—down to nuts and bolts, suspension geometry, spring and shock absorber rates, and individual tire characteristics. Then there were all the "field test" records kept by Chaparral. Every time the vehicle ran, whether testing or racing, pages of notes were made concerning location, time, temperatures, pressures, laps, laptimes, corner times, driver, positions, chassis setup specs, and subjective impressions. And, at many tracks, a continual recording was made of speed and lateral acceleration all around the track on one of the fastest practice laps.

So what was left unknown? That was just the beginning then the vehicle had to be analyzed as a complete entity. A special tilt-table was available to measure the height of the center of gravity, with and without full fuel tank—a very important and usually unknown dimension. Similarly, the vehicle polar moment of inertia was determined by rotating it on a torsional turntable. It was

The Chaparral photographed at one hundred mph, with cotton tufts taped on the skin to observe airflow direction and condition ... whether smooth or turbulent. The wire above the wing is the instrumentation transmitter aerial.

also necessary to determine rotating inertia of all the driveline components from crankshaft pulley to wheels and tires, since that adds an effective weight component under acceleration.

To learn the net tire/vehicle capabilities, it was run on a skidpad to measure the maximum lateral traction without aerodynamic influence. And it was accelerated from a standing start and braked down from high speed, while heavily instrumented, to measure pure longitudinal traction coefficients. At the same time, the test-track coefficient of friction was measured at various locations.

A considerable amount of time was spent just determining aerodynamic characteristics of the running vehicle under different attitudes of the wings and chassis. Because of the unknown rolling drag of race tires at high speeds, total drag was measured at a number of speeds and a curve fitted to the data by computer. From the curve, an equation was derived to indicate the amount of drag caused by chassis friction, tire drag, and air drag. Because of the great influence of aerodynamic downforce, it was measured at front and rear axles, and also at many speeds to find how it varied as a function of velocity. Airflow in the ducts was noted for future reference, both in cubic feet per minute at a given speed, and the distribution across the opening. To better understand the effect of specific body shapes, airflow pressure (positive or negative), was measured on every square foot of the body—top and bottom, front and rear. Then wool tufts were taped on and their direction and turbulence photographed at speed to illustrate airflow.

To serve as a check on mathematical predictions, the suspension was tested, also. Ride rate, or spring rate of the chassis, was measured front and rear, and lateral roll rate was measured, as well. Total suspension dampening was considered important, and then, bounce, pitch, and roll frequencies were measured without damping. Brake temperatures were recorded during a specially formulated series of stops, for correlation on the brake dyno, and brake line pressures were recorded front and rear.

Then, after all the running tests were completed, the lab tests began. The chassis stress rig was used to measure the amount of deflection at the wheels, due to the extremes of high "g" loading. Changes in camber and toe were recorded at both front and rear suspensions under simulated racing conditions, because deflections of a few thousandths of an inch mean errors in tire alignment of as much as one degree. And then, the entire vehicle was twisted, from wheel to wheel, to learn how much *it* deflected in use.

All that information is too time-consuming and expensive to gather for mere idle curiosity—it was absolutely necessary for many reasons. Most obvious is the premise that you can't move forward in any great steps unless you know exactly where you are standing. Then, if something still goes wrong, it's possible to return to the baseline and find out *why* it went wrong. This was demonstrated time and again, but most often, fortunately, in components and systems that never reached the public eye. Some good bad examples are the Camaro independent rear suspension, the Corvette that floated its front wheels at high speed, radiators that wouldn't cool, anti-skid brakes that skidded, and so on. Then, conversely, there was the Chaparral 2H, but even it almost taught enough lessons to make the "sucker car" a success.

The most educational toys that Chevrolet R&D ever produced, by far, were the electronic instrumentation systems. To any engineer who wanted to know anything about what he had done, or was doing, or ought to do, they were indispensable. In spite of the fact that Winchell abhorred any electrical device that had more than two wires leading into it, and had a basic distrust of all the "electrickery" specialists, the "little black boxes" were the most respected and requested tools in the department. Certainly, there are few things that can't be measured or analyzed mechanically, but aerospace electronics has produced the hardware to more accurately and more efficiently record it, especially in moving vehicles.

The very first device was simply a tape recorder that could be carried in a race car to record speed. This was done by wiring it to a digital magnetic pickup on a front wheel, which produced electrical impulses, the frequency indicating speed, and the sum indicating distance. Playing it back in the lab, of course, would merely produce an indecipherable warble, except that it was wired through calibration devices into a chart recorder. The resultant charts were then snipped off at one-lap lengths and compared to other laps on which a vehicle component had been changed. Therefore, not only was the effect of a change on laptime known, but the exact areas in which it increased and/or decreased speed could be noted. Many times a vehicle change will do that— improve performance in, say, a corner, while decreasing it in the straightaway.

A velocity transducer being mounted to a front wheel of Donohue's Camaro. This is a digital pickup, which not only can record speed, but distance traveled. The cable leads to a two-channel tape recorder in the car.

The entire 10-channel instrumentation calibration, modulation, and transmitter box mounted in the passenger seat of the Chaparral 2F. The cylinder mounted on the front is a transducer to measure lateral acceleration.

By studying the precise performance, sometimes it is possible to accentuate the positive and diminish the negative effects.

But then more information was requested. Such as where and how hard was the car cornering? So an accelerometer was installed, and a second frequency was superimposed, to be proportional to lateral acceleration. This really produced unintelligible sounds, but as two-channel recorders are common, both parameters could still be drawn on one lap sheet. This was considered the bare minimum, and over a period of years, accurate, top-speed lap recordings were taken from sedans, sports cars, and racing cars at perhaps two dozen American and European race tracks. From Laguna Seca to Indianapolis to LeMans, the maximum speed at any point on the track was on file in a cabinet full of strip charts, to be referenced before the next car was prepared for the next event. That should clear up the mystery for all those race-watchers who have wondered about the odd front-wheel hub with wires leading to a black box, seen on Chaparrals and Camaros.

Naturally, the most practical test course to use was Rattlesnake Raceway, for its privacy and ease of access. But being 1600 miles from the track to the office made time a major obstacle, so testing was done over the telephone. Data lines are available through the phone companies for the continual transmission of data. By having an extension at the track, and an extension at the chart recorder in the office, the data could be instantly accumulated in the office. Also, by that time, the on-board recorder had been superseded by a smaller, short-range radio transmitter with a receiver at trackside. With this arrangement, the information could be read out of a small single-channel recorder at the track, while simultaneously being recorded on the more elaborate and more accurate devices in Michigan.

Even the most blasé engineers must have felt part of the space age, as one would stand there next to the recorder with earphones on, talking to the technicians halfway across the continent, while information on what the car was doing poured across the analysis table. "He hit 1.35 g's in the double 90°s ... should be pretty fast down the straight. Yeah ... shifting earlier ... he's doing 140, 150, 160, 170 ... 2 ... 172 in the straight ... let's watch the speed up the front straight." All accompanied by a whistling and clicking and paper spewing out of the machine.

The system even had a valuable safety aspect in testing. On a track that is over two miles around, often the car can't even be heard, much less seen. And enough safety personnel to cover the entire track just are not practical. But with telemetry, any variations from the normal are instantly noted in the pits, as is the location of the car, and assistance can be dispatched before the car has even come to a stop. Another valuable fringe benefit is that after the emergency, the cause can often be uncovered by analysis of the recording immediately preceding the event. Even in the heat of disaster, the machine never forgets what happened.

But then, even more information was requested. Suspension travel became important in handling studies, vertical acceleration figures were needed for shock absorber and chassis design, aerodynamic force measurement was necessary to evaluate new devices, and soon two channels of information were not enough. That's when Gates began work on the greatest tool of all, the instrumentation van, or "truck of knowledge."

There is no great difficulty in recording any number of channels of information if size and weight of the instrumentation is not limited. In testing high-performance cars and race cars, though, space and weight are critical. Also, there are environmental problems of heat, vibration, and engine electronic interference. Since it was decided that six channels of continual analog data and four channels of digital signals were the absolute minimum for complete analysis of a vehicle in any maneuver, and the most precise and legible recorder system was as big as a steamer trunk, telemetry was the only answer. Through the use of surplus miniaturized aerospace electronic equipment, the in-car hardware was reduced to a 15-pound shoe-box-size "signal sorter" and transmitter, plus the required measurement transducers and assorted wiring, and an antenna. At the receiving end, a Chevrolet step-van was outfitted for all the reception, printing, and readout, plus storage of all backup and calibration equipment. Because of adverse conditions at many test sites, it was also equipped with wall heaters, air conditioning, refrigerator, stove, and a stereo FM radio and tape deck to suppress the noise of instrumentation—and vehicles being abused. All in all, the setup was almost a takeoff on a "Mission Impossible" caper, with the inconspicuous van (and its 30-foot antenna) parked discreetly away from the track while engineers came and went, studied graphs and instruments, and conversed over two-way radios.

It was strictly business of the highest order, though. With the proper transducers, any combinations of forces, displacements, velocities, accelerations, temperatures, and pressures could be conveniently and accurately measured up to three miles away. Also, in one channel, there was the capability of time-sharing eight additional signals where transient conditions were not significant (as with temperature), and the recorder output rate could be based on either distance traveled or on an accurate time reference. At first, Hall and Donohue were skeptical of all the "gimmickry," but after a demonstration of the speed of setup, dependability, accuracy of output, and quantity of output, it became a highly requested piece of hardware. It was considered so valuable, in fact, that when Penske switched from Camaros to Javelins, he had an economy two-channel version (like the earlier Chevrolet equipment) built for his engineers.

When the telemetry van was completed, one of its first uses was in a press preview of the 1969 Chevrolet "high-performance" line, where a Z/28 Camaro was completely instrumented and given to the press to drive around a slalom course. The information transmitted was velocity, lateral acceleration, longitudinal acceleration, steering-wheel angle, throttle position, and brake temperature, plus digital signals for time, braking points, and the start/finish line. It all tended to upstage the new cars, however, as the press was more awed by this technique of studying and comparing their *own* performance.

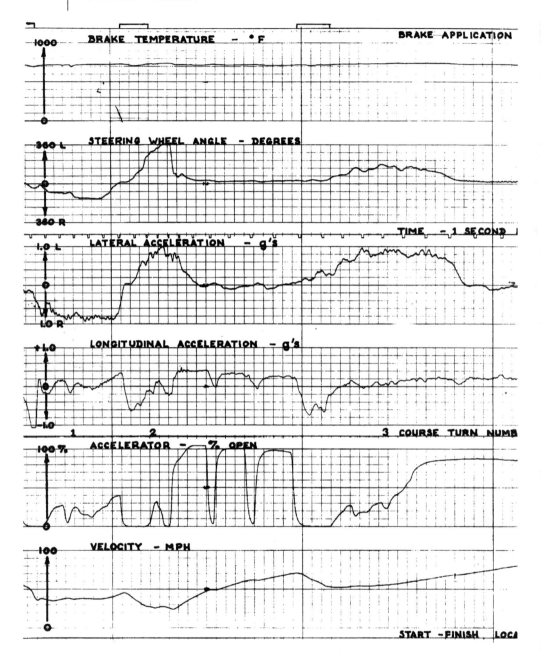

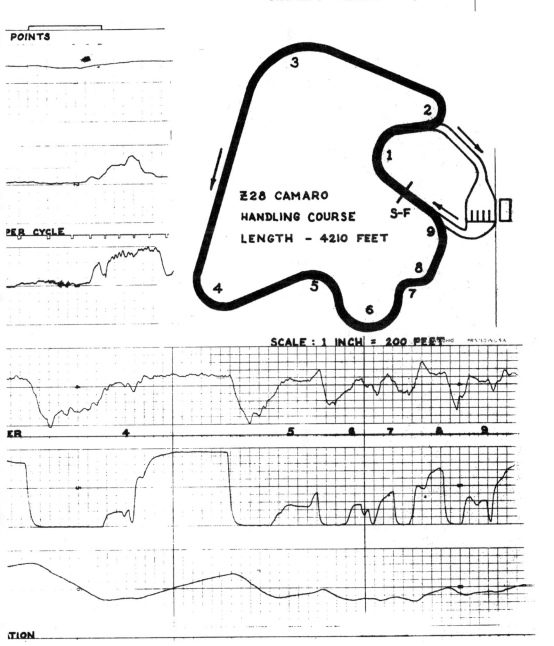

POINTS

PER CYCLE

Z28 CAMARO
HANDLING COURSE
LENGTH - 4210 FEET

S-F

SCALE : 1 INCH = 200 FEET

ER

TION

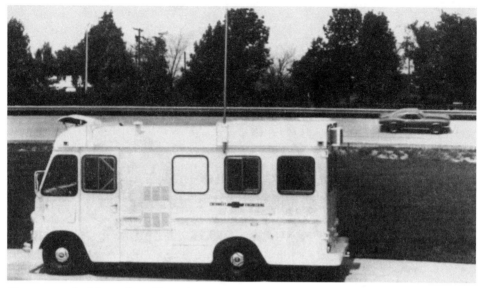

The most valuable tool in Chevrolet R&D—a portable instrumentation laboratory, seen here inside the GM check loop with a Camaro. The antenna can be extended far enough to receive signals from over three miles away.

The guts of the instrumentation van. From the left: an automatic-winding analysis table; the ten-channel strip-chart recorder; the radio receiver and signal demodulator; Don Gates and a portable calibration reference box.

The setup was not wasted solely on the press, however. It was a very few days later that the very same equipment was mounted in another Z/28 Camaro. Only this one was blue, had very wide tires, a roll cage, and wrapping paper taped over names and numbers on its sides. And *that* car, and its famous driver, produced invaluable knowledge. Of all the uses for the telemetry van—studying vehicle dynamics, pinpointing problems, quantifying design changes, etc.— one of the most interesting was studying driver techniques. It was possible to record exactly what the driver did at any time, and the consequences, from a reduction in laptimes to a complete spinout. And when the driver is gone, or the test engineer has forgotten, all that information is still permanently recorded and on file for future reference.

But the most valuable use of all those numbers, as it turned out, was in the verification of DK-4. After many years of successively more-sophisticated vehicle dynamics programs, and the successively larger computers required to handle the information, they were all pieced together into one gigantic and nearly unworkable unit called DK-4 (which is merely a sequential code designation).

The first, most basic program was merely a simulation of straight-line acceleration. By inputting all the vehicle characteristics, including engine torque curve, gear ratios, vehicle drag, tire friction, etc., an acceleration run could be made, reading out time, speed, and distances. This was used to study engines and transmissions, particularly automatics. From there, braking performance was simulated, and it became possible to run the math model down a given length straightaway. By selecting a beginning speed and an ending speed, the acceleration and deceleration curves could be worked toward each other, and matched at the brake point. Computer simulation stagnated there for a few years, for the lack of knowledge of what the driver and car did in the transient stage of cornering. For an approximate simulation, the track performance recordings were used to input velocity points in corners, and they were merely upgraded or degraded by percentages to allow for changes in tires or aerodynamics.

Using this approximation, any track on which a performance recording had been made could be rerun repeatedly with different driveline characteristics in the vehicle, and the optimum selection made. Most often this was used to predict the proper top gear ratio in the fastest straight, but it was also useful in selecting intermediate gear ratios for the slower turns and straights. After a few years of this, with constant feedback from the outside race teams for correlation of conditions versus laptimes, the prediction of laptimes became very accurate.

In the meantime, however, chassis and suspension programs were being improved, based on the latest comprehensive tire data. With these programs,

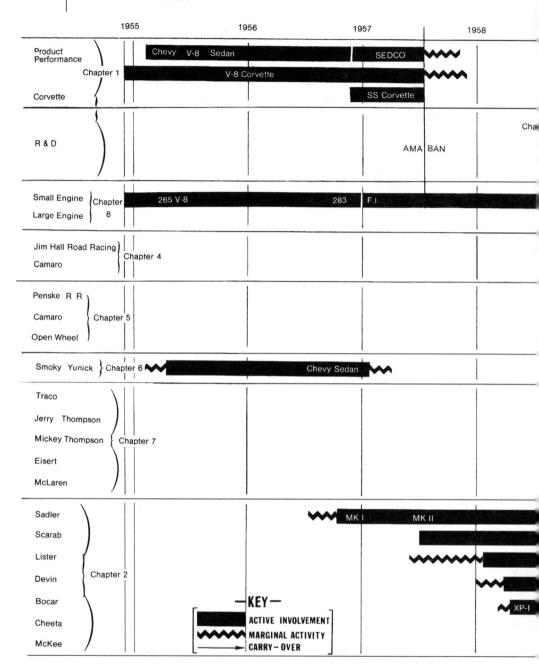

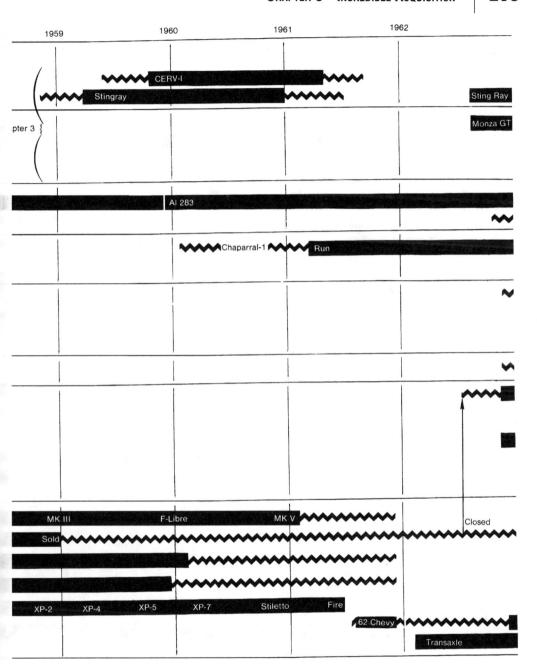

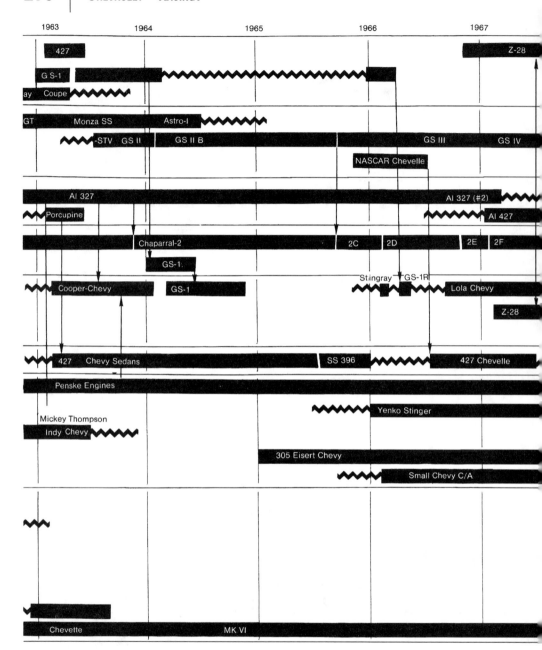

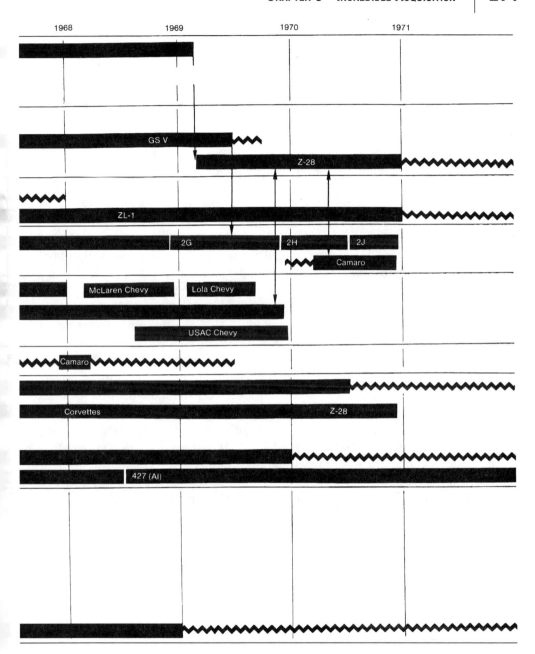

the cornering actions of a vehicle could be predicted before it was built, by inputting all the suspension parameters—tires, shocks, springs, anti-roll bars, geometry, c.g., tread, wheelbase—and simulating a critical vehicle control input. For example, the "car" could be running at a constant high speed and the steering wheel suddenly cranked over 180°. If the computed output sheets or graphs indicated a spin, different tires or springs or anti-roll bars could be tried, and the simulation run again.

With this type of tool, a different vehicle could be built and tested every day. Or many small changes could be run successively to evaluate the general characteristics of component variations. Some of the more interesting studies were: the effect of total vehicle width on cornering speed (balancing weight transfer versus path radius); the effect of wheelbase on transient response; the importance of c.g. height; and the effect of variable spring rates and shock rates.

And yet, the system was still not sophisticated enough. There was straight-away performance, there was a cornering model, and there were racetracks on file. All this was incorporated in a computer library of data on various engines, vehicles, converters, transmissions, tires, and tracks, which were detailed down to corner radius, grade, banking, and lengths. But one vital ingredient was missing—the driver.

About that time, the famous "wing ban" hit, and the department was unsettled as to what its next act would be. There were many rumors of four-wheel-drive racers from Europe, and that looked like the most profitable area of investigation for an automotive R&D department. The 4WD prototype (CERV II) that Duntov had built four years earlier hadn't done too well, though. In the first place, its weight was intolerable for the engine it carried. It was at *least* three hundred pounds heavier than the current rear-engine Chaparral, which ran the same basic engine and yet had no particular traction problem. Another difficulty was that the proper selection of front/rear torque split was not well-understood at the time. At "face-off" against Hall's Chaparral in Midland, in the summer of 1964, the CERV II didn't fare at all well, and research in that particular layout of 4WD was dropped. After exhausting tests and develop-ment, the car was ordered to be scrapped, but through some oversight, all that was destroyed was the paperwork covering its existence, and it was rediscov-ered in an obscure garage at the GM Proving Grounds. Progress in tires had obsoleted its suspension, however, and considering its basic driveline deficien-cies, it was decided to study 4WD mathematically instead.

At that point, steady-state (constant-radius) cornering simulation was easy, and the transient programs gave a good indication of response, but the empiri-cal track cornering data couldn't be extrapolated from 2WD to 4WD. That was the question we were trying to answer. If the actual control inputs a race driver went through for optimum performance were known, a complete mathematical lap could be simulated, but the consensus was that humans are too complex to be replaced by equations. The converse turned out to be true.

The theoreticians wanted a driver with "eyes," a "feel" for lateral acceleration, "foresight," and "learning," to steer around a corner on the optimum line
at the maximum speed. As the only experienced race driver/engineers in the
group, however, Don Cox and I sat down and brainstormed out the simple truth.
A racer doesn't drive from a straight, through a turn, to a straight. Instead, he
drives from an apex, through a straight, to an apex. Coming out of an apex is
relatively easy—it's merely like balancing on a tightrope—but going into the
apex is a little worse—it's like leaping onto the tightrope blindfolded. On a
computer, however, time can be run in reverse, so it was possible to work from
both apexes toward the middle, selecting the absolute optimum braking point.

Based on this theory, and the other known tire and vehicle conditions, it
was relatively straightforward to complete the driver control simulation,
although the mathematical equations took months to formulate. Representative paths had to be modeled within road boundaries, and they had to have a
smooth transition from the minimum radius to a straight. The front- or rear-tire
traction limit (understeer or power oversteer) had to be computed at each inter-
val. The mathematical selection of proper front/rear torque bias in a 4WD had
to be resolved. (Could that be the famous "Ferguson 4WD Formula"?) Optimum
acceleration had to be limited at the point where the engine was at full throttle.
Et cetera. The basic equation, with every term substitution included, was a
quadratic which could be written out on one line that was over seven feet long.
But the computer swallowed it and spit out the answer. Plots of time and speed
versus distance for the existing 2WD car, and the projected statistics on a 4WD
car were compared in different types of corners. Four-wheel-drive on a road-
racing car is not all bad—but it wasn't good enough, even at optimum development, to justify building at that time.

We were still up in the air. Turbine engines were a recent sensation, but
the technology was just a little too far removed from Chevrolet R&D's experience or facilities. Then, too, they would detract from further development of
the bread-and-butter V-8 engines. Anti-skid braking was a strong possibility
for investigation, and Hall was under construction on his 2H, with its anticipated giant step in drag reduction.

And so, after a few day's worth of deliberation, we decided to begin apply-
ing systems analysis to management of our efforts. Gates had been studying
the aerospace management techniques of PERT (Performance Evaluation
Review Technique) and Critical Path Flow Systems, and had gotten us all on
the kick of logical problem solving. Meanwhile, out of idle curiosity, I had
been running an interesting exercise on the performance prediction computer,
called the Relative Value of Parameter Variations. By making step-by-step
improvements in various race-car parameters on the computer and reading
out the reduction in laptimes, it was possible to plot performance improvement (in percent) versus change in vehicle (in percent). The investigation
covered: power increase up to 20%; weight decrease down 20%; drag reduction

DRIVER CONTROL INPUTS, AND

TIME (SEC.)	STEER ANGLE (DEG.)	DRIVE TORQUE (LB.-FT.)	BRAKE PRESSURE (PSI)		AIR DRAG (POUNDS)
			FRONT	REAR	
2.50	4.3	95.	0.0	0.0	62.
2.51	4.3	95.	0.0	0.0	62.
2.52	4.3	95.	0.0	0.0	62.
2.53	4.3	95.	0.0	0.0	62.
2.54	4.3	95.	0.0	0.0	62.

VEHICLE LOCATION, VELOCITY,

TIME (SEC.)	C.G. LOCATION (FT.)			C.G. VELOCITY (FT./SEC.)			C.G. (F]
	X	Y	Z	X	Y	Z	X
2.50	129.98	72.77	1.38	63.10	1.56	0.0	0.2;
2.51	130.26	72.85	1.38	63.09	1.56	0.0	0.2;
2.52	130.54	73.35	1.38	63.09	1.56	0.0	0.2;
2.53	130.82	73.92	1.38	63.08	1.56	0.0	0.2;
2.54	131.10	74.49	1.38	63.08	1.56	0.0	0.2;

SUSPENSION POSITIONS, VELOCITIES, ANGLES,

TIME (SEC.)	WHEEL RIDE POSITION (IN.)				WHEEL VERTICAL VELOCITY (FT./SEC.)				RF
	RF	LF	RR	LR	RF	LF	RR	LR	RF
2.50	1.73	-0.90	1.91	-0.59	-0.36	-0.34	0.17	0.20	12.9
2.51	1.73	-0.90	1.91	-0.59	-0.36	-0.34	0.17	0.20	12.9
2.52	1.73	-0.90	1.91	-0.59	-0.36	-0.34	0.17	0.20	12.9
2.53	1.73	-0.90	1.91	-0.59	-0.36	-0.34	0.17	0.20	12.9
2.54	1.73	-0.90	1.91	-0.59	-0.36	-0.34	0.17	0.20	12.9

TIRE SLIP ANGLES,

TIME (SEC.)	SLIP ANGLE (DEG.)				SLIP RATIO (PERCENT)				NORMAL FC (LB.)	
	RF	LF	RR	LR	RF	LF	RR	LR	RF	LF
2.50	3.6	3.6	2.6	2.5	0.1	0.0	2.1	0.8	42.	774.
2.51	3.6	3.6	2.6	2.5	0.1	0.0	2.1	0.8	42.	774.
2.52	3.6	3.6	2.6	2.5	0.1	0.0	2.1	0.8	42.	774.
2.53	3.6	3.6	2.6	2.5	0.1	0.0	2.1	0.8	42.	774.
2.54	3.6	3.6	2.6	2.5	0.1	0.0	2.1	0.8	42.	774.
2.55	3.6	3.6	2.6	2.5	0.1	0.0	2.1	0.8	42.	774.

Typical computer output for the mathematical simulation of an imaginary vehicle being driven by an imaginary driver. Each of these four pages of data (in total)

AERODYNAMIC FORCES

WING ANGLES (DEGREES)		TOTAL AIR DOWNFORCE (POUNDS)		SIDE GUST (POUNDS)
FRONT	REAR	FRONT	REAR	
10.5	15.0	10.2	30.5	0.0
10.5	15.0	10.2	30.5	0.0
10.5	15.0	10.2	30.5	0.0
10.5	15.0	10.2	30.5	0.0
10.5	15.0	10.2	30.5	0.0

ACCELERATION, ANGLE, AND ROAD SLOPE

ACCELERATION (./SEC./SEC.)		VEHICLE ANGLE (DEGREES)			ROAD SLOPE (DEGREES)	
Y	Z	X	Y	Z	GRADE	CAMBER
32.20	30.74	3.03	0.14	64.51	0.10	1.60
32.20	30.74	3.03	0.14	64.78	0.10	1.60
32.20	30.74	3.03	0.14	65.06	0.10	1.60
32.20	30.74	3.03	0.14	65.34	0.10	1.60
32.20	30.74	3.03	0.14	65.62	0.10	1.60

AND TIRE ROLLING RADIUS

ROLLING RADIUS (IN.)			CAMBER ANGLE (DEG.)			
LF	RR	LR	RF	LF	RR	LR
12.6	13.6	13.4	-3.0	-0.0	-1.0	-0.0
12.6	13.6	13.4	-3.0	-0.0	-1.0	-0.0
12.6	13.6	13.4	-3.0	-0.0	-1.0	-0.0
12.6	13.6	13.4	-3.0	-0.0	-1.0	-0.0
12.6	13.6	13.4	-3.0	-0.0	-1.0	-0.0

SLIP RATIO AND FORCES

RCE		LATERAL FORCE (LB.)				CIRCUMFERENTIAL FORCE (LB.)			
RR	LR	RF	LF	RR	LR	RF	LF	RR	LR
377.	1077.	42.	771.	352.	978.	0.	1.	79.	83.
377.	1077.	42.	771.	352.	978.	0.	1.	79.	83.
377.	1077.	42.	771.	352.	978.	0.	1.	79.	83.
377.	1077.	42.	771.	352.	978.	0.	1.	79.	83.
377.	1077.	42.	771.	352.	978.	0.	1.	79.	83.

epresent no more than one-half second of actual vehicle time. The equations are so com-
lex that the simulation of one minute of driving takes two hours of computer time, at ten
ollars per minute. But it is still far faster than an actual build and test.

of up to 50% (approximate goal of the 2H); and increase in aerodynamic downforce. The results were very interesting—and are still valuable, for that matter. From there, knowing the approximate cost in dollars and man-hours to produce the different gains, it was possible to make a rational decision as to the proper direction of our efforts. And to make it stick when confronted by higher policy-makers.

That is when we began to design the world's first successful (?) vacuum-traction race car.

Radically different systems concepts don't just spring full-blown from the engineers' minds and become reality. Past experiences had taught the value of the words "research" and "development." Also, they had shown that difficulties increase with the square of complexity. Since there was no previous engineering work on vacuum-traction, it was necessary to do research from scratch. Efficient axial-flow fans were common and well-developed, but air seals rubbing against asphalt at 200 mph ... that required some development. Over a period of months, a number of seals were tried in the wind tunnel and on the road, with all sorts of hinges, actuating mechanisms, and materials. Most worked adequately—for as long as they lasted—but they pointed up other development problems such as lateral and vertical stability. The first rigid skirt seal worked too well ... it yanked the car down on the pavement so hard that it couldn't be moved. The first system that could be driven on the skidpad increased cornering power by an unexpected ten percent, but it only lasted about three laps before it ran over its own skirts and ripped them off. Not only that, but it was both the world's loudest road-racing car (like standing in front of a jet fighter inlet) and the world's ugliest. Even the final experimental prototype looked as though it were put together inside out. Its fans and drive motors and skirt-actuating mechanisms were all tacked on the outside of the old STV, which was grotesque enough as it was. Only the leading-edge skirt was hidden, which was in part due to the fact that it was the key to success. At the front, combined problems of sealing, wear, and ground clearance were the big holdup until Gates schemed up a complex hinged skirt which was automatically controlled by frontal air pressure.

By January 1969, a number of us had driven the test system on the skidpad, and it was a phenomenal sensory experience. It takes a number of turns around a skidpad circle before you realize just how incredibly far you can push a vacuum-traction vehicle, and as you approach the limit, the forces on your body are totally disorienting. A lateral force of up to 1.5 g's—in addition to the normal 1.0 g's body weight—tend to cause a driver to lose comprehension of which way is "down." The feeling is very much like racing around a steeply banked track, or inside a giant cylinder ... although the track is perfectly level. There was no denying the fantastic increase in performance, and even before prototype development was completed, Cox was designing an all-new race-car chassis strong enough to take the loads.

The Chaparral drafting (and trophy) room in Midland, Texas. On the left are Chevrolet employees Don Cox and Paul Van Valkenburgh (the author), and on the right, Chaparral employees Troy Rogers and Mike Pocobello.

Development of the "sucker" car points up another valuable aspect of Chevrolet's R&D team—the exchange of esoteric knowledge. A lot of credit is due the specialists in other GM divisions who could be called upon at any time, concerning any scientific project. Air pumps and fans, for example, are a technology in themselves. So GM Research was scoured for an expert in that area. As it happened, not only did he have just the right size fan lying around, he had also worked on the opposite principle—air bearings for moving large objects (Ground Effects Machines).

The same was true in many other areas: converter design, fuel injection, structural materials, wind tunnels, wheel design, etc. And the information flowed out, also. Representatives from as far away as GM's Australian facilities would visit Chevrolet R&D for consultation on high-performance vehicles. Information seldom flowed sideways, however, to such places as Pontiac or Oldsmobile, for whom there seemed to be a little too much sibling rivalry.

To the race-car engineer, the concept of all that specialized technical knowledge accumulated under one roof is staggering. Knowing what is there makes it more than a little discouraging to imagine coming up with a productive new idea in racing, or trying to develop it without GM's facilities and experience. Of course, the scoffers are saying "Oh yeah, if you're so smart, why weren't you first—every time?" Well, Chevrolet couldn't win, because Chevrolet wasn't racing. And from the same fortunate standpoint, Chevrolet couldn't lose, either. Private and sponsored teams have always raced Chevrolet products, some with advice and hardware from Chevrolet engineering and some not, and if they finish first—fine. But Chevrolet in itself never claimed to be a racing team, and perhaps could never have won a single race without the Chaparral or Penske organizations, because the primary goal was always the accumulation of technical knowledge, and at that, the company was unbeatable.

10

Engineering Spin-Off

Although intensive research into racing is probably dead forever at Chevrolet, the engineering benefits will continue to crop up in production vehicles for years to come. And that is not just wishful thinking or lame, unsupported justification. Most other auto manufacturers who spend gross budgets on direct competition or financial sponsorship have used "improvement of the breed" as an ethereal vindication, when in fact, exposure and advertising are the major interests. It is rather doubtful whether the 4-cam Indy Ford project ever benefited any production sedans, and Chrysler's omnipotent drag hemi engine is no longer even manufactured. Lotus's successes in Formula 1 racing do not give the marketed products any better reputation for reliability, and until recently few Ferraris were at all practical for everyday use. For those who build race cars by the "cut-and-try" method, the end result is simply a race car and nothing further—although in many cases the end result may be very successful in its own environment. Therefore, racing ought to be gracefully accepted for what it is—a form of entertainment for those who follow it, a personal challenge for those who participate, and a very effective form of advertising and promotion for those who underwrite it.

But Chevrolet was not going racing. It was not the advertising and promotion department at Chevrolet that was showing the interest. It was the engineering people, individually and as a group, who saw a challenge.

Your ordinary automotive engineering department is an incredibly dull place to spend a career. Very few persons ever reach the point at which they can "design an automobile." Instead, the typical type of assignment may be to reduce the cost of the trunk latch, or improve the torsional rigidity of the subframe, or design new window winders for next year's new doors. Engineering evolution in the bread-and-butter products is not much fun. But engineering revolution, engineering discoveries, in a game where your creations go into hardware immediately and are soon proven or disproven in direct competition—that is interesting! In the first case, the engineer simply puts in eight hours a day, whereas in the second case, enthusiasm and gratis overtime produce results beyond expectation. And, after all, what do you expect from a group called Research and Development ... new colors of paint and rear-seat television? Yet high-performance and competition knowledge was never the department's principal interest. At any time, over all the years, most of the people were always involved in other areas: cost reduction, sedan prototypes, plastic applications, production problems, fuel economy, emissions, crash protection, etc. However, if they had the normal amount of adrenaline and were not prone to heart attack or nervous breakdown, those engineers and technicians usually envied the high-performance group.

At any rate, it is time to forget the hackneyed assertion that the rear-view mirror is racing's only contribution to automotive transportation. In Chevrolet R&D, "racing" contributed to useful technological advancements.

It could be that the Corvair was responsible for Chevrolet's most serious interest in racing. When the first Corvair lawsuit came up in court, Winchell was in charge of Chevrolet R&D. But as a former transmission specialist, he was uneducated in automotive vehicle dynamics. So when the corporation lawyers came to him for advice and support, he had to learn fast, and one particular approach was obvious. Corvairs had rear engines and independent rear suspensions, and they could be rolled over. The fastest road-racing cars in existence had rear engines and independent rear suspensions, and could *not* be rolled over. Why? Why not?

The vehicle dynamics of a four-tired automobile is a very complex study. If it had only three wheels, it would be statically stable, but the redundant wheel makes an analysis far more difficult to comprehend. Even under the urgency of court dates, it took Chevrolet man-years to produce an honest and comprehensive Corvair defense—and more important, to produce it in a non-engineering language that the witnesses, lawyers, and juries could understand. During this stage, the interplay between expert race drivers, and race cars, and inept drivers, and sedans, and engineers, and test cars, fairly well-educated everyone as to the abilities and disabilities of each. And the more the engineers studied racing, the faster the race cars got.

Race drivers such as Moss, Fangio, Shelby, and Hall were easily qualified as "expert witnesses" and their testimony was highly respected. It was also highly appreciated by the engineers as a subjective evaluation of their efforts, and led to further objective studies of vehicle dynamics. The advanced vehicle dynamics knowledge was then fed back to driver/engineers who could comprehend and use it, such as Hall and Donohue. And finally, the success or failure of the theories was fed back again to research and production engineers for practical application. So it is hard to say just who was helping whom the most—everything just sort of fit together.

Along the way, while Chevrolet was expanding its knowledge of (and teaching lawyers) the difference between oversteer and understeer, and the difference between static stability and dynamic stability, racing safety techniques were being applied in testing. Cars that were to be *forced* into a rollover (and practically any car can be, under the worst circumstances, even if it means tire pressures low enough to dig a rim into the pavement) were completely equipped with all the latest safety hardware. Roll bars were built per SCCA specification, fire extinguishers were installed, flammable upholstery removed, and all glass removed and the windshield replaced with unbreakable plastic. And, of course, the test drivers always knew enough to securely strap themselves in with double shoulder harnesses, and they wore the very best crash helmets. Sometimes it seemed as if a privileged few test drivers got *all* the interesting work.

Along that line, we come to another "chicken-or-egg" question concerning the interests of production safety and racing research. GM has been rolling and wrecking cars for decades, but only in unobstructed open fields where there was enough room for observer safety. The problem was that in all the hundreds of miles of test tracks, none left enough room between trees or guardrails to have a safe, planned accident. On the other hand, dirt was hardly a representative surface for accurate, pre-rollover vehicle dynamics, and the flying dust tended to obscure high-speed filming.

There were other equal interests among the high-performance engineers. When you have a vehicle that is capable of over 150 mph, where do you take it to study what it does in a critical situation at that speed? Anyone who has ever seen a race car go out of control and ricochet off the walls on a high-speed track such as Daytona or Indianapolis, knows that there is not a track in the world that is wide enough to allow such a car to skid unimpeded. At least there wasn't until Winchell decided he needed more room in which to test his various rear-engined cars—Corvair and otherwise.

The GM Proving Grounds at Milford, Michigan is a road-racers delight. It has every imaginable type of surface, grade, bank, and corner, from Belgian blocks to 150-mph "hands-off" banking, all winding through a heavily wooded two square miles. Inside one large loop, however, there was a small, dense forest. There was. Within a very short time, a budget appeared, and lo—the trees parted and a sea of asphalt was laid before their very eyes. Sixty-seven acres of unobstructed asphalt, one-third of a mile square, with high-speed access roads coming in at each corner. It soon became known as "Black Lake," since during rainstorms it does not drain very rapidly, in spite of a 1/2-degree slope, and ducks tend to make poor landings in its 1/4-inch depths.

It is not hard to imagine the uses such a surface can be put to. There were sedans skidding sideways (intentionally) at 100 mph. There were Toronados running huge, continual figure-eights at wide open throttle, with blue smoke billowing from the front wheel-wells, and the wipers on full to keep the rubber dust off the windshield. An inter-city bus might be thrown into a "J"-turn at top speed to see if it would fall over. And there were "slalom" courses—

high-speed handling courses—painted down and marked with pylons on which to evaluate ordinary transient response. Even when it rained, there were still cars running at top speed, investigating tire aquaplaning characteristics. All without the fear of a sudden stop against an immovable object, as the trees had even been cleared away for a hundred feet in all directions from the asphalt.

With all this activity going on, how did GM seem to be so far off-guard when the federal government stepped in with safety standards? To understand the problem, means understanding the difference between accident avoidance and accident protection. The government started demanding protection, ignoring the fact that for the entire history of the automobile, the industry has been concentrating on accident avoidance—which is certainly logical. The manufacturers were after the *cause* not the effect. Accident avoidance means concentrating on control and handling, an area that is beneficial throughout the life of the car, not just in one tragic instant. It means greater dollar value to the customer, and it may be more important than protection devices when it comes to saving your skin. Certainly, GM has made some mistakes, but the almighty U.S. Government makes some mistakes too, which are just as costly in terms of human lives. But whatever GM's errors were, they cannot compare with the advances in automotive accident avoidance through better handling over the past 70 years. And the race car has always been the ideal model of accident avoidance. Race cars have better brakes, better visibility, better acceleration, greater traction, and are more controllable. Where else would you go to learn how to make production cars more driveable?

The conditions under which a race car is operated mean that the engineers and mechanics have to be gravely concerned with the safety of the driver. If the driver has the slightest doubt about the durability of a component—it gets strengthened. If he is unsure about the operation of a new system—he makes the final decision whether or not to use it. A typical example was the wing actuation system on all Chaparrals. Although there were more efficient means of changing the condition of the wings from low drag to high downforce, Hall specified the fail-safe technique. In this case, if anything went wrong with the linkage, the wing would stay in the downforce position. And there was never any question about giving him what he wanted for safety's sake.

In spite of the concentration on accident avoidance in racing, however, people make mistakes and accidents do happen. But for any given automotive accident, there is no safer place to have one than on a race track. The conditions are carefully controlled and there are expectant, trained rescue personnel immediately available. What is of equal importance to the engineers, though, is the fact that each accident is usually carefully observed by many qualified persons—if not recorded on film or videotape. The vehicle failure or driver error can then be resolved with some confidence, and engineers and racing sanctioning bodies make it a crusade to ensure that the serious accident never occurs twice for the same reason. A great number of race-car specifications are established this way—roll cages, window nets, five-point belts, helmet standards, etc.

Racing, or high-performance vehicle engineering, is not a killer's game. It really is a proving ground for safety innovation. Practical and efficient safety innovation—primarily in accident avoidance, but also in accident protection. When Hap Sharp went off the road in the race at Nassau in 1966 and broadsided a tree, the car was destroyed. The aluminum structure and gasoline-filled bladder absorbed the blow, and yet he was unharmed. The information gained from that accident and the one in which Hall went end over end at Las Vegas, at least produced lessons in driver protection during violent impacts. Both of those chassis were built in the same department where General Motors' first impact-absorbing bumper/frame/engine layouts were built and tested.

During the studies of vehicle maneuverability, a course was designed to evaluate the response of driver/car combinations. It consisted of three straight lanes with red and green lights over each, or an expendable obstruction which shot out from either side, blocking any combination of lanes. As a car was driven down the center lane, a last-minute decision situation was presented—whether to swerve right or left or brake. With its electronic controls and recording systems, it not only proved which vehicle designs were best at evasion, but which drivers could not cope with emergency situations. It became a standard accident-avoidance test, and it was created by the high-performance group.

When General Motors' separate Accident Safety Group was formed in 1968, it relied heavily on the talent and experience of Chevrolet Research and Development. That was where the background in vehicle dynamics, accident avoidance, and structural collapse came from. Everyone else had been concentrating on comfort, and durability, and styling, and option gimmicks—the stuff that *sold* cars.

The value of race-car technology in safety research, however, is merely one of the more ironical cases of engineering spin-offs. There are many more examples in almost every area of design. Consider the computer models that were created to simulate a vehicle so that future performance could be accurately predicted. They were developed in Chevrolet R&D primarily to safely study vehicle dynamics at the limit of stability, as in accidents or racing, and yet they were verified using both race cars and production sedans. As such, the computer simulations became frequently demanded by many other diverse engineering groups within Chevrolet. Fuel economy of comparative engine and vehicle combinations was predicted by computer, and the results used to select areas of concentration. Use of the computer in this instance eliminated all the uncontrollable variables such as driver, weather, and track conditions, and allowed the engineers to recognize the smallest gains. Large numbers of radical suspension designs were evaluated by computer simulation of vehicle dynamics before they were built, or to explain why a particular design under test was not performing correctly. The first use of all this vehicle dynamics theory in production was in the suspension design of the 1967 Camaro, and every new Chevrolet passenger car since has been "proofed" by computer. Eventually, even crash dynamics were simulated—the actions of a car leading up to the impact or rollover, and the following structural performance and passenger movement. It is hard to imagine any department other than the "race group" asking for, or initiating, or being able to justify, the hundreds of thousands of dollars in development and verification of such a valuable analytic tool, regardless of how widely it came to be used.

A similar case could be made for the instrumentation van, with its capability of telemetering ten channels of engineering information from a distant test car. To the race-car evaluation group it was invaluable—it *had to* be created. But it was not until it was demonstrated to them that any of the production groups recognized its potential. However, at the time, the system had capabilities greater than were needed to solve production problems.

Then, because it existed, it became needed. The fact that the transducers and transmitter were light and shock-proof, and that there was no umbilical cable needed from test car to truck, meant it could be used to record data from high-speed unmanned rollovers. And the ease with which it could be set up and calibrated made it far more popular than the previous systems. If a suspension system that looked good on paper failed to perform properly in practice, the fastest way to find out why was the instrumentation van—if it was not being used by someone else. Wheel hop on acceleration? In one day you can find out what frequency, what amplitude, what direction, and what location—leading to solutions that are almost guaranteed to work.

Although no components from a racing-development-car chassis were ever applied directly to a production vehicle, the engineering certainly was. Generally speaking, the suspensions on the late-model Corvette and Camaro were products resulting from the knowledge obtained by studying race cars. And sometimes the optional heavy-duty equipment available for the Corvette and Camaro is the same as is used on professional race cars. Equipment that is available to improve the response of your everyday sedan only because it was developed and put into limited production to satisfy the needs of professional racers and sanctioning bodies. Those persons who need the parts, whether for repeatedly braking a police car from 120 mph or towing a house trailer over the Sierras, find the parts. All they have to have is the need, the knowledge of what is required, and money. The only people who find out about the optional disc-brake rear axle for the Camaro, or the list of optional spring rates for the Corvette, are the people who write to the Engineering Center and ask for them. It doesn't matter whether they are Highway Patrol or drag racers, they get what they need.

But there are specific examples of how racing research has improved production handling. One is the use of compliance in cornering stability. Compliance means the deflection of components under stress, such as the bending of suspension links due to lateral forces. In racing, it is of primary importance to eliminate this deflection, so that the movement of the suspension can be rigidly controlled. That is why all rubber bushings are eliminated in race cars, and at that, the "rigid" links still allow up to a degree of unwanted camber change. However, the rubber insulators are very important from a ride and noise standpoint in a production sedan, so they have to be compensated for. That is why Chevrolet has begun converting to steering arms *ahead* of the front axles. With the old standard layout, all that deflection meant added steering angle under the stress of cornering. Or in other words, it contributed to oversteer, an unstable condition. Now, of course, the unavoidable deflection works the other way, adding to understeer at the limit—a stabilizing condition. It *is* possible that the theory and principle could have been established without the press of competition, but when?

That is merely one of the more easily described contributions to passenger car control and stability. The many more esoteric engineering breakthroughs are hardly understood by the production group that has to apply them. It is not just a matter of race cars demonstrating the value of a low center of gravity. The race-car program demanded an intensive understanding of where, when, how, and why all the various suspension systems worked as they did, even though it took computers to grasp the entire system.

Ten years ago, probably 99 percent of all drivers were content with the average American car's handling. Today 99 percent are probably still content with what they have, but now they would not tolerate what they were used to then. What about tomorrow? The suspension that is good enough on production cars today is not good enough for race cars—*nothing* is ever "good enough" for race cars. So the racers will continue the development, and thereby continue to produce the technology for tomorrow's product.

The same can be said for brakes, from both a durability and control standpoint. Some manufacturers apparently still do not understand the principles of proper front-to-rear brake balance. If they tried to race their cars, they would have to learn in a hurry, and the results might soon be seen in their production models. Perhaps the average driver either brakes at low rates, or locks them all up at once, but the skillful, educated driver should be given a well-tuned package with which he can modulate the brakes for a quicker, controlled stop. The ultimate in brake control, the new anti-lock systems, may owe their development to production requirements, but Chevrolet's race engineers were studying the application many years previously.

Brake durability is another matter. There are few cars on the road today that can maintain adequate braking under severe use. That is to say, their capacity for producing horsepower is greater than their capacity for dissipating it through the brakes. The car may be able to accelerate from zero to a hundred all day long, but it will not take ten hard stops from a hundred in rapid succession. Perhaps the only exception on American cars is the optional heavy-duty package that is available on the Corvette and adaptable to the Camaro. This package has undergone many stages of improvement since four-wheel discs were made available in 1967, but it was only because of the extreme requirements of competition. Better pad materials were developed, the components were stiffened, and insulators were designed to eliminate fluid boiling. And now those optional production brakes can tolerate maximum deceleration stops on a 3200-pound race car for as long as the friction material lasts—or about three hours under constant severe usage, the equivalent of a hundred thousand highway miles.

Are they worth the cost and time of development? No—not unless they are on a car that is being pushed at high speed down a long mountain grade by an overweight trailer. Then, the fact that they were developed primarily for competition is quite irrelevant.

The role of racing in the development of better production tires is obvious, although Chevrolet can hardly claim credit in this area. However, high-performance interests were responsible for the broad adoption of the standard wide rim and tire. When it comes to the selection of tires for production installation, the cost group had been opposed only by the tire manufacturers' load recommendations. But the performance engineers' demands finally started carrying some weight. Very early in the study of the effect of wide wheels and tires, it became obvious that there was no known practical limit to width—except for the ability of the tire companies to manufacture tires. But even yet, it is difficult to get the production designers to allow enough fender clearance, and to get the engineers to design suspensions to clear the monster tires that are available. Finally, however, they are coming around to the realization that the fat tires do not just mean a racy image—they allow surer cornering under all conditions and a much shorter stopping distance in panic braking. Providing the original vehicle design allowed for them, that is. Considering that aspect, and trends in automotive safety legislation, it is a safe bet that eventually we will see production sedans engineered to take the sizes of tires that are used on Can-Am race cars of today. And the tire companies will be producing them in tread designs and durability suitable for everyday use.

Serious research into race-car aerodynamics began in late 1963, and it was little more than a year before the knowledge was applied successfully to a production sedan. Solving the nose-lift problem on Hall's first mid-engine Chaparral was largely an intuitive cut-and-try operation. But putting an air dam, or spoiler, below the nose was so effective, that as an answer, it almost went looking for other problems to solve. The first one was the Corvair. Wind wander on the highway led to wind-tunnel tests of its stability, during which it was learned that *lift* was the problem. At speed, crosswinds not only pushed the nose sideways, they created lift on the front end, which actually lifted the car sideways. The transfer of experience from the Chaparral was obvious. A small two-inch plastic spoiler was adapted to the underside of the nose. It was not too obvious, but it helped considerably.

The next production interest in aerodynamics was a 1966 Chevelle. Smokey Yunick was preparing his race car for Daytona, and Chevrolet was asked for anything that might help aerodynamics (which the company could offer as an option). The plastic spoiler from the Corvair was tried, but extremes were also examined. Although none of those devices ever reached production, that background helped considerably when the new Camaro was announced and the optional Z/28 package had to be prepared. This time, the acceptance of the production group was considered, and a more conservative but less efficient set of spoilers was adopted. Whether the Camaro spoilers are considered as a valuable production benefit from racing research depends on how fast the car is driven on the highway, but the fact remains that they *did* improve handling, and they would not have been built if not for competition needs.

The production body design group still had not gotten the word, however, and the new Corvette body that came out the next year had critical nose lift at high speed. It was so bad that going over a rise at 140 mph, the front wheels were almost floated. Again, R&D instrumentation and the nose spoiler to the rescue. Another problem with that body was that it could not pass enough air to cool the engine. So many accessories had been crammed under the hood that the air had no place to go, once past the radiator. The first approach to a solution might be to experimentally start cutting holes in the body. However, to study airflow on race-car bodies, R&D had developed quick and accurate methods of measuring the pressure at many points on the inside and outside skin surfaces. Finding the proper locations for vents, therefore, was simple. Getting the stylists to open them up was impossible.

One interesting exchange of information, which has only benefited an experimental prototype so far, was the development of the rear-mounted radiator. When the Chaparral 2H was being designed, there were doubts whether the radiator duct above the engine would collect enough air. It was important to answer the question early in the design phase, although it was mid-winter in Michigan and no sports-race cars were operational, anyhow. But there was one coupe available for mockup and testing which very roughly approximated the height and shape of the proposed 2H—a Ford GT 40, which had been bought, evaluated, and set aside. After it was appropriated, and a non-functional radiator core mounted above the transaxle, I spent weeks running up and down the test straightaway in freezing weather, gathering data. Ducts of every size and shape were evaluated for air flow and distribution, to ensure not only cooling capability, but a low air-drag figure. Shortly after that, the first mid-engine Corvette prototype went into design. Because of problems with passenger cooling on the previous *rear*-engine (bustle-type) prototype, which had a conventional front radiator, the race-car data was used to justify the radiator installation on the car, which was later known as Astro II. Radiators may forever remain in the nose of even rear-engine sports cars, but it will be because of needed "crush-space" for the safety engineers and not because a better-engineered package has not been proven for the rear.

In the area of engines, the contributions from racing research to production were largely discussed in the chapter on engine development (Chapter 8). To generalize and summarize, however, is to look at the end result of production Chevrolet engines. The basic smallblock Chevrolet may be the most dependable V-8 engine in the world—if not the most numerous. There may not have been *any* production pieces in the 327 Chaparral engines, but that development certainly created the background for production design. And independent amateur racers all over the U.S. will testify that that development and the available components has made it one of the easiest and cheapest engines to modify for competition.

The bigblock engine was little different. Because of the accumulated knowledge from the smallblock in competition, the production cast iron 427 engine was a relatively trouble-free design from the start. Of course, the aluminum-block version did not reach the public for some time, but when it *did* become a production engine, it definitely had all the right pieces. Even in Can-Am racing, practically every component within the block and heads was the same as was available in a ZL-1 Corvette—although each component had been carefully inspected, measured, and remachined to closer tolerances.

The failures that are discovered in the stress of competition tend to produce an engine that is infinitely more reliable for everyday use—as long as it is basically the same engine. Of course, racing is not "necessary," since any sort of schedule can be simulated on a dynamometer for testing. But there are two intangible factors to consider. First, are the automatic benefits of the initiative as engineers and technicians strain to surpass the last horsepower reading or the last endurance record. Second, is the constant challenge from the racers. When a typical race lap is duplicated on a dynamometer, the engineers are always astounded at the sort of stress expected of their product. This is why Chevrolet engineering has always concentrated on the development of engines suitable for road racing, instead of drags, superspeedways, Indy, or formula racing. That is the challenge that is most applicable to public use. When Granatelli shocked Indianapolis with his Turbine, there were considerations among Chevrolet engineers to develop a turbine for road racing. But the idea was stillborn for the lack of any possible production relationship. The alleged unwritten rule of Chevrolet, "race what you sell, and sell what you race," would be more accurate and acceptable if it read "develop what you sell, and sell what you develop—to racers."

Automatic transmission research and development could not work exactly that way because of the specialized purpose of the package, and the individual tailoring required to match each engine, vehicle, and track. The Chaparral automatic was totally unsuitable for anything but a lightweight racing car, and yet, because it was a combination of automatic and manual, it provided a research tool for both. Lessons from experiments with the automatic, as well as the engine and chassis, benefited engineers from such diverse GM divisions as New Departure, Saginaw, and Engineering Staff. The constant drive to get the maximum durability for the absolute minimum weight, provided them with a need for—and a source of—education without equal in the field of metal fatigue. It is merely a matter of scale (the "safety factor") between a race car and a production car in this area, as racing demands a far more precise knowledge. That, plus the experience in ultimate gear strengths and design, shift mechanism durability, extreme pressure lubricants, and the effect of temperature on seals, lubricants, and metals, is already improving the efficiency of all GM transmissions, and will for years to come. The Engineering Staff specialist in hydraulic converters, Don Harshman, probably designed, built, and tested more different specialized torque converters than anyone else, ever. The accumulation of first-hand engineering data in such areas as blade design, efficiency, precision control, and construction techniques, is part of the reason that the GM Turbo-Hydramatic is one of the smoothest, strongest automatics in the world.

This chapter is not as long as it ought to be, because the story of "Engineering Spin-Offs" is not complete yet, nor will it be for many years. Competition cars and their innovations are always years ahead of public acceptance or production realities. Therefore, the total results of the racing research involvement lie in the future. *Research is partly a quest for answers before the problems occur,* and racing pushes problems before the engineers far faster than anyone would voluntarily find them. In previous chapters, many innovations and solutions were mentioned which have not, as yet, found production application. But by looking in the past, it can be seen that the expensive, specialized racing technology of today becomes the production technology of tomorrow. Who knows, someday we may even see vacuum-traction vehicles in everyday use, first on emergency vehicles, and then perhaps as an emergency assist system on your everyday sedan. Right now, other departments, other divisions, are requesting assistance or advice from the specialists who were forced to explore advanced technologies due to the pressures of direct, immediate competition. If not hindered by pride or envy of all that "impractical blue-sky thinking" behind the locked doors of Research and Development, many more production engineers could learn a point or two in areas such as suspensions, transmissions, performance analysis, aerodynamics, and materials, especially lightweight alloys and plastics.

The AMA racing ban of 1957 may have been one of the best things that ever happened to Chevrolet. Because at that point, they stopped racing—

they stopped building and maintaining and campaigning race cars. They stopped racing and started thinking about *what* and *why* and *how.* And then they produced the knowledge and the pieces that relatively autonomous, efficient racing teams could test and/or race with.

Does automotive racing improve production cars? No one at Chevrolet is in a position to authoritatively answer that question. But Chevrolet *has* shown that racing *research* most certainly does.

11

The Final End

A ssuming that Chevrolet's activities were a success—if not attaining many championships for the company, at least at producing knowledge—then the reason behind that success is that there was always the right number of the right people and there was always enough money to do the job right. Perhaps the former was more important, because the people always seemed to be able to arrange the money. But because there was not a specific goal, such as "Win LeMans" or "Win the Manufacturers Championship," the duration of the program was always in doubt. The manufacturers who raced their products always had a specific race or series of races to challenge them, whereas at Chevrolet, the goal was general research. Individually, of course, every engineer, executive, and technician was fired up to do his damnedest to see that every Chevrolet product won every race it was entered in, but that was not the "company line." Whether the work was being done under the engine group, Duntov's group, or finally R&D, the budget could be cut off or reallocated at any time the review came up, whether in the middle of a season or the middle of a race.

As the economy dictated, there were frequent budget juggles within Chevrolet. And every time, each department fought to justify its own value and diminish everyone else's, especially Research and Development's, and especially their most obvious activity—the "Competition Program." But if other department heads had sat in on the R&D evaluation reviews to learn what was going on below the surface, they might have been a little less critical. Certainly, as in any financial operation, some questionable activities were "hidden" under vague research projects, such as the automatics being under "Transmission Development," or chassis construction under "Materials Research." But there were always a number of obvious expenditures and consultation fees that had to be accounted for.

Whenever a review was scheduled, the preceding week might be spent accumulating the specific discoveries, accomplishments, and developments that had accrued through the last period. And the quantity would be so great that by the time "show-and-tell" day arrived, the presentation for management would have to be tightly condensed to get it all into the allotted schedule. In addition to the monologues by the head of the department and project engineers, there was an endless stream of hardware, such as new vehicle components and test equipment, filmstrips and slides, engineering graphs and statistics, and more engineers waiting in the wings to clarify detail points if necessary. But competition was seldom—if ever—mentioned at those sessions. An executive might jokingly ask, "Then why didn't the Chaparral win at LeMans?," but all that was expected was an *engineering* explanation. Actually, the word "race" probably does not exist in Chevrolet's entire engineering and budget paperwork system. If a particular event was significant enough to mention in any correspondence, it was always referred to as "field test event, date - place," as though it were any other field test at any other outside test site. For example, a report might simply read, "6/16/66 - LeMans - Bonnier - car #3 - 400 miles - trans #12-A jumping out of gear." Further explanation of the specific problem and how it was solved would be covered in an engineering summary of the particular component being evaluated.

Perhaps the presentations were "overkill" from the standpoint of real jus-tification, but no one ever even implied, "Give us money because we will win races with it and that will develop a strong image which will sell more cars." It is quite possible that no one involved in the project even believed that to be true. For fourteen years, the continuation of high-performance projects depended on what was to be learned from them. At the end of every review, the current responsible executive would smile, thank everyone for doing his job well, and walk out of the meeting with perhaps a parting reminder to "Keep your nose clean." Everyone else would then exhale, and the budget would continue for another indeterminate period. As long as research was the desired product—and racing was a byproduct.

In spite of the fact that a budget was so crucial to the programs' existence, death and dissolution was not due to the sudden lack of money. It was much more subtle than that. If anything, it could be attributed to the continual loss of the necessary people. Every time a key man was drawn off for higher purposes, the team would shudder a bit, reorganize, and carry on as well as possible, or try to break in a new man. Of course, the first great loss was of the instigator and prime mover himself, Frank Winchell. In early 1966, GM upper management recognized the results that Winchell was producing in the Corvair lawsuits, and the force with which he attacked every problem—and person—that stepped in his way. Perhaps he wasn't subtle enough to become the next general manager of Chevrolet, but it was obvious that he knew how to get results in hardware. So, he moved over to the management of GM Engineering Staff, the corporation devel-opment branch as distinguished from GM Research, a more esoteric division.

When he left, he took as many of his best men as he could to support him, and many even volunteered. But Jim Musser, the next most influential man in keeping the competition research program alive at Chevrolet, was promoted into his old position, and Ray Gallant took charge of the "racers." There wasn't much doubt among the team that Musser would fight for whatever his old group needed, because competition was in his blood, whether within the company or in his offspring on the track. However, he was such a fighter that he couldn't last. Before the year was out, he also had been promoted out of the department, and a new man, Bill Route, was brought in from Passenger Car Transmissions.

So many men have been responsible for the racing research activities in R&D, that perhaps it is necessary to clear up the sequence and levels at this point. Many at the management level received ample credit within the organization for the work of the team, and yet have not gotten as much credit in this book since they weren't directly involved in specific projects. Winchell and Musser have been well-mentioned because they laid the groundwork. Following them, Ray Gallant was responsible, although he never received the recognition he was due—especially for keeping the activities alive in those difficult years when no one upstairs cared. Then there was Bill Route, and then Charley Simmons, and with each there was a smaller percentage of interest in outside competition activities. (Or perhaps better said—there was a larger percentage of interest in more pressing sociological problems.)

The size of the project was also strongly dependent on the relationship between these managers and the project engineer, and the strength of both individuals in the department. The sequence of project engineers was: Musser, Mrlik, Pocobello, Clark, Gates, and Piggins. The rate of turnover is a good indication of the "dirtiness" and thanklessness of the position. No one stayed very long, and if they couldn't move up fast enough, they moved out. Musser moved up. Jerry Mrlik moved over to engineering staff. Pocobello moved out. John Clark moved up. Gates moved out. And finally, Piggins had the major effort move out on him. Under each of these men, the project had its own distinct characteristics, reflecting the personalities of the department head and project engineer. In later years, the cool, logical managers began to replace their competition fanatic predecessors—and the program had to start working a little tighter.

Musser stayed at Chevrolet for the next few years, though, as chief design engineer on the new Vega, and because of interdepartmental conflicts, he was given the additional reassignment to coordinate all the departments that had any outside high-performance activities. As such, he was able to spend a little of his time promoting those activities among the other executives. But that couldn't last either. Through Winchell, he had made an impression on Bunkie Knudsen. After Bunkie rose from Chevrolet to GM, shifted to Ford, and was deposed, he used his capital to start a recreational vehicle company called Rectrans. Early in 1970, Musser joined him as vice president of the company. From that point, there was no one at any influential management level who really cared about high-performance at Chevrolet. Actually, everyone else had become slightly antagonistic toward the program from a budget allocation standpoint, and besides, they all had problems of their own. The project engineers in R&D were left to fend for themselves.

Even at that, they might have survived at a more covert level within the locked doors of R&D, if it weren't for certain attitudes shifting outside Chevrolet. A few people were becoming disenchanted with the way they had to handle their racing activities.

Everyone wants to be associated with Chevrolet in some way or another. After all, they are the biggest automobile manufacturer in the world, and they can certainly spare a few hundred thousand dollars for sponsorship of a sure-fire racing team. Those who *were* affiliated, however, knew how little was actually available, and for what reasons. To the businessman in racing—the promoter—there are benefits other than money or parts, though. There is the inestimable *status* of being affiliated with the giant. As long as you don't stand too close—and get eaten. No one knew that better than Roger Penske. From the beginning of his professional racing career, he used his inside relationships to the fullest. It may seem odd that Hall preferred to be considered independent of Chevrolet, while Penske wanted it to be known, but perhaps it has something to do with the way they started. Hall began big—he put millions of dollars of his own money into his operation and he wanted that fact recognized. On the other hand, Penske started on a relatively small budget and drew in sponsor's capital, and to do that he needed contacts. He made the contacts, he cultivated the contacts, he multiplied his capital, and he grew. The trouble was that he grew faster and further than Chevrolet's participation could.

When Penske heard about the vacuum-traction vehicle being experimented with in R&D, he tried every ploy to get the car for his own Can-Am campaign. The Can-Am and Trans-Am activities were still somewhat politically segregated at Chevrolet, however, and so Hall and Penske were implicitly constrained to a race series for each of them. Roger wasn't too happy about that decision, and as it turned out, he probably would have been a better person to develop and capitalize on the value of the "sucker-car." That was 1969, and as Penske wrapped up another sedan championship with his Camaros, he began feeling out Chevrolet, with the Can-Am rebuff in his mind.

His year hadn't started out too well, but by spending enough time and dollars, he had come from behind to catch the Fords. It had not taken the same effort that Ford put into the series, but it still required such luxuries as flying cars across the country to allow time for rebuilding, development, and testing. Then, going into the last two races, with the title still unresolved, Penske had laid out his cards. To develop and campaign the Camaros had cost him well over what he had been paid for engineering services, and he wanted to be reimbursed for the expenses incurred. Musser was caught between Penske and the accounting department. He tried reasoning that Penske was not operating at a deficit—that his sponsorships were guaranteeing him a profit—but Penske argued back that that was his business and Chevrolet owed him for engineering services performed. To finish out the series, Musser arranged payment for a fraction of what Penske requested—and the matter was settled. But then Musser went on vacation—and the accounting department took it upon themselves to reduce the payment even more. Unable to reach Musser, and certain that he had been deceived, Penske began looking around to see what he could get elsewhere. When Musser came back and found out what had happened, he was highly disappointed, but he had to admit one fact—if Penske had been shopping, he was gone, because there was no way Chevrolet could match anyone else's offer. Roger Penske's racing enterprises were growing and Chevrolet R&D racing research was merely holding its own.

The other camp, in Midland, Texas, held out a little longer.

After the poor showing of the Chaparral 2H in 1969, some of Hall's bigger sponsors pulled out—to the tune of a few hundred thousand dollars. At the same time, Chevrolet management started losing interest in development of the automatic/manual transmission and the aluminum-block engines. Accident protection and emissions were taking more and more of their resources.

The last complete engine that was shipped from Chevrolet to Midland was for the 2H, just prior to its demise at Texas International Speedway. From then on, every Chaparral engine, including the 302 Trans-Am engines, was built in Midland by Gary Knutsen. The automatic transmissions were of no value to Chevrolet anymore, so instead of scrapping them, Musser agreed to send all the pieces to Chaparral. But that was no great help, because there were practically no shifter sleeves left—the part with the highest wear, and the most difficult to machine. The turbine shafts were also going fast, as even the "conservative" 465-cubic-inch engine was twisting them.

Gates had moved in with the 2J sucker car in September, however, and it looked like a good possibility for the '70 season. In addition, there were discussions concerning an engineering program on a new plastic sports car based on the Vega, and Hall had brought in Cam Argetsinger from Watkins Glen (later to become Director of Professional Racing for the SCCA) to operate the company. Then, when Penske pulled out of the Trans-Am development program, it looked like Chaparral had the whole show for 1970.

There was just one little drawback. There still wasn't any outside support money. It cost over a third of a million dollars to run a two-car program through an entire SCCA professional series, and now Chaparral had two series. In addition, the economy was sinking, and even a multimillionaire like Hall could feel the pinch. But Chaparral went ahead, expecting to win, and confident that sponsorship was imminent. The Trans-Am program started out a little rough, however. Chaparral had never built racing sedans before, and the team had far more enthusiasm than practical experience in that field. Also, Chevrolet had just come out with the all-new chassis, which meant an all-new development program was necessary. Don Cox had already started developing the '70 car at Chevrolet, because as a race car, it was somewhat less than the previous model. Both aerodynamic drag and lift were worse, the weight was up, the center of gravity was higher, and the engine was further forward. In short, it needed time to become competitive.

Hall's physical condition was also a handicap. Since his disastrous accident at Las Vegas a year and a half before, he had recovered far faster than expected, but his strength was still down. He had been driving test laps at Midland for some time in the development of the new cars, but that is far less than the strain of a two-hour sprint race. To help, power steering had been adapted to the sedans, and that was just one more headache.

When it became obvious that the Camaros were in trouble, all of Chaparral's resources were channeled in that direction. After all, Chevrolet was still helping to some small degree, and production cars were their bread and butter. That may not have been the primary reason for the one-sided effort, though. Jim was anxious to make his comeback as soon as possible, and if he couldn't manage the sedan, the sucker car, with its tremendous traction, required even more strength to control it. Besides that, the 2J was sort of an unwanted child when it arrived at Chaparral. Everyone there was a little sore about the failure of the 2H, and no one particularity wanted the 2J to show them up. After almost a year's research in the principle at Chevrolet, R&D had all the information they cared about, and so Gates was fairly well on his own. Only Tom Dutton was open-minded enough about the thing to devote his eighty-hour weeks to it, which meant that one engineer and one experienced driver/mechanic had to handle the entire development program.

And that was when General Electric joined the team. The Trans-Am was more or less lost by then, and the SCCA and track promoters were screaming for the 2J to return, so Hall's men were put to the project just weeks before Road Atlanta.

But it was too late. The principle was sound, and everything worked well enough—well enough to set lap records at Road Atlanta, Laguna, and Riverside, but the car was just too *different*. There were not enough man-hours left to make each new component and system reliable enough to last an entire race. The fan motor overheated and vapor-locked, it broke a crankshaft, the drive belt was chewed up by track debris—and at Laguna Seca, the main engine was destroyed because old, fatigued connecting rods had been accidentally installed in haste.

Chaparral's 1970 race season was enough to make any man hang up his helmet. Jim decided that it was too long a road back to being a competitive driver, and halfway through the series he relinquished his seat in the Camaro so that he could devote more time to the Can-Am. When that also produced nothing but disappointment and frustration for the team, dissention split them into small, hostile groups. So when the FIA brought up the question of whether fans could be used to generate downforce in future races, Hall offered no resistance, but let them set the law. There were other vacuum downforce systems which Gates could have still used if the regulations were worded slightly differently, but Hall was through arguing. If he couldn't drive, and if the sanctioning bodies wouldn't let him innovate, he was through.

There had always been a large turnover in personnel at Chaparral, so there weren't a lot of tearful goodbyes. Hall retained two of his most loyal mechanics, Troy Rogers and Franz Weis, to maintain the shops and track, and to restore and store the remaining running race cars. They hadn't gotten racing out of their blood, however, and spent their spare hours preparing the old Indianapolis chassis (GS-III) for Formula A racing for Franz—which he subsequently destroyed in an accident at Mid-Ohio. Gates, Argetsinger, and Rutherford had bonded together under a common cause, and they decided to stick together in a new racing venture which Hall blessed by buying a small percentage of stock in it. Marshall Robbins, a wealthy amateur racer who was close to Chevrolet Engineering in Detroit, managed to get one of Hall's Camaros, and campaigned it with some distinction and factory advice throughout the '71 season. But even the meager interest and support that had remained at Chevrolet slowly disintegrated through the year.

The aggressive people were gone. The motivators, the promoters, the racing fanatics—they had all found their way up or out. The right people at the right levels could still keep racing research going under the justification of handling, instrumentation, materials, accident avoidance, engine or transmission development, but it doesn't appear that those people are ever going to reach those levels again.

There was another significant occurrence in the summer of 1970 that insured it. In practicing for a Trans-Am race, Jerry Titus was killed while driving a Pontiac Firebird. Unlike Hall's accidents, no one was certain of the exact cause. In other words, it could have been a vehicle failure, and it could have been connected with General Motors. It *wasn't*, but it was a little too close for comfort. At the same time, the economy was suffering and there were layoffs and budget cutbacks. Anyhow, for one reason or another, corporate auditors swept through the accounting divisions of Chevrolet and Pontiac, asking some very pointed questions.

Soon after that, a very important corporate officer got in touch with deLorean, and said, in effect, "We don't know exactly what you are doing over there. But *stop* it!" And, according to the rumor, deLorean's response was a request to reallocate any questionable funds into the *advertising* budget. If true, this makes a lot of sense, considering the current upper management of General Motors. In the last few years, financial people (the "bean-counters") have become more powerful than those with engineering backgrounds. A dollar justification carries far more weight than an engineering justification anymore.

Then, within a month after Titus's accident, a memorandum was sent to certain department heads throughout the automotive divisions. It was from T.A. Murphy, the vice president of Finance, and it was therefore very influential. It was obviously not related to any particular incident, but the message was clear. Any overt or covert deviations from the AMA racing ban decision would be dealt with ... strongly. And it went on to repeat the AMA statement verbatim. Still with no loopholes, and now with some teeth in it.

Not that it made much difference at that point anyhow. It was a little stronger than the previous clampdowns, such as on the "porcupine engines" and Grand Sport Corvettes of 1963, but this time most of the "funny stuff" had already ceased. Penske was "out," Hall was "out," the GS cars were gone, Corvette had grown into a "touring" car, and R&D was busy on other matters. Only the customer performance-advisory group remained, and its name was hastily changed from Product Performance to Product Promotion. Their activities were restructured, and now they handle such projects as Clean-Air Runs, Economy Runs, and the flashy decal kits for Chevrolet Blazers.

What about the knowledge, however? And what about all the "little people" who innovated, researched, and found the answers? So much information was gathered, and so many advanced racing technologies were explored, that they could fuel any other racing team for years. To any race-car engineer or developer around the world who has any comprehension of the data, the theories, the analyses that are stored there, it must be quite a dream to imagine having unlimited access to it. Even Chapman, or Ferrari, would certainly find some great benefit from the knowledge. But the ironic thing is that there are few engineers left at Chevrolet who even know it exists, much less where it is. Anything that was ever researched or developed in Chevrolet R&D was recorded on paper, and it is still there, although scattered almost randomly in cabinets, files, and personal libraries—under component categories. The problem was that there was never a "race technology" category, and so there was never a central clearing file or organized method of reporting. Over the years, so many people passed through the program with their own systems of control or noninterference, that few people really have a comprehensive picture of what was really, totally accomplished. Nor does anyone care anymore, which is why no one has put it all together into "How To Build the World-Beater Race Car." Not yet, anyhow.

Another point of irony was the naivete of everyone involved at the time. Because of isolation from the world of racing at Chevrolet R&D, everyone naturally assumed that all the other racing teams in the world—such as Ford, or McLaren, or Lotus—already knew, at least intuitively, the things we were trying to research. It was only after the dissolution, when everyone spread out into other areas such as USAC and Formula 1, that it became obvious how far ahead in race-car engineering Chevrolet actually was, although at the expense of many lost races due to the lack of at-the-track observation and fine development in many areas.

So much for the data—what about the people? Chevrolet R&D was only a name, it wasn't an organism that created ideas and knowledge. When the guard came through and checked all the locks at midnight, R&D was not producing anything—unless some of the more dedicated people were still there, finishing up a test or running data on the computer. When the team disintegrated, then, R&D didn't care what happened to the people. Only the individuals cared, and they took care of themselves fairly well.

First the mavericks took off. The decline was visible, and the more observant ones left early. Of course there weren't many places to go outside the company. There weren't many race teams that knew of the capabilities and accomplishments of anyone from the "inside," and there were fewer yet who could recognize or accept that level of engineering. Also, once an engineer had become accustomed to Chevrolet's facilities and talented associates, anywhere else was "down." But the mavericks couldn't surrender their racing enthusiasm, and most of them chafed under the corporate system anyhow.

The first of the hard-core racing engineers to go was Mike Pocobello, though the end was not yet in sight and his reasons were more personal. Hall needed to replace his last in-house engineer, Paul Lamar, and Pocobello was the most qualified candidate. He was the current project engineer in charge of all Chaparral research projects, he didn't require any specific racing training or familiarization, and he didn't create a new security problem. Mike was more than willing—and not merely for favorable financial reasons. Political and management stresses of the program were causing him some serious internal problems, and it appeared that in Midland he could negotiate for fewer sixteen-hour days, not going to races, and no responsibility for the normal, immediate, week-to-week competition panics. He would simply design and build a completely new race car, and then handle some new production ideas to be marketed by Chaparral. When the 2H was finished, however, he found himself back in the same old pressure grind, and he left for General Motors' Engineering Staff. There he was able to drop race cars and pick up buses and Wankels—until Gates tapped him for Antares Engineering. To some people, the strain of racing is as tragic an addiction as there is.

When Penske pulled out for American Motors, Donohue put the finger on one of the brightest "hardware" engineers in the group, Don Cox. Penske wasn't particularly interested in any theory—the "what" or "why"—he just demanded results, and Cox had given him just that in the late season development of the '69 Camaros. There were a lot of engineers with stronger specific knowledge, but Cox had a broad background in many areas—and he had the necessary Penske "clean-cut college kid" image. Knowing where he was going, and what he would be doing, Cox naturally made sure that anything he might be able to use was in his head, and that he could get people to build the necessary instrumentation that he was giving up. After all, it was obvious from the inside that they wouldn't be competing with Chevrolet for very long. Now, if Cox is still not visible behind Penske and Donohue, at least his accomplishments in development are obvious—the Javelin in Trans-Am, the McLaren in USAC, and the Porsche in Can-Am. Penske the engineer, Donohue the engineer, and Cantwell the engineer, will all be glad to admit who really handles the engineering.

Jim Hall also became aware of who and what he needed as Chevrolet began tightening up. Not only was Don Gates the current project engineer responsible for all competition activities at Chevrolet (and the former boss of Don Cox), he was also talented at management, and the most knowledgeable engineer on the suction-traction project. So the 2J and Gates went together. Growing conflicts at all levels over all issues prevented Chaparral from any great success even with all the new talent, but racing wins weren't the primary reason Gates had taken the position. He had greater plans, and he needed experience in a small business. Although the only man with any real power was the man with the money, enough experience—and enough contacts—were obtained so that after Chaparral folded, it was possible to open another racing-oriented engineering firm. Antares Engineering started with a contract for an electric truck, but before long, the racing world caught wind of who and what was available, and the next project was to build five Indianapolis cars. With Gates, Argetsinger, and Rutherford from Chaparral, Hall's investment, and more talent from Chevrolet, including Mike Pocobello as chief engineer, it could someday become the equivalent of Chevrolet R&D's performance group.

As for myself, I got what I wanted, also. I was permitted to trade three and one-half years of imagineering for an incomparable education in race-car engineering and development. Even at the time, it was obvious that Chevrolet R&D must have been the world's greatest graduate school in that field. When I caught up with all the available information and the sources began getting pinched, there was no great incentive to stay, and the climate of California overruled the fact that there were no race engineering operations there that could accept our degree of accumulated knowledge. Which is why I had to turn to *writing* about race cars.

When Winchell and Musser set out from Chevrolet, they took what talent they could, both engineers and technicians, although fortunately not the irreplaceable specialists. Some of the well-trained specialists became so valuable to the racing game that when Chevy stopped, they continued profitably on their own. Most notable were the engine builders such as George Foltz, Bill King, and Jim Kinsler, whose names are becoming well-known among the independents in Can-Am.

Then there were those who opted for the security of a regular, known paycheck and a guaranteed future at Chevrolet. Not that they can be criticized for that—they may turn out to have made the wisest decision, as automobile racing declines in profitability. Certainly, everyone made his own decision as to what was best for himself. Those who stayed are using their developed talents and accumulated knowledge to produce a better product—in whatever way the public, and management, and the government decide is better.

But where are they now—all the rest of those Chevrolet engineers who wasted their time on competition research? What good did it do them? Frank Boehm, the GS-II suspension and wheel designer is now in charge of the light truck design group. Joe Kurleto has all materials research in R&D. Jerry Mrlik now has complete vehicle design at GM Engineering Staff. Tom Goad went to Forward Planning at Pontiac. John Clark, the last project engineer over GS development now handles cost and function analysis in Value Engineering. Ray Gallant split a group off R&D to cover all Special Vehicles. Leonard Kutkus and Fred Porter are using their engine experience on the Wankel and Vega engine development. And Jerry Thompson is on his own lateral training program, from engines to suspension development on the Vega.

It's not that competition research was the accumulation of the most talented engineers, by any means. Instead, it was a gathering of good people with extraordinary drive and enthusiasm. Research and Development was a tantalizing department to anyone who had any idea what was going on there, but membership was by invitation only. For example, while Don Cox was in drafting, he was building race cars at home, and he kept bugging R&D with questions about tires and suspensions. So finally they took him in—so he could find the answers himself. As for my own case, when I heard how rare it was for me to be hired directly into R&D, I asked how it happened. The reason turned out to be very simple: I didn't know all the answers. But in my interview, I had shown that I did at least know the *questions*—and how to *find* answers. And that is what R&D is all about.

There was another quality demanded of R&D engineers involved with competition research, though, and that was … invisibility. There is a popular saying that no great car was ever built by a committee, and perhaps it is true that no "great" car was ever built by Chaparral or the Chevrolet racing enthusiasts. But every one of them was built by a team of relatively anonymous people who were expected to maintain that invisibility. Still, "recognition" is one of the basic needs of man, and although it was exchanged within the tightly-knit group, it was sometimes difficult to accept the idea of one or two individuals gleaning the world's acclaim for a team's effort. One of the original reasons for this book was simply to balance that inequity—to prevent all those invisible people from passing from oblivion to oblivion without at least one high point of recognition for their efforts. Even at that, to include *all* those who contributed their diverse talents would make this book read like a telephone book, which is why a separate listing of many of those people was included. But if someone whose name is not listed claims he was involved, also, believe him, because at one time or another, hundreds were at least indirectly involved, and no one knows all of them.

Of course, there are some advantages to being "invisible." Such as the ability to appear in odd places and quietly learn confidential information. For example, it was possible for Chevrolet R&D engineers to attend races anywhere, and learn by either overhearing a team's conversation, or by discreetly measuring and photographing the cars—without anyone getting excited. Under such circumstances, a weekend at a NASCAR, Formula One, Can-Am, Trans-Am, or USAC race was as valuable as months of in-house research. However, it was necessary to be cautious.

One R&D engineer lived near Roy Lunn, the director of Ford's LeMans effort, and he always watched for whatever odd creation Lunn would drive home. One evening, he was driving past just as Lunn was pulling up in the new GT 40 coupe, and so he stopped to "chat." This was before the public had seen any data on the car, and so this "anonymous passerby" began asking casual questions. One of the questions was, "It sure looks tiny. Do you know how much it weighs?" To which Lunn proudly replied, "Less than 2300 pounds!" That should have been enough information, but the engineer automatically responded with, "You mean with half-load and driver?" Lunn stared at him for a moment, and at his Chevrolet, and then pulled the GT 40 into his garage and closed the door without another word. Only a *race*-car engineer commonly uses the term "half-load and driver."

There is another occupational hazard of doing research on race cars, and that is the accumulated stress of immediate and direct responsibility. At Chevrolet there was the additional complication of corporate bureaucracy and the need for absolute secrecy, which could be blamed for the frequent turnover in authority. One of the most immense problems in race cars is logistics—getting the right people and the right pieces in the right place at the right time. Airfreighted engines and components would get lost with such regularity that sabotage could have been suspected. And being "invisible" doesn't help a bit when you try to find them.

But the worst stress, especially under Frank Winchell, was waiting for the Monday morning "weekend report." Winning or losing was up to the outside race team, but the failure of an R&D component ... that was *inexcusable!* If things went badly enough, it would even prompt a Sunday night phone call and harangue. Kutkus and Kurleto, the senior engine and transaxle engineers, perhaps survived longest because of their heavy European accents. As Kurleto puts it, "H'ile nefer forget tose Montay morninks. But our dialect was very strong ten, und Frank wut tink we chust misunderstood each utter."

There was no consolation for the major disasters, however. When Hall crashed at Mosport in 1964, no one at Chevrolet was too involved at the time. But by 1968, when he was critically hurt at Las Vegas, it was different—it was a major shock to everyone. Not only because he had become a good acquaintance, but because it brought the realization of just how much responsibility was carried by each individual. Every man quietly reviewed his own possible contribution—although no one was to blame. Race-car engineering and construction is not a job for the insecure.

The engineers who have stuck with racing activities—Gates, Cox, Pocobello—have to admit that the projects they are working on now are based almost totally on what was learned at Chevrolet. Even Winchell and Musser, even the other engineers who stayed, might all agree that their intensive experience under the stress of competition taught them lessons that might not have come any other way. The list of specific examples is endless, but the list of general lessons from either firsthand experience or direct observation is worth contemplating: How to overcome organizational obstructions. How to avoid overengineering. How to anticipate failures. How to plan and schedule accurately. How to open dead ends. How to identify the problem and solve it—fast. How to identify or find the right and wrong people to work with. The proper allocation of time and money. The relative value of various efforts. The absolute necessity of teamwork. The proper degree of attention to detail. And many more that are more subtle. You can't run any racing team or engineering team efficiently without knowing all those techniques, and nothing could have taught them faster or more vividly than they were. That's not to say that there won't be all-new problems and mistakes, but the experience has improved future performances.

Then there is another thought that is interesting to consider. It seems that as long as Chevrolet allowed certain valuable persons to indulge their interest in racing, Chevrolet was able to draw upon their talents in related areas—brakes, instrumentation, engines, management, or what have you. But when they stopped allowing that luxury, they lost those persons. It's as if the competition activity was a fringe benefit for irreplaceable employees.

At any rate, wherever any two or more of the old group gathers anymore, there is a common fascinating nostalgia: After all the following years of experience, what if all the original team could be reassembled under the same roof with the same budget—all the R&D engineers and technicians, Penske, Hall, Donohue, and their teams. It might be unbeatable in any race series in the world. Hall was close when he had the 2J. Penske is even closer right now, and he may do it yet. Antares Engineering is a strong dark horse. But "what if's" don't win races.

There doesn't seem to be any reason to ever get the old group together anyhow. Research-related-to-racing generated such enthusiasm and results, that Chevrolet is still far ahead of most other manufacturers in high-performance engineering knowledge. Not that Chevrolet could rapidly assemble an all-new Formula 1 car that would take the World Championship the first time out, but there are few people who would gamble against them doing it after a little experience in that area. If there is little left to learn, there is less remaining to prove. If the public has not realized that professional racing is more of a competition between professional teams than the equipment they use, it is because the spectator wants to believe that there is some great difference between a Chevrolet, a Ford, and a Plymouth. In fact, as normally purchased and used by perhaps 99 percent of the population, there is simply no way to functionally distinguish them. It's only at the rarely approached fine edge of competition that any differentiation will stand out. At that point, however, statistics frequently indicate that in any fair fight—showroom stock to showroom stock—it is hard to beat a Chevrolet product.

Another point that the public is not recognizing, is that another sort of competition is rapidly growing behind the chrome and lacquer facade. Competition with the federal government. If the public had expressed as much interest in accident protection as accident avoidance, the manufacturers would have been fighting it out on the crash barriers of America already. *Whether* protection is more important than avoidance is debatable, but what is happening now is an inescapable reality. The American government has gone into competition with the world's largest industry. If anything, this has brought all the companies closer together, as the government fails to identify collusion or monopolistic tendencies with anything that falls under the current accepted definition of the "public welfare." Those legislators who would like to see General Motors split up into more "controllable" independent units are going to have to acknowledge one point. Only such a colossus has the facilities to develop the safety systems that are being demanded, in the time that is allotted. If the government operates under the illusion that nine women, laboring for one month each, can deliver a baby, it is because they have never been in direct competition with such an underrated industry.

It is possible that part of the government's interest was in bolstering the idle aerospace industry—although things didn't quite work out that way. When the Department of Transportation asked for bids on their Experimental Safety Vehicle, it was intended to leave out the current automobile manufacturers, because they were prejudiced with vested interests. However, it was politically impossible to reject General Motors' offer to compete for *one dollar.* When the aerospace companies heard who else was in the race, few wanted to get involved for any price. For all their advanced technology, systems analysis, engineering personnel, and facilities, they couldn't compete with GM's experience and efficiency. But not only did GM's strategy get them on the mailing list for changes in the contract specifications, they were also able to get a more reasonable delivery date of 12 months after the aerospace companies—which allows time to incorporate any positive results from the initial acceptance tests.

There never was any question at GM whether they could outperform the DOT, anyhow. It may not be so easy to meet arbitrary overzealous standards, but when it comes to matching results to results—small worry. Who else has a computer simulation of loss-of-control vehicle dynamics or structural crash dynamics? Who else has hydraulic crash simulation sleds and 67 acres of unobstructed asphalt and tire analysis machines and unlimited test vehicles and a long history of previous crash tests and hundreds of experienced automotive engineers? You could hardly expect any real competition, if merely because all the necessary personnel are internally trained in Detroit, and few could be induced to switch their allegiance. Even for money and security. They know where the knowledge and rationality are. And they had been challenged again—just like in racing—to prove what they could do if someone cared, or goaded them.

It's not all that simple, though. There are some unwritten rules to the game. To prevent the suspicion that they have been restraining knowledge of accident protection, GM needs to be revolutionary in concept. Their safety car ought to be loaded with recently patented innovations that are unrelated to the current design technology. And yet, they have to face the fact that as winners, they are likely to be forced into mass-producing the vehicle—and no *other* vehicle. So, for production reasons, the design ought to be merely evolutionary. We are sure to be staggered by the announced cost of development in dollars and engineering man-years, and yet even if the dollar value is twice that of the government/aerospace version, it still has to be economically feasible. If that incongruity weren't enough, a total competition elapsed-time of almost three years means that the starting rules are going to be somewhat different than the rules at the end of the first period. There will be changes in administrations, society, goals, technology, and the market. Who knows, maybe there will be a mass consumer revolution, demanding nothing more than basic, casual transportation such as the ever-present Volkswagen.

There is also another race going on—between the industry and public ecology enthusiasm. The government is acting as middle-man, by setting quantitative requirements in parts per million of specific pollutants, but the industry has such an economic influence that the government cannot demand "unrealistic" cleanliness. The population still decides how much they are willing to pay for clean transportation. A corporation may not have a conscience, but if it wants to make a profit, it has to respond to public conscience. At the moment, that seems to mean cleaner air, less congestion, longer vehicle life, and more functionality. Not, surprisingly, better impact protection. Perhaps the public recognizes that personal responsibility is more practical than "absolute protection" from the market or from "inevitable" accidents.

Contrary to what the doomsayers imply, the large automotive corporations are not omnipotent or inherently evil. One largely overlooked point is that they are indeed in competition—with the world economic community. Today, at least. The legislative branch of our "corporate-state" is trying to isolate them by taxation on European or Japanese products, and so the worst may happen, but right now we still have an ever-more-limited choice. Our corporations are still in a race to satisfy public opinion.

Perhaps this book may strengthen the faith a little in the possibility of individual freedom under corporate rule. It is not a story of General Motors, or of Chevrolet, but of strong people within who had their way. General Motors as a corporation may be good, or may be bad—I am not one to judge. But GM is not all wrong in exploiting technology. The heroes are those within who used that technology to express their freedom, adventure, creativity, skills, and power in the face of the awesome machine, although it may turn out that it was the last act of individualism we will ever see there.

Is Chevrolet involved in racing? No. Unequivocally not ... today. There are still relatively free, powerful individuals remaining, such as Mitchell, Winchell, and DeLorean, but they are involved with competition of another sort. There are even more race fanatics on the lower levels, but they are not sanctioned or organized. "Things are pretty slow right now."

What about the future? It doesn't look like there is one, unless auto racing again demonstrates a definite purpose. "Engineering development" is unlikely while the interest in safety and ecology is more important than handling or speed. Advertising or promotion are possibilities, as racing grows into acceptance as valid entertainment instead of a "blood sport." It could even be reestablished as an intercorporate sport for the engineers and technicians—as a fringe benefit, or to generate employee loyalty, or simply to improve the product.

Surreptitious automobile racing had a long and stormy life at Chevrolet. Fourteen years, more or less. It grew slowly and it died slowly—it had neither a birthdate nor a death date. It was not stopped by government influence, or by AMA decision, or by corporate mandate. It could only be stopped by replacing it with another kind of competition—a more humanistic kind. It didn't go out with a bang, or a roar, it just sort of faded away.

Epilogue

A reprint of a historical document almost demands an epilogue. However, in this case it seems like the writing of an epilogue to Darwin's *Origin of Species*, There's no middle ground. Either it would be an immense undertaking, trying to find what happened to the 227 people mentioned, the subsequent racing programs, and where each of the race cars ended up over 28 years. Or, I'd have to say that the results and consequences were so publicly obvious, especially those people who rose out of the program, that describing it was superfluous. A few, like Penske and Jim Hall, went on to greater glory. A few, like Donohue, died in race cars. Most left Chevrolet to be entrepreneurs, or retired, and/or died. Of the 74 race cars and prototypes mentioned, many have been restored and are in museums or are still running in vintage racing. And some of the racing venues have flourished or died.

Other books have been written to expand on various aspects, such as the Can-Am, the Trans-Am, the Camaro, Chaparral cars, and my biography of Donohue, which is also about to be republished. The racing technology has moved forward, although not in any great leaps. It's hard to think of many great advancements since that era, except for onboard computers (and none in NASCAR). Astoundingly, in spite of Chevrolet's ventures in production and racing of overhead cam V-8's, the basic "smallblock" still dominates in American racing, as it has since its inception in 1955.

But the greatest irony, is that GM now has a high-level department officially called the "Raceshop." In the late eighties, Chevrolet came "out of the closet," when they changed the name of the Product Performance group to Chevrolet Raceshop. The driving force was Herb Fishel, who has become one of the most powerful forces in American auto racing, and when he was given responsibility for all of GM's competition activities, he carried the group name with him. They still don't run any factory racing teams, but they do have scores of engineers running competition programs for each GM division, and designing and distributing components and even chassis—*and they promote it in the press!*

An epilogue of a satisfying length would make it the tale that wagged the dog. Instead of an epilogue, my feeling is that Chevrolet's subsequent racing activities deserve a multi-volume collection of sequels, covering 1970 to the present.

Index

Persons

Cars

The Companies and Series

About the Author

From the First Edition:
Paul Van Valkenburgh has been involved in motorsports since his high school days—first making engine swaps, then restorations—and he built the second deDion axle sports car in the United States. Van Valkenburgh's mechanical and aeronautical studies took him to Kansas University of Engineering, and then on to Douglas Space Systems before he went on to work at Chevrolet Research and Development as an aerodynamicist. While there, he became a specialist in competition vehicle dynamics and was promoted to research engineer. From there Paul went to *Sports Car Graphic* as a technical editor and developed one of the most complete and accurate road test programs.

Update:
Since publishing the first edition of this book, Paul has written four others, including the definitive *Race Car Engineering & Mechanics* and *AUTO 2010— the Car Magazine from the Future*, as well as over 300 magazine articles. He has also been an engineering consultant and lecturer on the dynamics of cars, trucks, trailers, motorcycles, snowmobiles, motorhomes, tour buses, 3-wheelers, bicycles, human-powered vehicles, electric cars, and race cars. Currently he is the editorial columnist in *Racecar Engineering* magazine, and occasional feature writer for *Road & Track*. He also earned an advanced degree in Human Behavior, and is beginning a second career in neurological disorders. For more information, see www.wryt.com.